D1115215

AUTO FOCUS

Previously published as
The Murder of Bob Crane

Robert Graysmith
Illustrations by the Author

BERKLEY BOULEVARD BOOKS, NEW YORK

AUTO FOCUS

Previously published as *The Murder of Bob Crane*

A Berkley Boulevard Book / published by arrangement with Crown Publishers, a division of Random House Inc.

PRINTING HISTORY
Crown hardcover edition / June 1993
Berkley edition / July 1994
Berkley Boulevard edition / October 2002

Copyright © 1993, 1994, 2002 by Robert Graysmith
Book design by Kristin del Rosario
Motion picture artwork and photography copyright © 2002
by Sony Pictures Classics Inc. All rights reserved.

Visit our website at
www.penguinputnam.com

ISBN: 0-425-18902-3

BERKLEY BOULEVARD
Berkley Boulevard Books are published by
The Berkley Publishing Group,
a division of Penguin Putnam Inc.,
375 Hudson Street, New York, New York 10014.
BERKLEY BOULEVARD and its logo
are trademarks belonging to Penguin Putnam Inc.

PRINTED IN THE UNITED STATES OF AMERICA

10 9 8 7 6 5 4 3 2 1

*For David Martin Smith,
a wonderful son, gifted
mathematician, and future teacher,
for his excellent advice
and never-failing encouragement.*

ACKNOWLEDGMENTS

First and foremost I wish to thank Lieutenant Ron Dean of the Scottsdale, Arizona, Police Department for his generous assistance in explaining the complex Bob Crane case to me and enduring over three years (often several times a day) my phone calls and questions. Without his help the Crane book in its present form would not have been possible. Thanks to Dennis Borkenhagen, Dean's able partner, to Richard Romley, county attorney of Maricopa County, Pete Noyes of KNBC-TV news, and Werner Klemperer, Robert Clary, and Richard Powell of *Hogan's Heroes* for their insight.

I am indebted to the following for their encouragement, moral support, willing ears, and friendly smiles during the rough times: Aaron, Margot, and my mom. Thanks especially to Eric Lenaburg of Scottsdale, journalist, writer, and researcher, and his wonderful family—Marybeth, Brett, Siavonh, Inez, and Pasqual.

I would be remiss if I did not mention two names out of my past who have been a constant inspiration and example to me in my writing and drawing life—Carl Barks, immortal creator of "Uncle Scrooge" and one of the great cartoonists of the twentieth century, whose kind letters of twenty-five years ago I still treasure, and Nancy Imlay, my high school English teacher in Tachikawa, Japan, who encouraged me.

Gratitude also to Linda Meltzer, Wolf, Kathleen Derby, Penny Wallace, Mike and Hope Wallace, Al Morch, Uncle Sol, Jeffrey Adamsky, Elaine Birnbaum, Christine, Danny Stewart, and to the Hendricks family: Kelly, Stephanie, Becky, and Sarah; and the Cooper family: Bob, Peggy, Benjamin, Nicholas, and Danny. Emily Ann Nilsson, Stephen Taylor, Zac Wilson, Mark Devito, Jason Lily, John C. Alves, Mary B. Martin, Tony Castro, Jim Delasandro, Elaine Greenberg, Shayne, "Spy on a Bike," Lou Grant, Donna Gould, Gene and Kathleen, Somerset and Paris, and the gang at the Owl and the Monkey: Justin, Maggie, Eric, Tami, Jenny, Jenn, Carey, Diana Austin, Lon, Maggie, Laura, Karen, Lita, Richard, Kelly, and Ali. Also to Paul Vietzke, Mark Gentry, and Ann Rasmussen; Jody Frandle, Greg Tarter, and Stacie Kizziar, Jerry and Marcia, Kent Taylor and Janine Kennedy, Sarah and Martin David. And to Al and Sheryl Stafford, Gavin Grow, Robin Smith, Brad Konkle, Dan Herbon, Dr. Michael Payne, and Gayla Faahs; David Birnbaum, the Bushe, Kinner, and Barrett families, Natalie Finnegan, Frank McGinn, Bob Lynch, Norma Luquin, Kevin Anderson, Bob and Valerie Wooldridge, Bob, Diana, Adam, and Audie Crug, Napoli N. Lehnert, Lee and Charles Brady, Jim Toland, Christina, Candace, Victoria, Jennifer, Don, Sonia, Adrienne, and Steve. Mike McAlary, William K. Rashbaum, Pete Bowles, Virginia Byrne, Kieran Crowley, Mary Garofalo, Joseph McNamera, Jim Walsh, Teresa Allen, Paul Olsewski, Bruce Bellingham, and Roger Cooper.

Finally, but certainly not least, I owe a great debt to my agent, Dan Strone, at William Morris, and to the only editor I've ever had (or for that matter would ever want)—Richard Marek.

Television is not the truth. Television is a goddamn amusement park. Television is a circus, a carnival, a traveling troupe of acrobats, storytellers, dancers, singers, jugglers, sideshow freaks, lion tamers, and football players. We're in the boredom-killing business.

—Paddy Chayefsky, *Network*

Has any one supposed it lucky to be born? I hasten to inform him or her, it is just as lucky to die, and I know it.

—Walt Whitman

I know nothing. I see nothing. No-*thing!*

—Sergeant Hans Schultz of *Hogan's Heroes*

PROLOGUE

Wednesday, June 28, 1978: 10:27 P.M.

The vast parking lot beyond the stage exit was darkened by an elongated rectangle that shrouded the few cars clustered there. Its illumination emanated from the blazing light securely mounted on the south wall of the Windmill Theatre near its east corner, but the effect was of shadows and gloom. For the last three weeks the cast of *Beginner's Luck*, which was playing at the Windmill, had often complained that the lighting was "very poor at best."

On the last night of Bob Crane's life, the popular actor and his best friend, John Carpenter, felt the wall of hot dry air from the surrounding desert as they left the air-conditioned playhouse. Crane's energy level had been low, and he had caused the play, and the autograph signing that followed, to end late. Thus, he arrived at the lot much later than was his routine.

A beam of thin light struck the right rear side of his leased Monte Carlo, and the whitewall of the steel-belted tire gleamed in the dimness. Crane saw that the tire was flat.

"Nuts!" he snapped, and then to John: "There goes our time. I'm supposed to call Patti when we get home." Patti was Crane's estranged wife.

Crane looked warily around the lot. He was edgy. Only a month earlier in Dallas, he had lunched with a young woman named Roxy Pace Smarzik and poured out his divorce woes. "Scotty, my son," Crane had said, "wrote 'Fuck Daddy' on the wall of my home. My wife, Patti, accused me of showing Scotty dirty movies."

Roxy had just had her palm read and in an amateur fashion began to read his in order to change the subject. She saw that Crane's lifeline was short, and she told him his life would be brief.

Crane laughed. "I'll be happy if I can make it to my fiftieth birthday." Now, as he stood in the lot with John, Crane's fiftieth birthday was only sixteen days away.

Not long after Roxy's reading, Tamara Rand, a professional psychic in Los Angeles who was dating Crane, had also predicted "danger" for Bob. Most recently, Brenda Broyles, another lover, had left Bob's bed in a state of panic and told Julie Sue Brinker,* another bed partner, of the terrible dream that had come to her while the trio slumbered. "Something bad is coming," she had cried.

These unsettling intuitions, along with the menace of the night, were enough to cause Crane to act unpredictably. Instead of kneeling in the darkness to change the tire, he slid behind the wheel and waved John into the auto. About three hundred yards across the open lot toward the front of the theater Bob had observed a brightly lit service station on the corner. Crane rode the rim of the flat to the station, pulled to a stop by the second row of pumps, and waited for the attendant.

Twenty-three-year-old Kevin Landrith was working the

---

*This name has been changed.

late shift at the Arco Station at North Scottsdale Road and Shea; his partner, Steve Wilson, was preparing to leave. Both Landrith and Wilson recognized the actor but did not know the man with him. Later they described Crane's companion as "a stocky man with long, dark brown hair over his ears." Both thought the dark, iodine-skinned man was Spanish or Mexican and later agreed he was wearing a mustache. The odd thing was that John Carpenter did not have a mustache.

Bob asked Landrith to change the tire, and the attendant watched Carpenter get the spare out of the trunk before Landrith could. "The tire didn't get chewed up that much, I don't think," said John.

Landrith used the station tools to change the tire, leaving the equipment in the Monte Carlo untouched. When he had finished, Crane asked him, "Could you fix the flat? I can be back here to pick it up tomorrow."

"Sure," said Landrith, and he watched the Monte Carlo turn south on Scottsdale Road and disappear into the night. Wilson left the station just ahead of Crane, also headed southbound, and he watched the Monte Carlo in his rearview mirror until it turned east onto Chaparral.

Back at the station, Landrith started to patch the flat, but on closer examination he observed that the valve core stem was almost completely loose. It appeared to him that someone had "deliberately loosened the valve core." No other holes were in the tire to account for its condition. He was certain that the loose valve stem was the sole cause. "I've worked with tires for approximately five years," he said later, "and I've *never* known a valve stem to work loose, especially as loose as this one was. I'm *sure* it was tampered with."

Landrith was so suspicious that he placed the tire under lock and key. Afterward the authorities would come to the conclusion that the tire had been flattened in order to strand Bob in the darkened lot and signaled a failed first attempt on his life.

PART ONE

The First Prison: The Cell

HOGAN: Search me.

HOCHSTETTER: That, Colonel Hogan, is exactly what I intend to do—search you. And every inch of Stalag 13.

HOGAN: Well, gentlemen, if that's all, I'll be on my way.

HOCHSTETTER: You're most anxious to get out of here.

HOGAN: If there's going to be a search, I don't know about you guys, but I've got things to hide.

CHUCKWALLA

1

THE VALLEY OF THE SUN

Wide shot—Camera term that calls for framing that is some distance from the object being photographed and relates it to its surroundings.

There was not a breath of air near Scottsdale. In the surrounding desert, the clear, burning light that had scorched away the last remnant of ragged cloud magnified distant objects through wave after wave of shimmering heat. Far off, brown dunes rippled as knee-high winds rushed over them.

Poised on its toes in the shade on a flat, dry rock, away from the afternoon sun, a chuckwalla lizard stirred its tail lethargically, following the shadow of a towering saguaro.

Nearby in the hardscrabble were forests of jumping cholla, whose barbed breakaway spines stuck tenaciously to any passerby at the slightest contact, graceful ocotillo plants, and red-blossomed Joshua trees whose otherworldly arms twisted toward the lofty Mojave to the west of Phoenix.

Phoenix, the heart and capital of Arizona,* beats within the Valley of the Sun, cradled within ten dry surrounding Maricopa County cities—Tempe, Mesa, Chandler, Litchfield Park, Glendale, Wickenburg, Sun City, Cave Creek, Carefree, and Scottsdale. More than half the population of Arizona lives here. The valley stretches from Apache Junction west to Gila Bend and from Chandler north to Wickenburg and in turn is surrounded by parched mountainous land.

Once past Wickenburg the faded blue mountains and the blinding glare of the sun-baked desert land of the harsh Sonoran to the south of Phoenix combine to create inverted mirages and ghostly images on the evening horizon. A vast and holy silence holds sway here, interrupted only by the howl of a coyote or the sudden violence of a dust storm.

The northern face of the state sports an expression approaching abandon—from the mile-deep, eighteen-mile-wide gash of the Grand Canyon to black gorges, high, bleak mesas, narrow buttes, natural arches and bridges, surrealistic stone spires and needles, petrified forests, and red-and-lavender rock formations. Here beneath snow-capped mountains, jagged black rivers that once were lava beds are edged by meadows of bright flowers.

But down around Phoenix the state wears a different face—its plains are simple and unadorned. Its four mountain ranges huddle close together, separated only by steep narrow valleys. Whether the simpler geography and sameness of climate make for less complicated passions is open to debate.

In these parts rain falls always where it is least needed—over thirty inches in the highest mountains, only five inches in the thirsty desert. During the July and August rainy seasons late afternoon thunderstorms often mix with dust to

---

Ali-shonak—Papago Indian for "Place of Little Springs." Arizona is host to fourteen Indian tribes. One-seventh of all Native American Indians live here.

form eerie dust devils, which are held by the Indians to be symbols of danger and bad luck. With only two brief rainy seasons, finding a solution to the water problem had been essential for the desert dwellers.

The Hohokam (Those That Have Vanished) Indians have been gone so long that no one knows when they lived or where they went, but "the Departed Ones" were North America's first irrigationists, and the lifeblood of the valley is pumped through arteries they established during the Pueblo period approximately six centuries earlier. In 1911 Theodore Roosevelt Dam was completed, the capstone of the nation's first great reclamation project. With this tapped water came a bonus, abundant hydroelectric power.

Soon the Salt River Valley was revived through a series of broad canals that coursed westerly and southwardly and made the sands flower. Water was brought from east of Phoenix, and the city rose from the desert as an oasis, one of the richest agricultural regions in the country, irrigated by the Salt and Verde rivers and numerous laterals and ditches.* It is one of these canals, the Arizona, that plays an important role in Bob Crane's story.

The meandering Arizona Canal cuts sluggishly through Scottsdale, describing the gray shape of a backward seven through the center of the city and down into the Salt River Pima Indian Reservation. In places the canal is broad and deep and lined by thin rows of telephone poles and brush. At times water roars through the stone canal, and at times it is dry, its state dictated by turning on or shutting off the flow at Granite Reef Dam.

Just where the canal turns southward, it pauses at the northwest corner of Chaparral and Miller roads, where the Winfield Apartments stand. The Windmill Dinner Theatre chain had leased apartment 132A two years earlier at $365 per month for the stars of their productions. Joseph Cotten

---

*Canals such as the Grand, Arizona, Highline, Western, Tempe, Consolidated, and Eastern. Dams such as Cave Creek, Horseshoe, Bartlett, Granite Reef, Stewart Mountain, Mormon Flat, Horse Mesa, and Roosevelt in the Superstition Mountains.

had been the first performer to stay there; JoAnne Worley and her husband, Roger Perry, followed. Now the apartment was Crane's.

On Monday, June 5, 1978, just as Scottsdale was cooling off (the temperature plunged, at least at poolside, to ninety-five degrees), Bob Crane pulled himself from the small, circular pool at the rear of his apartment, shaking the water from his head. Briefly, a wind swept off reddish-sandy Camelback Mountain, which dominates the area to the west where Scottsdale meets Phoenix.

The breeze rattled the palms poolside, brushing the treetops above the red-tile-roofed bathhouse, and Bob could smell dust, sage, and oranges. Arms crossed over his chest, he stood quietly in the falling light.

The setting sun highlighted his upturned nose, the laugh lines around the brown and vaguely Oriental eyes, his high cheekbones. Almost six feet tall, a muscular 187 pounds, with a full head of curly, dark brown hair only now growing gray, Crane at forty-nine was a smooth-talking, gum-chewing, jut-jawed man who exuded confidence. There was an appealing quality to his insolence, and the characters he usually portrayed were brash, resourceful men in command.

Since his enormously successful television program, *Hogan's Heroes*, had gone off the air seven years earlier, Crane had been doing dinner theater around the country for the Windmill Dinner Theatre chain. "I've always had an extraordinary amount of luck," Crane said, "being in the right place at the right time."

Brimming with exuberance, nonstop gab, bright wit, and apparent self-esteem, Bob impressed the critics. One *TV Guide* writer described his conversation as "a compulsive torrent of affable showbiz talk, facts about his multiple careers, his problems, his aspirations, his convictions, all mixed up in an articulate-chaotic, joke-studded stew."

"I take over," Crane admitted. "I don't really mean to, but I dominate. A tornado is let loose. It happens when I'm interviewed. On *The Merv Griffin Show*, Merv looked as if he'd been hit by a flounder.

"Mike Douglas's producer said I was 'pushy.' I *was* pushy. I know it. I come on like a Sammy [from the 1941 Budd Schulberg novel *What Makes Sammy Run?*]. But I'm not a Sammy. I hate the Sammy Glick type, myself. I try not to be pushy, but I come on too strong. I *exhaust* people."

Yet, in fact, Crane had the thinnest of skins. Imprinted on his mind was virtually every critical line and paragraph ever written about him. It was just this spring that the *National Enquirer* had printed gossip about him with quotes attributed to his recently estranged wife, Patti. The article had agitated Bob beyond words.

"I'm as thin-skinned as Jack Paar," he admitted in an interview. "I'm easily hurt . . . conflicts scare me. They really do. I run from a fight. . . ." Many of his friends had recognized his strong aversion to weapons of any kind.

"I'm not well educated," said Bob, "I'm afraid of intellectual snobs. I'm afraid of being put down. People bring up cultural subjects, I have to walk away like a dummy. I can't argue with people. Tony Randall scared me. He talked about *opera*. Puccini! All I know is Dave Brubeck. I didn't open my mouth for fifteen minutes! . . . I joke. It's a comic's defense. What makes Robert run? If they get you in a corner—throw a funny line and run! . . .

"I'm hip, flip, and cocky. That's the thing I *loved* in Jack Lemmon, when I first saw him. The Jack Benny braggadocio that I love. I recognized myself in it. That's *me*, I thought."

As the former "King of the L.A. Airwaves" at KNX, the CBS-affiliate radio station, and a star of two Disney films, Crane was presently starring in *Beginner's Luck* at the Windmill Theatre in Scottsdale. You're on shaky, very shaky financial ground, his business manager, Lloyd Vaughn, had suggested. This was in spite of the fact that the comic actor had been toiling thirty weeks a year on the dinner club circuit, making anywhere from $110,000 to $250,000 annually, including his royalties from the syndication of *Hogan's Heroes*. (For the year 1977 this royalty was $96,000 in one lump sum.)

Crane owned *Beginner's Luck* and was the unofficial director of the play. A romantic comedy written by Norman Barasch and the late Carroll Moore, it told the story of a couple's reconcilement in two acts, eight scenes, and four characters, two men and two women. Crane had first taken it on tour in 1973.

Perhaps the play's theme of reconciliation struck a chord in the actor, given his own troubled marriage. But these feelings were ambivalent, and just as often he would strengthen his own resolve not to return. After the failure of a long first marriage and the pain of a second, Crane obsessively sought someone he could care deeply about. He had come to tally his own worth by the number of women he slept with each day. Fearful of being alone, the star had taken to prowling relentlessly, excited more by the chase than the conquest. It was common for Bob to reject a woman for any subsequent encounters.

Crane rubbed some tanning lotion on his nose and dove gracefully back into the water. His portable radio blared the jazz he loved so much as he floated in the pool; a row of empty yellow sun chairs and huge tilted umbrellas stood silent audience. Bob routinely spent four afternoons a week sunbathing, bobbing around a pool, and listening to music, welcoming the extra time to contemplate his life and the direction in which it was headed.

There were a few bright prospects—Crane was only weeks away from signing a contract with ABC-TV to do a movie of the week; he was buying a new house with his elder son, Bob Jr.; and after Scottsdale, *Beginner's Luck* was scheduled to open in Austin, Texas, on the Fourth of July for a month's run. Reviews of the comedy in Dallas last month had been favorable.

Earlier in the day the entire cast of *Beginner's Luck*— Crane, his brand-new leading lady, Sandra Giles, and supporting actors Jack Schultz and Victoria Ann Berry had arrived on the same morning plane from Los Angeles. Since Victoria had been in the Dallas production and had her ten-to fifteen-minute part down cold, she had been exempt from the previous week's run-through.

Jack Schultz, who was also new to the cast, thought the preliminary rehearsal in Los Angeles had gone well, but as soon as the quartet arrived in Scottsdale it became obvious that there were going to be some serious problems with the new leading lady. "Sandra never really got the part down," Schultz recalled, "never really memorized her lines properly, so that she could not handle the part when we got here."

Giles was an old friend of Crane's from the mid-sixties. However, this was the first time she had done a play with him. Although there were no blowups between the two, Crane realized that Giles could not continue in the role.

After the rehearsal, Crane had gone over to the Casa del Sol complex in Phoenix, where the dinner theater chain had leased apartments 214, 216, and 219 for the supporting cast, to be certain that Sandra, Victoria, and Jack were settled and comfortable. He had even rented TV sets for the women. Later, when it appeared that *Beginner's Luck* would be canceled a week early, he would offer to pay the remainder of the rental on the sets.

Bob had made arrangements to rehearse with Victoria and Sandra at his place that night and then had returned to his large two-bedroom apartment at the Winfield to unpack and take his swim. From the pool he went back to his apartment, following the path under the dappled shadows of tall trees to his front door. His apartment's poolside arcadia door was inaccessible, blocked by balls of wires and an array of the video equipment that was Bob's passion.

Crane unlocked his door, threw the dead bolt, and strode into his bathroom, where he dropped his towel on the floor and hung up his trunks to dry. The heat had given a coppery patina to the rooms. The Windmill Theatre provided no maid service, and the visiting stars were expected to clean up after themselves. Bob, though, was notoriously messy.

Crane brushed his teeth, rinsed out a twin-blade razor, shaved, splashed on Chanel aftershave, and ran a comb through his hair. He wandered into the kitchen, where he poured some orange juice and then downed an antihistamine pill and a handful of vitamin E tablets.

("How many vitamin Es are you taking?" John Carpenter, his traveling companion, used to ask teasingly, in a reference to the amount of stamina Bob needed to satisfy the women in his life. The idea of Crane taking drugs was inconceivable to John. "Not a thing," said Carpenter. "He never took drugs, never smoked dope. In fact, when somebody would pull out a joint Bob would more or less back away a little bit. As many years as I've known Bob he's never taken a hit off a joint that you've seen passed around. I don't smoke, but he don't smoke, either, and I've never seen him take a pill other than a vitamin . . . nothing illegal.")

After he dressed Bob left to pick up Victoria and crossed the long, open lot to his leased car. Camelback Mountain faced his apartment, and the sun was setting directly behind it. The desert town was washed in pink. As he drove, eventually only a pale, prolonged, and tallowed orange brightened the horizon.

After dinner Crane brought Victoria back to his place, expertly navigating his way around the small town. They had shopped for groceries together earlier in the day. Because they were waiting for Sandra, Victoria left his front door standing wide open. She sensed that the open door bothered Bob, but he didn't say anything.

Eventually Sandra arrived, and they rehearsed most of the night. "She didn't know her lines at all," Victoria said later. "I ended up sleeping the night on Bob's couch." As she dozed off, the sounds of crickets and passing traffic in her ears, a blue key to the apartment caught her eye. It was made of lightweight metal, the kind used to make copies. Bob had all his keys on the same key ring, an ignition key and a trunk key for the Chevy, both silver-colored, a bronze dead-bolt key, and a blue front door key.

In the days ahead Bob would give her the blue key often. "Where I was staying," Victoria recollected, "our pool was closed every Monday, quite often more than Monday, and I went over to his place a couple of times to use the Winfield pool, and he'd always give me a blue key, the blue key. I think there were two blue keys, but Bob only gave me one each time, and that would unlock the door. That single key."

Months earlier the lock to Bob's rooms had been rekeyed and a dead bolt installed because over the years some keys had been lost. The theater wanted to be sure that its high-priced stars were protected. One key was kept with Jean Reed, the Winfield's manager, one in a locked drawer at the Windmill, and one in the possession of the visiting celebrity. Bob Crane, for some reason, had taken both the theater's key *and* the star's key.

At the Winfield Crane developed a pattern for locking his door. Later it would be of great significance. Each time he left the apartment he habitually locked both the dead bolt at the top and then the knob below, which was locked by pressing the knob inward and twisting. When Crane returned he always unlocked the door in reverse order. Once inside, without fail, he would shoot the dead bolt home.

Crane's oldest son's stepfather, Chuck Sloan, remembered the day Bob had become obsessed with locking his doors. "He told me of a situation," recalled Sloan, "it may have been in Chicago, where Bobby and Karen, his kids, were with him and someone had come into the room and rifled the wallets and taken some money out. . . . He always locked his doors since that day."

Tuesday morning, June 6, Crane had another rehearsal. Opening night was hours away, and this run-through went as poorly as the previous night's. In the late afternoon Crane went for a dip and videotaped the pool area behind his apartment, recording a woman in a dark swimsuit with bold white stripes. She did a fashion pose for Crane. "Seems to me that I remember that pose," he said into the microphone.

Bob began to get ready for the short drive to the Windmill and put on the only stage makeup he used, a little Cover Girl. He fingered the drumsticks on his dresser, a complimentary gift from a band in Scottsdale. An accomplished drummer himself (Bob had played with the Connecticut Symphony Orchestra), he beat out a staccato rhythm on the dresser's edge. In *Hogan's Heroes* he sometimes worked his drumming into the story line.

After he had buffed his shoes with brown polish, Crane picked up the white photo album that he often kept on the living room coffee table. It was twelve inches long and six inches wide. Inside the back and front covers were small plastic pieces of film, two to each envelope. The entire book contained black-and-white Polaroids of women both with and without clothes, their names written at the bottom of the pictures. When he showed off the photos, and he often did, Crane would explain where the women were from and what sex acts they had performed with him. When you lifted one photo you could see another on the back side. Crane had similar albums at his place in Los Angeles.

"Bob was not shy about showing you his photo albums," Victoria recalled. "He was very open about that. He would show you even if he didn't know you. If you were visitors here and he stopped by and you were my friends, if he was sitting here right now, he'd say, 'Hi, how are you? I've met this girl.' Sometimes I used to shrink under the table, he was so open. He would say, 'I took these films, this goddess-love thing on the camera.' But that's the way Bob was. You know he would never force a girl to do anything."

Crane took the album into the master bedroom and stowed it away in his large, black overnight bag. He did have his secrets, and it was understood by his friends that this "mystery bag" and the items it contained were off limits.

Bob left for the theater in his leased Monte Carlo and, as always, arrived at the theater only fifteen to twenty minutes before the performance began—a practice that drove stage manager Chris Roberts to distraction. In the weeks ahead Roberts would take to standing outside the theater in the dark, wondering whether or not there would be a show that night.

Almost everyone saw Crane as relaxed, laid-back, an extremely passive personality. But some, such as Roberts, sensed the deep tensions that smoldered just beneath the surface—the insecurities, the eagerness to please, the search for perfection. "Bob could be quite volatile," Chris said. "He was generally a fun-loving person, but he could become very upset if something went wrong. For example, if somebody screwed up in the play while rehearsing. But this was not common. Bob seemed to be quite to himself emotionally. And lonely."

Roberts additionally felt that Crane was not emotionally

stable. "He was unhappy due to his work," Roberts said later. "He felt it was second-rate compared to what he had been doing in the past—his TV series and other shows. He apparently felt that the play circuit was lower than where he should be."

Victoria knew Bob never argued with anyone or was rude unless it was connected with his work. "He's very strict about the work," she said. "Work was work!"

Bob went directly to Sandra and Victoria's dressing room, bypassing Jack Schultz's. Although Jack's dressing room adjoined the women's, Bob rarely spoke to him.

After packing *Beginner's Luck* around the nation in 1973 and 1978 to Florida, Houston, Cincinnati, New Orleans, Long Beach, Hawaii, Dallas, and Scottsdale, Bob had the two-act play running precisely—curtain up at 8:05 P.M., down at 10:05, 10:15 at the latest, depending upon the evening's energy. Then all four players would take their bows and everyone except Bob would exit.

Bob would stay onstage with the lights up and do a fifteen- or twenty-minute "after show speech." Often the audience found it to be the best part of the show, "open and funny," said Bob Crane, Jr. "The part of the performance that made a really tight play work," said one of Crane's friends. After his monologue, Bob would invite the audience to the lobby to chat with him and, if they wished, get his autograph. It was an opportunity for Crane to meet the women who were interested in him. It well may have been his favorite part of the evening.

As all had feared, opening night was a complete failure. Bob wrote in his appointment book: "PHOENIX OPEN AWFUL!"

"Oh, yes," Victoria said later, "terrible. Read the reviews. It was a disaster. Bob did a whole monologue onstage opening night because Sandra didn't know her lines or anything, so she was replaced after the first two nights."

So on Thursday, June 8, Bob and Victoria drove Sandra to Sky Harbor Airport. Victoria could tell that Giles had no hard feelings about her firing, held no grudge against Bob, and was concerned mainly with any bad publicity that the firing might generate in the media and the effect it might have on her career.·

At the same time they dropped off Giles, they were able to pick up her replacement, Peggy Walton, arriving from Hollywood. Peggy had been the female lead in Texas and would be able to fill out the remainder of the week, four more days and five more performances, until a suitable replacement could be located. Peggy had worked a lot with Crane and on his suggestion was booked into the Sunburst Motel half a block away from his own apartment. Bob placed many of his friends and business acquaintances there because it was convenient.

Bob's vague fears and worries over his impending divorce cast a pall over the evening. The trio went to a little place to eat where Bob planned to meet a former Playboy Club waitress he had been with years ago. As they waited he said, "God! She's probably real old by now." But she was beautiful, Victoria remembered.

CAMELBACK'S "PRAYING MONK"

2
BRENDA

Episodic series—A television series with continuing characters whose different adventures an audience follows from week to week. Each episode is a self-contained unit, a complete teleplay.

Crane had a policy of taking the cast out for drinks and dinner during the first week of an engagement so they could get to know a little bit about the town they were in. In Scottsdale he took them to the Playboy Club, B. B. Singer's, Bogart's, and Friday's Restaurant Disco, all jazz places, since he had a passion for music.

"Bob loved people, and it was very important to Bob to have people like him," said Victoria. "It was a very big need in him. I remember him saying, 'Gee, it's beautiful to have people like you.'"

"The only other place that he took us once," said Jack Schultz, "was the Sunburst Motel, which is right near his apartment there on Scottsdale Road. And then after the first week he doesn't do anything with the cast. He then goes off after the play and socializes on his own."

Schultz found Bob to be outgoing, honest, friendly, and forward; but he could not penetrate beyond the professional level. At least Crane's highly developed sense of humor helped Jack's performance.

"I guess," Schultz remembered, "I would describe him as a person who had a lot of fun in life, enjoyed life, enjoyed acting in front of an audience, a very humorous type of person. He had a very active mind, very sharp, and that's all I know about him. But that's only the surface. There's a surface Bob Crane and someone else hidden under that."

During the first week, Crane also went out with Chris Roberts, the stage manager. Often he took Roberts to his favorite hangout, Bogart's. It was here that Chris became aware of just how straight certain aspects of Bob's life were. Not only did Bob not use any drugs or smoke, he generally drank only grapefruit juice. Chris noticed that the actor always had a group of friends around him, yet he couldn't shake the feeling that Bob Crane was lonely.

Crane's evenings took on a pattern—usually he went out to a quiet dinner and then, according to Chris, "looked for action, went out to pick up some ladies." Bob was a high-energy man, always on the move and always on the lookout for women. A late-night person, he was usually up until four or five in the morning. He needed very little sleep. Often he would bring a new date to the show as his guest. It was Chris's job to seat these women at the VIP table nearest the stage at the Windmill.

Most of the time Roberts was with Crane in the company of friends, but one morning around three he found himself alone in Crane's apartment with the star. Mournfully Bob told Chris of his divorce troubles. During this period Crane had mixed feelings about the topic. "Right now," he said, "I'm doing better than normal with women, and going back into the marriage would make me feel too tied down. I was married to my first wife for seventeen years, my second wife for eight years. I was entirely faithful to Anne, my first wife, for the complete seventeen years, then with Patti I went the other way—almost to the point of excess. This meant going out with many women, different women, just about every night."

Embarrassed by Bob's openness, Chris looked around Crane's littered room and listened to his host in the late-night heat.

"I've been very concerned about how Scotty is going to take the separation," Bob continued. "We're very close. I'd been seeing a psychiatrist though not because of my wife's complaints that I'm not quite fit to be a father. I'm seeing him so that I can be a *better* father."

According to Bob the marriage difficulties with Patti apparently revolved around Bob's mother, who lived in the house with them. Crane told Chris that Patti had not treated his mother, Rose, very well. He didn't mention any fights over this situation, though.

"I'm a videotape nut," said Bob, changing the subject.

Roberts believed it. His eyes rested on the mountain of video equipment in front of the white curtains. This hardware had to be worth several thousand dollars, and it went with the actor wherever he traveled. Bob was also into photography and making audiotapes. "It's my hobby, and I spend as much time playing with it and experimenting with it as I can," he explained.

Bob's straight tapes were of shows that were broadcast when he was sleeping or at the theater and ranged from *Sanford and Son* to the *Tonight* show, from soap operas such as *Another World* to *Saturday Night Live* and news programs. All of these would be watched in the lonely hours. Of course, there were also rehearsals of *Beginner's Luck*, which he critiqued, and many, many episodes of *Hogan's Heroes*. Network programming was mixed in with homemade sex tapes, and periodically the tapes would be erased and reused.

"Bob would tape virtually anything from the *Today* show up to his group sex scenes," Chris said. "During my visit to his apartment, he showed me several videotapes, and some of these tapes included explicit sexual activities.

"On one tape the activities involved Bob and another male with two females. Bob told me that the male was his friend, John Carpenter. There was no sexual activity between Bob and his friend. Everything was heterosexual.

"Bob told me it wasn't uncommon for them to go out

together, pick up ladies, and bring them back to have a 'group scene,' or quite often they would pick up the ladies and go their separate ways. I don't know what his sexual habits were, but I'm sure he wasn't homosexual. It was highly possible that he was bisexual, though."

Friday night, June 9, Bob went out to Bogart's by himself and ran into Brenda Broyles, whom he had been involved with the first time his play was booked into Scottsdale in 1973. Like Patti, Victoria, and many of the other women in his life, Brenda was blue-eyed and blond, with "hair washed so thoroughly it sparkled in the light." When Bob first met the twenty-four-year-old she was in the midst of a divorce, and he took her to Ivanhoe's in Phoenix for the 1973 opening-night cast party. Later, Crane took videos and Polaroid photographs, and they had sex. He hadn't seen her since.

"Is your husband still in town here?" asked Crane.

"I haven't seen him since I left him."

"I've got a date tonight," he told her, "but let's go out for a drive."

They parked for a while, kissed and talked. These days Brenda had a common-law husband and a seven-year-old son. Recently she had grown very protective of him. Although she dreamed of acting, singing, and a career in music (she was currently attempting to master the synthesizer), she told everyone she was a model.

Just before Crane dropped off Brenda back at Bogart's, they made a date for the following night to get together to meet Brenda's friend, Julie Sue Brinker, who worked in the lounge at the Registry Hotel as a cocktail waitress.

Saturday night, June 10, Crane and Brenda went to Dr. Munchie's and afterward strolled into the Registry, where Brenda introduced him to Julie.

"We're going over to the Safari for breakfast," said Brenda, "and then over to Bob's. Join us." Crane almost always ended his nights at the Safari, which was open twenty-four hours a day. Brenda recalled that two years ago there had been a beating murder behind the Safari in the early morning hours, and as an amateur psychic this gave her a chill. Bob took a napkin, neatly jotted down his address, and handed it to Julie.

The two women were also sometime lovers. "Brenda and I are bisexual and have been girlfriends for a long time," Julie said later. She knew Brenda was heavily into the occult, witchcraft, and satanic literature.

Across the dimly lit lounge Julie saw her boyfriend, Carl, and the next time she brought drinks to customers she swung by and took his hand. "I'm going to have to break our date for tonight," she told him. "I want to be with Brenda. I haven't seen her for a while. I'm going to have breakfast with her."

The lounge was just closing as Crane and Brenda left. After work Julie, still in her uniform, went to the Safari, but there was no trace of the couple. She went on to the nearby Winfield Apartments, looking for them.

Meanwhile, Bob, at his apartment, was taping Brenda sitting on the couch and wearing her white dress. He then walked on camera naked, and Brenda was recorded performing oral sex on him. He then began taking Polaroid snapshots of her, saying, "Brenda, do you know how long it's been?"

"It's been five years."

The microphone picked up the sound of Julie knocking at the front door. She was let into the apartment. Both Bob and Brenda were nude now. Her entrance into the room was captured on videotape.

"Do you have anything there to drink?" asked Julie.

"She usually drinks whiskey or Scotch," Brenda said. Brenda drank as little as Bob. Her low blood sugar made drinking difficult; alcohol tended to depress her.

"I just moved in," Crane said apologetically, "so I don't have any liquor yet." Julie later contradicted this and claimed that she had been served Scotch on the first night.

The room was very, very cold. The air conditioner was going full blast. Julie began slowly to undress, while Brenda went into the bathroom. There she saw an elaborate photo lab that Crane used to develop his photos and make prints for friends and lovers. "Some of the photos were of other women Bob had affairs with," said Brenda, "and some were of his wife, both clothed and nude. He lost some of the photos [in December 1977] when his wife broke into the photo lab and took them for use in the divorce suit."

To those watching the videotapes later, it is obvious that Julie knew she was being videotaped. She can be viewed seeing herself in black-and-white on the TV screen across the room by the drapes.

Crane took Polaroid shots of Julie and then of her and Brenda together making love. "It's my hobby," he said.

"Could I have the pictures?" asked Julie.

"No," said Crane, "I'll get you copies."

"Don't hold your breath," Brenda snorted. "He was supposed to be printing copies for me of the pictures he took five years ago." She had last seen those pictures in two similar albums, among pictures of women taken in Texas, Florida, Hawaii, Ohio, and California, all places where *Beginner's Luck* had played.

Once more Brenda and Julie were engaged in oral sex on the broad-striped couch. Shortly Bob put his camera down and joined them. While the videotape machine and camera droned on, Crane had intercourse with both.

"Carl sure couldn't handle this," Julie said, giggling.

After the trio finished having sex, Crane rewound the tape and played back the encounter. Then all three went into the master bedroom. Bob lifted a piece of luggage off the bed and they all had sex again.

Around 4:00 A.M. Bob fell asleep on his stomach on the side of the bed closest to the bathroom. Brenda noticed that he seemed heavily asleep, but as the sky outside brightened he drifted into a light sleep and he would momentarily awaken at her slightest movement or noise. As she was getting up to dress and leave, Bob turned onto his right side and gave a grunt.

For a while Julie and Brenda stood in the living room discussing the things they had been doing since the last time they had been together. Abruptly Brenda told Julie that she had heard voices, as if someone were trying to get into the apartment.

"I'm worried about my house," said Brenda. "I've got to get home." She was trembling.

"No, Brenda, no," said Julie. "It's not your house that's being broken into."

After her friend left, Brenda began to pace, biting one nail on her hand. She was distraught. "It was late," she recalled, "but there was a disturbance in the corner by the door, and in the other corner it was quiet. Silent. Waiting. Voices, or a rush, or . . . it's hard to explain . . . like a cosmic shower. By the door between the bedroom and the bathroom by the closet. It was right there where there was a disturbance, really high."

Brenda rushed back into the master bedroom and snuggled in beside Bob. "I was in bed with him sleeping when I had a dream. There was a man and a woman involved, but she was at a distance. I dreamed that she would be his struggle. But in the dream she was me. I'm sensitive that way.

"There was a struggle. There was movement going from one place to another. And there had been some kind of fight or something. There seemed to be two other people there. And a third person, a woman, involved with those other two people. And moving from one spot to another and a fence with lots of hedges around it. Lots of growth around it. There was a house with a lot of stairs. It was . . . it was just a dream, but sometimes they pertain to the things that happened.

"Yeah, there was something silent in the other corner. It seemed to be a man, but it's very hard 'cause there wasn't any sound or any disturbance in *that* spot. It was just there, you know, something was there. It could have been Death waiting.

"In fact, every time I tried to plan something with Bob I would black out for a second and I would see something was in his way, and I guess it was trying to tell me that something was coming. . . ."

PHOENIX LOOKING TOWARD SCOTTSDALE, 1978

3

PATTI

Development—Elaboration of an idea or concept by work-
ing out the characters and plot structure and sequence
of a television play.

Peggy Walton's last performance was on Sunday, June 11,
1978. She checked out of the Sunburst the next morning,
and Bob and Victoria took her to Sky Harbor for her flight
back to California. Peggy's replacement, Joy Claussen, arrived the same day. Joy was *Beginner's Luck's* third leading
lady in less than a week.

After Bob had dropped Joy's baggage off at her Casa
del Sol apartment on West Northern in Phoenix, he took
her to the phone company, got her a phone, and installed
it.

"Then the three of us, he and Victoria and I, went out to
the movies," said Joy.

The movie they chose was *An Unmarried Woman*. At
one point Victoria looked over at Bob in the flickering light.
"Bob began to cry," she said. "I had just never seen Bob

cry. He cried and cried 'cause the movie reminded him a
lot of his relationship with his wife. That was a very big
thing. He had been morbid about the breakup."

After the film Crane took the two women to dinner. "He
talked a little about his business dealings," Joy said afterward. "He talked about stocks, but only because I had just
bought my first stock before I came. I know he was building
a house in California. A new one for himself and his son
Bob Jr. He was happy. He regretted getting out of the marriage only because of Scotty, but I think he thought he was
doing the right thing."

Crane drove them home, and Victoria and Joy talked for
a while. Later Bob dropped by with a TV for Joy and asked
if there was anything he could do to make sure she was
comfortable. "Bob was a very nice man," Joy said, "and he
never pushed anything of his whatever on anyone. He was
very open and liked to joke and kid about his social life,
and that's how I found out the little I do know. . . . Bob
liked women, but in my opinion I don't think he respected
them."

One night onstage Crane gazed out into the audience and
nudged Joy. "Did you see her?" he said. "Did you see that
big-titted whore out there?" Joy knew that Bob was especially partial to women with large breasts, and he had been
pointing out the date he had brought to the show.

"I know that Bob respected me as a lady," said Joy, "and
he was always very sweet with me, but a man to me does
not have to keep re-proving his sexuality that often, and I
don't think that he could respect himself that much if has
to keep going out and on, and on, and on.

"He would meet ladies in a coffee shop or he picked up
waitresses and then would bring them to see the show. Bob
had a big ego. He liked being Bob Crane. He liked people
to recognize him, and he liked to give people his autograph.
It was important to him on these levels to be approved, to
be loved."

Joy considered herself a "very old-fashioned lady." She
knew all about Crane's love of swinging and felt he was
headed for trouble. "When you go out like he did," she said
later, "you put yourself in positions where there are very

sick scenes. When you are that open sexually, you are that nondiscriminative in the way you pick people, you are liable to find some sick people. The people he chose to socialize with, or swing with, or have his sexual aberrations with—that is not *my* scene."

Tuesday evening, June 13, Bob took a woman out to supper, and before the meal was finished she jumped up, pushed back her chair, threw down her napkin, and snapped at some remark Crane had made. "Don't touch me!" she said. "I'm leaving right now!"

"Easy come, easy go," said Crane, who then drove by the Registry and obtained Julie's phone number and made a date to have breakfast at the Safari after she got off work. This time he made sure he had Scotch so she could have a drink if she wanted one.

When Julie entered Bob's apartment she noticed that the only item on the coffee table was a large photo album with a white cover. It was filled with sexually explicit photographs of Crane's lovers. As Bob showed them to Julie he explained where the girls were from and what sex acts they had performed together. He requested that Julie not tell Brenda that he had showed her the photos or that she had come to his apartment a second time. Julie thought it was because he thought Brenda might be jealous.

Walking in a circle, Bob took pictures of Julie while she was watching a videotape that had an episode of *Hogan's Heroes* on it. Crane pointed at the screen and said proudly, "That's me." His obvious pleasure at distant triumphs made Julie sad.

Bob put himself in the videotape. He was wearing only a shirt. Like a director, he had Julie enter the frame, sit down next to him, and take off her clothes. They began to have sex, but toward the end of the tape Bob can be seen getting up and turning off the lights. Automatically the film stopped.

Julie and Bob went into the master bedroom, where they had sex again. Bob washed scrupulously after sex the first time, but after the second time he did not. Julie dressed to leave. She thought it was odd that both times that she had been at Bob's the phone never rang and no one came to the door. Stepping out into the hot night air, she heard Bob lock the door behind her.

Her theory was that Bob felt he was going downhill and that he had to have a lot of women to make him feel important. At no time in her presence had he spoken of any family, and Julie was not certain whether he was married or not.

Later Brenda did learn of Julie's visit to Bob's and that she had seen the photo album. As Crane had predicted, she was angry. "She's lied to me before! She knew I'd get jealous 'cause she's always sneaking around behind my back. I'd introduce her to somebody, and the next thing I know she's going over to their place all the time. I'm not jealous, but I don't like the idea of her not telling me about it," Brenda said.

Thursday, June 15, Julie Smith, a waitress at the Safari, saw Julie, Bob, and another waitress from the Registry come in for breakfast at 1:30 A.M. It seemed to Smith that Bob and Julie were having some sort of disagreement. Julie was so upset that while she sat at a booth with Crane, she didn't speak. The three left, and an hour later Crane was back by himself. He slid into the same booth and sat quietly at the back of the restaurant, sipping a grapefruit juice— the loneliest man one could imagine.

Edith "Kippy" Lewis had heard that Bob Crane was back in Scottsdale doing a show and was excited at the prospect of seeing him again. Kippy was an old friend of Patti and Bob's. She had left a message on Tuesday for Bob to contact her at the French Connection Massage Parlor on Gilbert. Kippy had met Crane and his wife at a nightclub in Santa Monica six years before. A year later she had moved to Phoenix.

Crane's elder son, Bob Jr., knew Kippy. "I was in Hawaii with my father," he recalled, "and Kippy worked at a discotheque in the basement of the Sheraton Waikiki, where we were staying. She's dark-skinned, I think Hawaiian or Polynesian."

Crane called Kippy back, and at 3:00 A.M. she and her friend Linda "Burgandy" Budwit arrived at the Safari. Kippy and Crane embraced, and as the trio ate breakfast they talked about Bob's divorce.

"Patti asked about you two weeks ago on the phone," Bob told her. Now the actor was in high spirits, telling jokes and talking nonstop for the hour and a half they were there. Crane mentioned a girl with a light complexion and bright red hair who kept calling and bothering him.

Crane had also spoken of this woman to Chris Roberts. "She was a gal he had picked up several years ago when he was on tour through Phoenix," Roberts said. "They used to party a lot. He picked her up and the lady took him to a gay bar for women. Then she picked up a lady at the bar and left him stranded there by himself. Because she was 'really nice,' he wasn't too upset over the situation. She was quite a relief to him in the run of the play, and he had seen her a couple of times since he'd been in town this time."

"She's no more healthy than she was several years ago, psychologically," Bob told Kippy. "I talked to her on the phone, and we were supposed to get together one night, but she canceled out because of business she had to take care of. I asked her what business that was, and she said, 'I can't tell you.' I was kinda glad I wasn't going out with her, because I had bad vibes about her. Based on my knowledge and previous experience with the lady, I think her business might have been Mafia or underworld dealings. Besides, I decided she was a sickie and I didn't want to see her anymore.

"She knows you, Kippy," said Bob. "Come on over to the apartment. I'll show you a picture of her."

Kippy and Burgandy followed Crane to his apartment. It was now 4:30 A.M. At the Winfield Kippy didn't recognize the pictures that Bob showed her. Then he got out a photo album that contained more nude pictures of women. Neither woman recognized anyone in any of the pictures. Bob suggested that he take some photos of them.

"I was onto his scam," Kippy said later. "He had perfected a routine—he would begin by taking photographs of a girl, get the girl to shed her top clothing first, take some more photos, then the rest of her clothing would come off, then the next thing you know Bob would be involved in sexual intercourse with the girl. Not me. I didn't feel like giving anything out for free."

Crane began taking Polaroid shots of the two women, and then had Kippy take snaps of him and Burgandy and had Burgandy take photos of Kippy and him. The entire time the videotape camera recorded Bob taking photos of the women, who were kissing and hugging each other. "Kippy," he said aloud on the sound track, "Burgandy." Pointing to a girl in the album, he said, "I made it with Barbara." Gesturing toward another Polaroid, he said, "I ran into this girl while waiting for you to come."

Of the dozen photos taken Crane gave only one to Burgandy. "You seem to be having a good time," said Kippy, "but I want to go home. I'm tired."

As Kippy and Burgandy were getting ready to leave, Bob said, "Come again. Call between six-thirty and seven-thirty in the evening. I'm always home just before going to the show."

The women left in a hurry, but not before Burgandy made plans to contact Crane again to get free tickets to *Beginner's Luck*.

No conversation with Bob went for very long before the subject of his divorce came up. On Friday, June 16, just before Father's Day, Crane got a call from his seven-year-old son, Scotty.

"Daddy, come over for a swim," said Scotty.

"But Scotty, honey, you know I'm in Phoenix."

"Well, so am I."

Patti got on the line and said, "We're staying in a hotel. I booked us into the Camelback Inn."

"Well," said Bob, "this is silly. Come on over."

Crane took Patti and Scotty to dinner at Bobby McGee's. A waitress took their order of ribs and soft drinks. She

noticed that no one seemed very happy. At meal's end Bob
paid for the dinner with his American Express card, and
they left.

According to Crane later, Patti virtually forced him to
ask them to stay over with him that night. Bob was furious
because Patti had brought Scotty with her, and when he
came into the Windmill, he told Victoria how unhappy he
was.

"I'm a nervous wreck," he whispered just before they
went on stage. "I'm taking her back to the airport. I've got
someone coming in, and I don't want her to stay. I don't
like being surprised like this."

"Will you go back?" asked Victoria.

"No."

"I bet you do. I bet you do."

"I said *no*! I definitely don't want to ever go back."

"It's such a dumb thing to do, you know, just drop in
with your son when you're supposed to be separated," said
Victoria, "and use your son to call up." Victoria had noticed
how in Scottsdale Bob had seemed to be finding a sense of
calm and was starting to enjoy life once more. But now . . .

"She's driving me crazy," he said, "and I mean crazy.
She's crazy. She's insane!"

"Even little Scotty was under psychiatric treatment because their marriage was affecting him," Victoria said later.
"Bob told me a lot of things that were just unbelievable
between two people—fighting, incredible things, but then
that's not for me to say one way or the other.

"Patti has been a source of personal pain for Bob for an
extended period of time. He told me Patti is very distressed
and confused over their split. Bob told me their fights before the divorce action were of a violent nature."

Patti told Bob she had a boyfriend in Phoenix and that's
why she was there. But it was a fabrication to get a reaction
out of him. That night they had a terrible fight, and Crane
stormed out. It hurt him that Scotty was caught in the middle. At the Bombay Club and then again at B. B. Singer's
at 1:30 P.M., Crane was seen talking to a woman in her
mid-forties with red hair, but then he went home.

Bob Crane, Jr., thought the events of the last months

proved that his father was not going to reconcile with his stepmother. "The end is in sight," he said. "My dad and Patti are not going to get back together. They may get together sexually occasionally, but my dad, in the last couple of months, was a new guy—optimistic, new directions, he just didn't want to be part of that whole kind of slavery trip that he had been into in terms of her running the boat. This is kind of hard for her to accept."

Ronni Richards, one of Bob's closest friends and a former actress in *Beginner's Luck*, knew Patti. "Of course," she said later, "I'm not a psychiatrist, but Patti is really emotionally unstable, very disturbed. She's caused a lot of grief and a lot of pain for Bob. Bob has never struck anybody. But she struck him. I think it was in Florida. She threw something at his lip. He had to have stitches, it was so blown up. She was the one really doing all the stuff that she accused Bob of."

It was apparent to everyone that Bob was trying to start his life over—a new house with his son, a search for a lasting love, and a sense of commitment to someone.

Saturday morning Bob left the apartment early to buy cereal for Scotty's breakfast. By 5:00 P.M. he was driving Patti and his son to Sky Harbor. He walked them to the American Airlines counter to check in for flight number 561 to Los Angeles. After they left, Bob hung around the terminal for an hour. He was meeting a visitor from California—tall, twenty-three years old, Finnish, with shoulder-length blond hair: Liisa Kaponen.

At that night's performance Liisa was seated at the VIP table, and after the show she was joined by Chris Roberts and his neighbor, Rose Lange, nicknamed Terry.* They all went out to Bogart's, where Crane, still rocky from Patti's visit, uncharacteristically had two screwdrivers. Crane found himself enormously attracted to Terry.

It turned out that both Terry and Liisa spoke Finnish. Liisa asked Terry for her home address and phone number, promising to bring back a wooden spoon for her from Fin-

---

*This name has been changed.

land, where she was going on her vacation. Crane secretly asked Liisa to get Terry's number for him. As for Terry, she was amused by how completely unimpressed Liisa was with Crane's star status.

"I really like Terry," Crane whispered to Chris on the way out. "She's simple and easygoing."

"Terry's been sick for quite some time, and now she's unemployed," Roberts said. Chris himself would have liked to be her boyfriend, but the one time he'd tried to kiss her he had been rebuffed.

"Yeah," said Bob, "but I really like her company. I'd like to see her again."

Crane saw Liisa off the next morning and then went rafting on the Verde River with some waitresses from the Bombay Club.

On Wednesday, June 21, Bob asked a date to his play. After the show he was in the lobby signing autographs when a woman with long brown hair, "quite drunk," Chris Roberts recalled, tried to interest him in her portfolio. She was a club singer named Kathy Reid;* Crane had met her on a local radio show. Although she had been an entertainer for many years, she was only twenty-five. Crane drew her aside. "You should have told me you were coming," he hissed, "because I've got a date. Call me sometime later. I'll see your portfolio then."

At 1:00 A.M., Thursday, June 22, Bob's date drove him to the airport for a trip back to Los Angeles to attend his youngest daughter's high school graduation. There would be no performance of *Beginner's Luck* today. In the short time Bob had been with his date he had spoken "sorrowfully of his son and bitterly of the impending divorce."

Thursday afternoon, Chuck Sloan, Bob Jr.'s stepfather, sat next to Crane as they watched Karen graduate. "He just made loose conversation," remembered Sloan. "He told me that he was attempting to make as much money as he could during the year. He wanted to take at least the rest of the year off because of the home that he had bought for himself

---

*This name has been changed.

and his son. He said that his eyes had just opened up and he had seen many bright things. That was what he said, almost word for word. He indicated no problems."

Friday, June 23, Bob left Los Angeles at 2:35 P.M. on Western Airlines and by 3:40 P.M. was back in Phoenix. Chris and Terry picked him up. Bob took them to Friday's Restaurant for lunch and afterward dropped Chris off at the Windmill so he could use Roberts's car to drive Terry to her place, where he could be alone with her. At Terry's Bob stayed for an hour chatting and then left to get ready for his performance.

Crane's date that night was escorted to her seat by the stage assistant, George. She was astonished to find that the theater was only half-full. "How could they be making any money?" she wondered.

Over steak at Bogart's Crane spoke of his brother, Al, who had been hospitalized at the VA Hospital in Phoenix in 1977 but since January had been living with Bob's mother. They did not visit often, and "both pretty much stayed away from each other." Then for the next hour he complained of Patti's surprise visit.

After dinner Bob took her back to the Sunburst, where she had left her car. "Come on back to my apartment," he pleaded, "and see the Father's Day gift my son Scotty gave me."

Once inside Crane locked the dead bolt and the knob. The bed in the master bedroom was unmade, and his date could see brown print sheets hanging over the side. Against the drapes in the living room sat a videotape machine, a camera, and a TV. Bob made a pass at her.

"I'm chicken, and I don't do that kind of thing," she said.

She left the apartment at 1:50 A.M., and alone again, Crane called Terry, who was asleep.

"Can I come over?" he asked. Terry said yes, and Bob drove over and spent the night with her.

On Saturday, June 24, Lloyd Vaughn, Bob's business manager and attorney, sent Linda Sabattasse from his firm to have Bob sign the papers for his new house. Crane put her up at the Sunburst Motel, gave her tickets to that night's performance, and signed the papers there. He had just returned from his Saturday performance when the phone rang.

"Can I meet with you?" asked Kathy Reid, who sounded drunk. She and her friends had spent the evening at the Polo Lounge.

"Okay," said Bob. "Meet me at the Safari Hotel Coffee Shop at eleven."

Later Kathy and Bob drove back to his place for some coffee because Kathy felt she was still "quite intoxicated" and thought it would be a good opportunity to show Crane her portfolio and get some advice on furthering her career. The door was double-locked behind her as they entered, and soon Bob was taking Polaroid photos of her in the nude. After seven shots he took the photographs into the bedroom and put them in a drawer. Then he came back and, as Kathy later said, "began to make love to me. That portion of the visit wasn't planned."

Kathy and Bob left the apartment at the same time. He locked the door carefully, escorted her to the car, and left for an interview show on KOOL Radio at 1:00 A.M. Kathy listened to him on her way home.

4
JOHN

Cut to dissolve—End of scene, fade image out, new image fades in.

On Sunday, June 25, 1978, Bob picked up his longtime and close friend, John Henry Carpenter, who arrived from Los Angeles at 6:00 P.M. Over the years that Bob had known John, the "state-of-the-art video troubleshooter and salesman" had changed little physically. The straight thin mouth, brown eyes, strong nose, and iodine complexion remained the same, as had the pitted face. These days John was wearing glasses, his straight black hair worn with a feathered effect, parted on the side and to collar length. Victoria had described it as "a mane of black hair that almost looks like a wig." There was a gold bracelet on his wrist, and he had just received a watch for a birthday present. John had turned fifty the day before.

At five feet eight inches and 165 pounds, Carpenter was heavy around the middle, a fact emphasized by his wide belt and oversized buckle. He was depicted by Crane's friends as everything from chubby to well built. Although John was often taken for Mexican or Italian, he was actually three-quarters Native American. His mother, Molly, was Iroquois, and his father, Henry, was of Spanish and Native American descent. His father left the home in 1936, when John was only eight, and after that the boy saw him only once more, in 1950.

Before he had reached his teens, John was sent to the Morongo Reservation in Banning, California, to study. It was an unpleasant experience and he picked apricots after school. Married at the age of eighteen, John fathered a son, but by 1952, after he had completed his tour of duty in Korea as a tank commander, the marriage had failed. Fortunately, three years later, he met seventeen-year-old Diana Tootikian in a Los Angeles bar and they were married in Las Vegas in December of 1955.

Carpenter's career in electronics began with Hoffman Easy-Vision, a television set manufacturer, and from there he moved to Lear Aviation where he installed radios in planes. Eventually he went to Hughes Aircraft where he found time at night to play a roller-derby bad guy on television so convincingly that he was burned in effigy in L.A., his place of birth. Later he toured Japan with the New York Chiefs.

In 1965, about the time that John and Diana began a thirteen-year separation, Carpenter answered a newspaper ad and found himself working as a regional service manager for Sony and learning complex new technology. Within a short time Carpenter was teaching such luminaries as Alfred Hitchcock, Red Skelton, and Elvis Presley how to use a VCR, and so by the time he met Bob Crane he was accustomed to being around stars.

In his present position as national service manager for AKAI Equipment Limited in Compton, California, Carpenter was allowed a great deal of latitude in his job, and this enabled him to travel, juggle his hours, and spend time with Bob. Crane, with the overabundance of women in his life, was in the habit of sharing the extra females with John and, as an added inducement (as if being the closest friend of a

popular star wasn't enough), he would introduce Carpenter
as his manager. This rarely failed to excite interest in John,
especially among aspiring actresses. For this reason Carpenter would later characterize Crane as "the goose who
laid the golden egg for me, in terms of meeting ladies."

His various relationships and hopes of a new and more
fulfilling love affair were always on Bob's mind, even
though he was openly anxious about reprisals from jealous
husbands or boyfriends. In an interview for a singles magazine conducted by John Carpenter, Crane had expressed a
wish that all single people be compelled to carry identification that would verify that they weren't married "so you
don't wake up someday and find a gun to your head because you didn't hear footsteps." At one point an ex-
boyfriend of one of Bob's lovers taped a mutilated photo
of Crane to her back door.

Crane had once showed actor Richard Dawson hundreds
of pornographic Polaroids—most showing young women
performing fellatio on Bob—that were strewn around in the
rear of his auto. Carpenter would later claim that Crane had
gone as far as having his penis surgically enhanced with
implants so that he would come across as more photogenic
on the homemade porno tapes he made. By any account, it
was obvious that Crane was still obsessed with his hobby
of visually recording his sexual exploits.

On the way back from the airport Crane passed John a
white photograph album filled with pictures of nude
women. "Look what I got here. Look who I've had." He
laughed. "Look at this one. Look at that one!"

Carpenter was booked into the Sunburst Motel, which
was conveniently only a half block from Crane's own place.
Later they went to Bogart's and, after an uneventful evening, retired to their rooms. Carpenter rented a new car
from the Sunburst, but it was not as if he would have much
chance to use it. When you were with Bob Crane you got
driven just about everywhere.

The next morning, Monday, June 26, Bob and John went
swimming and then came inside to watch Crane's video-

tapes. Just then the phone rang. It was Kathy, still concerned about promoting her career. "I just want to bring over a vocal tape," she said. Of all the women whom Bob had been intimate with in Phoenix, she was the only one who was significantly involved with another person. Crane knew her boyfriend worked nights. Kathy insisted on bringing the tape at night.

"You know," he said to John, "this is bananas. She could bring it over in the daytime just as easily as she could bring it over at night."

"She was a vocalist," Carpenter said later, "and she had left an eight-by-ten glossy of herself, with her name and, I guess, her credits and her height and everything. He had already balled her once, and I guess he didn't want to hit on her again, for I don't know what reason."

Crane crossed the room and took down a tape. He skipped forward past shows, commercials, and the *Saturday Night Live* show for June 24, until he came to the setting for 538 through 720—his sexual encounter with Kathy. John watched as it ran. "Bob balling her. Her balling Bob 'cause Bob was sitting down," John said later. "And she was sitting on top of him."

"Oh, man," said Crane, "did she hurt me! Oh, man."

"Why?" said Carpenter.

"Because the cheeks of her ass were right there on my legs, and as she really got rotating it got just a little raw. God! I almost lost my hard-on."

"Yeah," said John, "you can see it on the tape."

Because it was Monday the Windmill was empty, and Bob, John, and Victoria took advantage of this to shoot Crane's third video of Victoria's performance. Back at the apartment, as they watched it, Victoria realized that the sound track was muddy, and Bob offered to help her redub it.

After they ate Bob disappeared for the rest of the afternoon, and when he returned Victoria confronted him. "Where were you? You had lunch and then you went."

"I was with Terry," Crane explained, "lying down. I nearly fell asleep on the bed. I really like her. I wish I could help her."

This was so typical of Bob, Victoria thought. He wanted to help every wounded little bird. "I really like the girl," Bob repeated. "I really feel sorry for her, and I'd be happy just seeing her one to one."

Victoria had never heard Bob say anything like this before. He had a different girl every night, and it was unusual for him to comment on a woman more than once. She figured he was actually trying to get his life together.

At four Chris Roberts was hosting a barbecue, and Victoria urged Bob to come. It was a quiet get-together of about thirty-five people. "It wasn't really a cast party," said Victoria. "Chris was throwing a party 'cause he was new at the theater and he wanted everyone to know each other."

Joy and Victoria got to the party about five, and forty-five minutes later Bob and John showed up. Joy finally got to meet Carpenter. She could tell John knew the Hollywood scene intimately and was acquainted with a variety of stars, including the cast of *Hogan's Heroes*. She gathered his profession had something to do with tape recorders and that he was fairly well-to-do because he talked so much about his cars and jewelry.

Bob and John left the party three times, once to go to a movie, but were back at 8:30 P.M. and stayed for the remainder of the evening, chatting with friends. Victoria saw that Bob and Terry were together for most of the evening.

Victoria and Bob posed for pictures on the couch as they ate, then he and Terry disappeared together and reappeared. By the time Joy and Victoria headed homeward, Bob had gone off with Terry again.

Tuesday, June 27, at 10:00 A.M., John Carpenter dropped in unannounced on Frank Grabiec and Ralph Tirrell, co-owners of Dyna-Tronics, an electronic equipment store. Although Tirrell had never met John before, Grabiec had known him for seventeen years.

Carpenter was thoroughly professional at his job, Grabiec knew. Whenever there was a factory warranty problem, Carpenter made "an immediate and proper decision." For the last ten years Grabiec's sole contact with Carpenter had been over the phone regarding their warranty repair work.

John wanted to look over the shop, check the books, and see if there were any problems he could help with. Service manager John Ayers showed him around the area where the equipment was repaired, and they discussed warranty problems and different types of equipment.

"I talked to him," said Carpenter, "about problems—service problems, national problems, and he asked me to be guest speaker at one of his outings." John, however, kept turning the topic of conversation to pornographic movies on videotape. He said he had a complete library of porno films at his California home.

Grabiec and Tirrell asked Carpenter to have lunch with them, but he declined. "I've got an appointment in the east end of the valley in the afternoon. Let's take a rain check." They decided to postpone lunch until the next day. John left at twelve-thirty, and he and Bob "goofed around for most of the day, running several personal errands."

Just before 3:00 P.M. Crane, clad in a beige denim shirt jacket and denim slacks, was on his way to get his photo taken. He and John strolled up Scottsdale's Fifth Avenue, admiring the boutiques, the kachina dolls, turquoise jewelry, Remington sculpture, and Indian rugs. First they turned in at Video World.

"Aren't you the actor that played on *Hogan's Heroes*?" asked Dorothy Lawson, the manager.

"Yes, yes, I am." Bob, who loved to be recognized, beamed. "We're looking for a videotape player." From their conversation it was obvious to Dorothy that the two men knew all about the equipment and how to operate it. Crane wanted a rental, but the $65 price was too steep.

Both Bob and John were in a playful mood and at 3:30 P.M. laughed their way through a portrait session at Ron Christopher's photography studio on Fifth Avenue. Most of the jokes were about women.

Back at the apartment Bob mentioned Julie to John for the first time. "He was telling me about a chick," Carpenter said later, "because I'd seen all the ones giving 'im head in his Polaroid book." John asked Bob, "Which one is Julie?"

"The one in the book," said Crane. "Go take a look at it."

"Where?"

"In the bedroom in the top left-hand drawer."

Carpenter opened the drawer, moved aside a pair of black socks, and uncovered the white album. "Which girl?" he asked.

Crane showed him, and Carpenter replaced the book in the same spot. It was the last time anyone would recall seeing the Polaroid book. In the late afternoon Bob rang up Julie and asked, "Would you like to go out with me and my manager? Do you want two guys?"

"No," Julie said firmly, and then with sarcasm, "You'll have to pay for any sex."

"Now I can't do that. I can't pay for sex. It would cause problems with my career."

Crane called his son next. Bob Jr. was in their L.A. house, in the midst of transcribing an interview he had conducted with Chevy Chase the day before for a magazine. "Happy birthday, son," said Crane. Father and son talked, and Bob concluded by telling him, "I'm with John."

Next Crane dialed blond-haired Carolyn Jean Baare, a waitress at the Golden Bell Restaurant in the town of Rawhide, near Scottsdale. He had met her through his hairstylist at B. B. Singer's. Bob wanted Carolyn to ask a friend to come as a date for Carpenter so they could double after the performance of *Beginner's Luck* that night.

Crane seemed unconcerned that the Windmill was only a half to one-third filled on some nights and that there were plans to cut short the run of *Luck*. He was happy he had met Terry and just as happy that he could return to Texas and the swinging parties he had so recently left.

After the show, Carolyn, Carolyn's friend Roberta Plunkett, Crane, and Carpenter went over to the Registry. Over dinner Carpenter joked, "I'm an Indian and if I ever went broke, I could always go back to the reservation and pick apricots."

Carpenter was displeased with his date, and he and Bob decided to leave the club under the guise that all were going home for the night. Crane planned on meeting Carolyn later. Plunkett and Baare left in Roberta's car, and the two men drove in Bob's car to Bobby McGee's.

It was 11:00 P.M., and the place was almost empty. Jack-Scott Lindsay, one of the two bartenders in the well, took Crane's order for a screwdriver and a grapefruit juice. Jack knew immediately who Bob was. Carpenter stood alone in the shadows some distance from the bar, and when Crane took the drinks to him they sat down.

Linda Robertson, a waitress at McGee's, noticed the two men enter. If business hadn't been so slow, she would not have paid the attention to them that she did. Dressed in her Daisy Mae costume, she waited on them. "Hi," she purred, "I'm Daisy Mae. I'll be your cocktail waitress this evening. How are you doing?"

They were very short with her, not a smile or anything. Usually I get at least a hello, she thought. They obviously didn't want to be bothered.

Robertson didn't recognize the former star of *Hogan's Heroes*, because her attention was captured by the striking appearance of Bob's friend. "He had dark hair," she said later, "real black, and it was parted on the side, and he had glasses on. He was pretty well built. He had on a black shirt and black leisure suit. He looked Indian to me."

She got Carpenter a plain ginger ale, collected for it, and went back over to the bar. Jack-Scott Lindsay told her whom she was waiting on. "So I glanced back over there," she said, "and indeed it was him. When they first came in they were tense toward each other. Tense is a good word 'cause it wasn't a loud fight. It was nothing that other people noticed. I noticed it because business was slow. It was something to do. You kind of notice how people are reacting toward each other.

"The Indian gentleman was sitting in the chair and Bob Crane was sitting against the wall." Because lounge cushions are soft, Linda knew how tempting it was to lie back against the cushions and just drink. Crane crossed his arms and leaned forward very close to his friend while he spoke. Carpenter had his legs crossed, and most of the time he was looking away from Crane over the back of his chair.

"It was not a relaxed conversation," recalled Linda. "It

was kind of a strained movement, and the voices got louder. I studied speech in school, so you can tell if it's relaxed. It's more smooth and soft, instead of abrupt. Without hearing the words I knew this was a tense conversation by the facial expressions and body language."

Linda could tell they were trying to keep the volume down. "When I went back to make sure the drinks were okay, I kind of heard they were discussing something pretty harshly. Not a fight, mind you, but not normal talk about their day."

"Do you want another drink?" she asked.

"No. We don't care for anything else."

Linda decided not to go back to the table again, but at McGee's the waitresses are required to walk their stations often. As Linda routinely swung by in her orbit she heard the tense discussion escalate. After fifteen minutes Crane got up and left. Carpenter kept checking the door, and after some time he turned around completely so he could keep a watchful eye on who was coming in and going out.

At 11:35 Bob came back with Carolyn, who had successfully ditched her friend. Crane had his arm around her and they sat down close to each other, whispering. Linda could tell that Crane no longer had that "tense and abrupt" look on his face. "Mr. Crane didn't say another word to this other man," she recalled, "and he just sat there and looked like he was kind of upset."

"Did you dance?" Crane asked John finally.

"No."

"Did you score?"

"No," replied Carpenter. "Everyone here is in cliques or is not very sociable."

Linda noticed that Carpenter seemed to be "pouting" as he ordered a Coke. It's because he hasn't made any contacts at Bobby McGee's, she thought. She brought the soft drink and noticed that Bob and Carolyn were still not talking to Carpenter. Soon she saw Bob and Carolyn leaving together, John trailing along silently behind them.

The trio stopped at B. B. Singer's and had breakfast. They left at 2:30 A.M. and headed for the Winfield parking lot, where Crane dropped Carpenter off so he could pick up his rental car. Then he took Carolyn home. At 5:00 A.M. waitresses at the Safari saw the familiar sight of Bob Crane sitting alone in a booth.

On Wednesday, June 28, Crane picked up a pair of glasses he had forgotten at a girlfriend's house, and then at 10:00 A.M. John called and the two men went to another photo shoot. Carpenter was on the lookout for a sunscreen for his automobile because they were unavailable in Los Angeles (sunscreens were outlawed in California at the time). The friends stopped by Western Auto Supply with no luck, so John got on the phone to find some alternatives.

By then it was time for their lunch with the owners of Dyna-Tronics. Carpenter had told them that he was bringing a movie star, and they were excited. Lunch was at Little Gregory's just down the street from the video store. "Of course," Carpenter said later, "the place went bananas when Bob came in. He was signing autographs, and he promised several waitresses pictures when he came back."

Grabiec got the feeling that John and Bob were very close, but the continual discussion of pornography grated on him. The remainder of the conversation between Crane and his pal concerned females they might date in Phoenix. Both men, it was apparent, felt that they had not been doing well, had been "striking out," and they were "a little bit upset" with that.

John explained that whenever Bob would go to different cities he would follow him if he had accounts for his AKAI Corporation warranty repair work. "This way," John explained, "I can be with my friend, make a few business calls, and charge the entire visit off to the company. Business with a little pleasure. Bob gets off work at ten-thirty at night, and of course my duties are all completed during the day."

Crane wanted to borrow a videotape recorder from Dyna-Tronics until Friday. He had an old-fashioned reel-to-reel tape recorder of his son's, and he wanted to take all the tapes he had and put them on the Betamax to edit. He needed two pieces of equipment so that the tape could go through one, be edited, and then get played back into the other. Grabiec loaned him a Sony SL-8200.

After they got back to the apartment Carpenter renewed his quest for a sunscreen, and while he was gone Crane incorporated the SL-8200 into his video system, getting the hang of the complicated equipment.

In Advance Auto Supply Carpenter bought a twenty-six-inch by six-foot sunscreen for the rear window of his Lotus back in Los Angeles and paid for it with his Mastercharge. "I came back and stuck around the house and did absolutely nothing, I guess, the rest of the day," John recalled. "I went swimming."

The neighbors at the Winfield observed John acting manically in the pool. One woman resident said, "He was doing strange things, giving karate chops to the water, acting very odd."

The woman was in the pool with John and he came on to her. Carpenter explained to her that he was a karate person. "I have to take karate because of this temper of mine that just goes beserk. I get tunnel vision," he said, "so my therapy is to take karate lessons and my instructor told me to always aim at a target beyond where you want to strike." As he was telling her all this John was demonstrating how to do the chops in the water.

When John was through swimming he dropped his wet trunks by the couch on the floor of Crane's apartment near the master bedroom door. He planned to pick them up later, along with Bob Jr.'s tape machine and a tape of *Saturday Night Fever* Bob was editing for Scotty to take back to California early the next morning. Bob had written in the appointment book by his bed: "John Leaves 10:00 A.M. Continental."

There was activity on the balcony of the level above Bob's apartment, where a new family was getting ready to move into 225A at about the time Carpenter would be leaving the next day.

Bob himself had gone over to Terry's. Once in her bedroom he quickly stripped and had Terry perform oral sex on him. After orgasm he lay down on the bed on his right side, hands curled up around his face, and went to sleep.

Bob slept in his undershorts as a rule, unless he had engaged in sexual intercourse; then he always slept nude. Terry noticed that he was a very light sleeper and woke easily whenever she moved in bed or got on or off the mattress. And he sat bolt upright at the slightest noise, she discovered when she opened the bedroom door.

When Bob and his son had shared a two-bedroom apartment, Bob Jr. learned how light a sleeper his father was. If he awoke first and opened the front door to get the newspaper, the mere sliding of the dead bolt would be enough to instantly awaken Bob.

"I woke him on occasion in our apartment," Bob Jr. said later. "I would walk into the bedroom for whatever reason. Generally, he'd be in his undershorts on his side. I would wake him up before even saying something to him. He would immediately jump up and go, 'Wup!' like that. I'd go, 'Dad, this is me.' "

Crane could program himself to wake up at a certain time and be alert; he needed very little sleep and was never difficult to wake up. "He was the kind of person who could capture ten, fifteen, twenty minutes, thirty minutes of sleep and be almost rejuvenated," Bob Jr. said.

Though Crane was a "pretty wide-open person," the doors in his apartments were always locked and the dead bolts thrown even when Bob was home and awake. As far as letting a stranger into his rooms late at night, Crane was "slightly sexist," his son admitted. "Let's put it this way," he said. "If he heard a female's voice on the other side of the door, he would tend to open it up without knowing the name, even at two, three, four in the morning."

Two hours later, when he awoke, Bob had intercourse with Terry again and then put on his clothing and left. Terry said later, "Bob appeared preoccupied, not as happy as he usually was. He didn't say what, if anything, was wrong, and I didn't inquire." One odd comment he had made to her was "John is not as popular as I am."

It was now 5:30 P.M. and while Bob had been gone, actress Ronni Richards, who had played Victoria's part previously on tour, had called him from New York. John answered, but Ronni wasn't surprised.

"Everywhere we've ever gone," she said afterward, "if there was a two-bedroom apartment, John always stayed with Bob. Always. I'd say every time since I've been doing the show that I can remember, he always came down. To Florida, to Dallas, where we played before, to Houston, to New Orleans. Every place.

"They'd known each other a long time because of Bob's videotape equipment. John would come over and fix it, I guess for nothing, and that's why Bob let him stay with him on the road for a week or two or whatever. They really didn't socialize, but they did fool around together with women. They always picked up girls together, but let me tell you something, Bob was straight. Bob was no way bi— at all, but John Carpenter was. I know because Bob told me and because John would boast about certain men and women he was involved with. As far as I know, John never made a pass at Bob, and Bob wouldn't have taken it anyway. He was just into girls.

"I asked for Bob, and John said, 'He's out.' I said, 'How you doing?' and he said, 'Fine,' and I asked, 'How's the show?' and he said, 'Great,' and that was about it. I said, 'Tell Bob I called. Have him call me tonight.' "

Crane was running late all day, and after he drove himself and John to the Windmill he complained to everyone that he was feeling tired. The cast could tell something was bothering him.

Onstage Schultz noticed Bob's performance was subdued, his energy down. "I would assume," he said, "it was because he was tired. Normally he's very energetic, very strong onstage, but he was a little done in. It probably wasn't noticeable to the audience, but it was to us in the cast."

Bob's passive and lackadaisical demeanor forced Joy Claussen to exhaust herself, carrying the weight of the scenes between them. As the cast went out for their curtain calls, Crane leaned over and whispered to Joy, "Boy, I sure was tired tonight. Were you, Joy?"

"I'm tired *now!*" said Claussen.

During the play, John sat alone at the VIP table until Victoria joined him after her short part. Bob usually told her of his plans, but this evening he had not done so.

At 10:10 Bob went to the front of the theater to sign autographs. At 10:26 everyone left the Windmill quickly. Bob and John headed for the Monte Carlo; the two actresses and Schultz went for drinks, as was their custom.

Bob and John arrived at the car a full ten minutes later than usual, and because of the flat tire it was not until after eleven when they got back to Bob's apartment. Crane said, "I'm going to call Patti," went into the master bedroom, and closed the door. At 11:06 Crane dialed her on Bainbridge Island in Washington State, where she and their son, Scotty, were on vacation. Recently Patti's cats had been sick, and Bob asked about that.

Meanwhile Carpenter waited alone in the living room, watching television. "Their conversation went on for about two or three minutes," John said later, "rather a monotone. Then all of a sudden there was a big argument, a huge argument, over the telephone. Bob was yelling and yelling and yelling, very, very loudly. Yelling so loud that I walked up to the window to see if anybody was on the patio [who might overhear]. There were two people sitting on the chairs around the pool. I don't know who they were. I could just see the backs of their heads.

"So I didn't say anything to Bob. I went back and sat down, and a couple of minutes later I heard Bob say, 'Patti, Patti, if you don't stop this, I am going to hang up!' Wham! He hung up."

The heated twenty-minute call between Bob and Patti had grown so fierce and loud that the neighbors in the surrounding units could make out the conversation. The walls were thin at the Winfield Apartments. In apartment 232A, which was directly above Bob's, Carol Klarfeld had just gone to bed when she heard Bob Crane yelling.

"I thought it was over the phone because it was a one-sided conversation," she recalled, "and I turned to my husband and said, 'If he keeps screaming like that, he won't be able to perform in the show tomorrow.' A few seconds later I heard a loud bang, which I believed was the phone being slammed down." Her husband then remarked, "It's all over. You can go to bed now."

Still upset, Crane called Ronni and told her, "No way am I getting back with Patti. I just had a tremendous fight with her."

Ronni said, "I heard she was saying you were going to get back."

Bob said, "No way. I'm not in love with her."

Ronni began to cry. Her husband had recently died, and she had just had to sell their music business. "Listen, Ronni," Bob said consolingly, "don't worry. You're gonna be living with my son and myself in the new house we're buying. No way in the world am I gonna get back with Patti."

Crane came out of his bedroom and said, "Let's go find some music."

"Okay," said John. "Where will we go tonight?"

"Well, let's go to Bogie's. That's a good place to meet people." Carpenter agreed, and they drove to Bogart's in Crane's car.

Minutes later Patti called back, but the apartment was empty.

At Crane's favorite hangout, the two friends got a couple of seats up front and ordered a tomato juice and a screwdriver. Crane looked at his watch. He had promised to call Carolyn Baare around midnight. After the argument with his wife, he did not want to be alone.

It was 11:55 when Carolyn answered. "I'm at Bogie's," Crane said. "Come on over."

"They'll be closed by the time I get there," she said.

"Okay," said Bob, "then let's meet at the Safari. Okay? In forty-five minutes."

After the call, two customers, Carol Newell and her sister, Christy, introduced themselves to Bob, who was now signing autographs. Crane stopped and took Carol's hand.

(When Bob spoke to a woman he almost always took her hand, gazing deeply into her eyes and leaning into her from the waist down.) Just then he was interrupted by a tall woman in black and a short, middle-aged, balding man with hair fluffed out above his ears, who invited him to a Jacuzzi party.

"Bob and I looked at each other," said Carpenter, "and figured we didn't like the way the woman in black was trying to push Newell out of the way when Bob was holding on to her hand. It just wasn't kosher the way she came in. Bob was talking to Newell even when he was listening to this conversation about the Jacuzzi party. We said no—and that was about it." Bob had declined without breaking the flow of his conversation with Carol. "We should go," he said, "because I have to meet this other lady. Would you like to come along?"

Carol found it impossible to turn down a charming celebrity who was asking her to breakfast, so she passed her car keys to her sister and at 12:30 the three of them left for the Winfield, where Carpenter's rented white Chrysler Cordoba was parked. Then John and Carol followed Crane to the Safari.

It was now 1:00 A.M.

The day's heat had battered the desert into stunned silence, but now, with a yellow-tinted moon dancing in the sky, heat lightning flickered in the distance and the stars glowed with such intensity that they cast shadows from small rocks and shrubs. Animals stirred.

"Bob was sitting by himself when we came in," Carpenter said later, "facing the door on the left-hand side. We sat down next to him. Fifteen, twenty minutes later the lady shows up so that the four of us are now sitting there. We had breakfast." John remembered the conversation as being casual, with some joking and laughing.

But Carolyn Baare said afterward, "Bob was visibly upset, and he spoke of the problems he was having with his wife and their pending divorce. He said his wife was extremely distraught, anxious over the breakup, and that she was overly jealous of him and even his relationship with their children [her daughter, their own son, and Bob's three kids by a former marriage]." Discussion about Crane's problems dominated the night's conversation.

During his KOOL Radio interview Bob had lamented, "Since we stopped filming *Hogan's Heroes*, I don't think I've been in the right place at the right time."

When John mentioned the Winfield, Carolyn thought he was saying that the apartment was both his and Bob's, but then Carpenter said that he was staying at the Sunburst Motel nearby. "I've never seen the inside of it," said Carol.

"Ah-ha!" said Bob. "Here's a chance for you, John. Here's your chance." He got up. "Well, I'm going to take Carolyn home or take her to my place."

"Whatever," said John, and he got up and went out to his car.

Bob paid his bill of $7.51 with his charge card. Judy Merlin, the cashier, said, "I sure would like to see the show, but I won't be able to make it until after July third."

"Sorry," said Crane, "it'll be closed by then."

In the lobby a man stopped Bob for a few minutes; Crane seemed to know him. This man, Andrew Gellart, was surprised that Bob remembered him. "We'd only had a few chance meetings on the set of *Hogan's Heroes*," he said later. "Our relationship had been very limited." Gellart's brothers had worked as extras on the show, and he had moved to Scottsdale in 1973. Through the heavy glass Carolyn was unable to make out what Bob was saying.

Crane and his date soon caught up with John and Carol in the lot, and Bob called out, "See you soon."

"I figured that I had met somebody at last," Carpenter said later. The minute he got Carol in his room, he made a pass at her.

"I got to go, I got to go. I got to get up early in the morning," she said. Carpenter lay down on top of her while her back was against the bed, and kissed her. Carol thought to herself, "How am I going to get out of this?" She tried to sit up.

"Gee, it's only a quarter to two," said Carpenter.

"I really got to get going."

"Aw, come on."

"No, really and truly," said Carol.

Carpenter said, "I figured—so anyway, the pass-off. So I said okay because I wasn't going to push, because she was a nice lady, and what the heck." John dropped his date off at her home on 78th and Camelback at 2:30 A.M. and started back. It was a seven-minute drive.

Before he had dropped Carol off Carpenter had gotten her to promise that she'd awaken Crane between 8:00 and 11:00 A.M. "If she doesn't want me," he said later, "I thought, maybe she'll want Bob."

In the meantime, Crane and Carolyn had talked for twenty minutes, Bob wanting her to go to his apartment or he to hers. She declined both offers and drove away in her car at close to 2:30. Bob returned to the Winfield, parked, sauntered across the open lot to his door, unlocked it, and stood for a moment in the hot night air before entering. Silently the door swung shut behind him. He slid the dead bolt home.

Carpenter would be one of the last to speak with Bob Crane, and here in his own words is what happened after he left his friend.

"Drove back to my place. Got in there, parked the car, locked it. Now, I packed my clothes. Took me about twenty minutes, half hour, to pack. Called Bob up to see if he was there. Bob was there and I said, 'Great. Are you alone?' And he says, 'Yeah, I'm alone. She said no way.' I said, 'What do you mean, Bob?' He says, 'Boy, she is a cunt.' And I said, 'What do you mean?'

" 'She wouldn't let me go to her place, and she wouldn't come to my place, and she comes up with this routine, "No way, Bob, are you going to come up, no way, Bob, are you going to come up." ' And he says, 'Boy, I don't need that.' And I says, 'Yeah, I can see what you are doing. I can see what you mean.' And I says, 'Well, since you have a speaking engagement tomorrow morning, tomorrow afternoon, I am just going to get up and leave, and I will call you from California, after you get back,' and he says, 'Okay.'

"I said, 'Okay, everything is fine. What are you doing?' He says, 'I am standing in my shorts in front of the video

recorder editing Scotty's tape [*Saturday Night Fever*].' So
I says, 'Okay,' and that's it. That's the total course of the
evening."

In the lot of the Winfield Apartments, near Bob's car, two
moving men employed by Louis J. Billera in 225A, an
apartment above and just to the right of Bob's, pulled to a
stop. In the desert a lot of heavy work is done in the time
just before sunrise, when it is cool. The two men made
themselves comfortable to wait. In the distance, some hours
later, a lone motorcyclist was heard fleeing from the Winfield complex, cutting past the Arizona Canal and out onto
Chaparral. It was soon lost in the night.

Out on the desert within the shelter of the towering saguaro, the cereus began to bloom, spreading their fragrant,
luminous white petals in the summer air. This happens, say
experts, only once in a single night each year at the end of
June and occurs so rapidly that the human eye can actually
follow its opening. By dawn the desert floor will be littered
with the gray fragments of flowers that have, between sunset and dawn, bloomed, withered, and died.

The stars faded, the silvery dawn broke. The desert was
as cold as it would be all day. On the pillow beneath Bob's
head, blood puddled, spreading and opening like a black
flower.

5
VICTORIA

Continuing characters—The characters in a television series who continue from episode to episode, usually the leads.

At the Sunburst Motel, in room 206, John Carpenter rose early on the morning of Thursday, June 29, and called Cathy Nugent, the day manager at the desk.

"I had an early call," he said. "I thought I had a reservation originally for the limo at ten, then I realized I don't have an eleven o'clock flight, that's my arrival time in California. That I had a ten o'clock flight. So I called up again. Is there any way I can get my limo at nine?"

"No," said Nugent, "there's no way. Nobody at the limo service to take your order now. You'll have to go by cab."

In the Phoenix area, taxis are hard to find at the last minute and expensive, two reasons Carpenter had rented the Cordoba from the Avis rental counter at the Sunburst on Sunday.

"We better call that cab now, Mr. Carpenter," said Cathy,

"because sometimes it takes a long time for it to get here."

"I've got to get to the airport," Carpenter repeated.

Cathy thought, Why is he making such a fuss? He's got hours to get there. What's the rush? The trip to Sky Harbor usually took twenty minutes.

Carpenter's understanding was that he should be at the airport "at least an hour and a half ahead of time" to be certain of getting his plane. Cathy called the taxi for him. By 8:30 A.M. John was down in the lobby, on the lookout for his cab. He went over to the Avis car rental counter in the lobby to turn in the Cordoba. Darla Preston was at the desk.

"You know," he told her, "I had considered turning the car in earlier because it had no taillights. It's a brand-new car, but when you put on the brake all the lights come on inside the car instead of outside. You should put a stop on the car or at least a hold until you get some taillights or least fix the wiring on it. That's one of the reasons I didn't put more than forty-nine miles on it. You should get rid of it. Get it towed out of here."

Preston phoned the Avis service lot and told them that the car was defective. They said they would send a man over at three to retrieve the auto.

By 8:40 John was in his cab, and he arrived at the airport by 9:15. He raced for the Continental Airlines desk to check in. When he got to the desk it turned out that his flight actually did leave at eleven, so the rush was unnecessary.

Back at the Sunburst, Cathy Nugent was puzzled. She thought that Carpenter had checked out "very hurriedly" and seemed agitated and nervous.

Meanwhile, Brenda Broyles was on the phone to Julie Brinker. "All day I've been feeling such remorse," Brenda said. "I know one of my friends has died."

At a little after 2:00 P.M. Victoria Berry, wearing a tight powder blue SCOTTSDALE T-shirt with a cartoon of a road-runner on it and a pair of dark blue hot pants with white piping, arrived at the Winfield Apartments more than a little concerned. Bob had not appeared at noon for a local Tele-

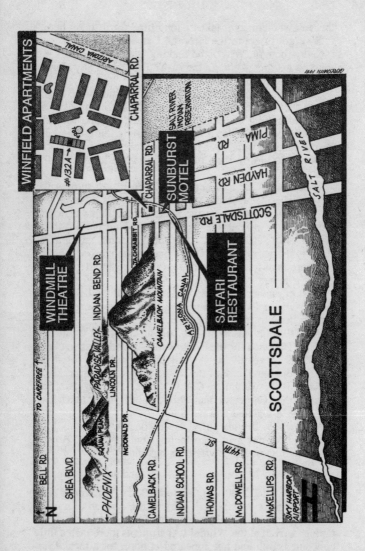

vision Academy luncheon, where the two of them were to
be interviewed, and it was out of character for him not to
have called if he had changed his mind.

There was a second reason for Victoria's visit—the
sound on the videotape Bob had made of her on the stage
of the Windmill three days earlier had been muffled, and
he had offered to help her redub the film. It would be useful
in getting her future work in Hollywood. Crane had also
promised to critique her performance.

Victoria saw Crane's leased white Chevy parked in the
assigned spot for 132A, so she assumed he was in. She
knocked once. Silence. A second time. Still no answer.
She gave the knob a turn. To her surprise the front door
was open. Cautiously she entered the apartment.

The heat of the afternoon mixed with the coolness of
Crane's room. Victoria could hear the reassuring throb of
the room's air conditioner. A stream of chilled air caressed
her cheek and filled her lungs. In the stillness of the room
the passing of afternoon traffic on Chaparral seemed loud
and abrasive, and she could hear people moving about in
the adjoining apartments. The room was dark; the curtains
were tightly drawn.

Victoria placed the bag she was carrying on the floor just
inside the door and called out for Bob again. A guest bedroom was to her left; the kitchen, which opened into the
dining and living room, was to her immediate right. A
photo of Crane's son Scotty looked down at her from a
bookcase, on a kitchen chair was a copy of *DrumChart*
magazine, and on the counter was a Nikon 35-mm camera
and a miniature tripod.

She continued into the living room, which was cluttered
with magazines strewn on the floor and stacked on all the
tables—*Playboy, TV Guide,* and *Esquire.* On the coffee table were Polaroid pictures Bob had taken of the pool area,
a Polaroid SX-70 camera with a flash, and an address book.
Papers overflowed the edges of the table; some had fallen
to the floor.

Bob's key ring, with the bright blue key, the dead-bolt
key, and the two keys to the Monte Carlo, lay on the large
rectangular dining room table. Victoria noticed that Crane,

used to living out of a suitcase on the road, had hung his white trousers over the sofa, which acted as a room divider. Sixty cents in change had fallen out of the pocket onto the floor. Near the fireplace were a pair of white jogging shoes, toes pointed inward, under a video camera on a tripod. The camera was pointed at the couch.

Bob's soiled brown military-style shirt was hung on a chair by the south wall. Three videotape boxes and the large box the Sony SL-8200 had come in were next to the sofa.

It occurred to Victoria that Bob might be out by the pool behind his apartment. She strode to the windows at the extreme eastern wall of the living room. She knew the curtains covering the windows were always drawn; arranged against them was an assortment of videotaping equipment—three videotape recorder players, a TV camera, and a TV set. A large number of black Beta videocassettes were stacked on top of the set. Victoria drew back the curtains slightly to look out but saw no sign of Crane or anyone by the pool. She turned back into the apartment, making her way to the master bedroom, at the northeastern rear portion of the complex, calling out Bob's name as she went. There was no answer. As she entered the bedroom she stepped over a videotape and a pair of swimming trunks.

Within the bedroom Victoria could make out someone stretched out on the double-size bed. A pair of pillows were at the top of the bed. Beside them was an apparently sleeping figure on its right side, knees slightly bent, in a semifetal position. The left hand was tucked tightly under the chin, the right arm stretched languidly along the length of the body. The bed was covered with a flower-print sheet; a second sheet was pulled up to the person's armpits.

An ominous, dark pool spilled from the area of the head and filled the well of the pillow, like long, flowing hair. Blood! Matted blood was on the side of the head, had dried on the face in long thin lines that had dripped downward, crossing each other.

Some blood was still moist; a trickle ran from the nose. More blood covered the upper half of the body, soaked into the sheets, and spattered the north wall above the figure's head.

"The wall was covered from one end to the other," Victoria stated later. "The blood was in a wide area, but not very high up." For a time she thought that she was looking at a woman whose hair was standing on end. "I thought it was a girl in his bed with long hair at first because it was dark—and when I looked again I still thought it was a girl.

"I remembered Bob telling me a story. I can't remember it in detail because he told me so many things—I remember once his saying that a girl had slashed her wrists and stuff, and he said, 'Oh! It was a horrible thing!' That flashed through my head. Oh, God! It's one of those crazy girls done something. Bob's probably gone out and gotten help. And I was going to leave a note and say, 'Bob, I can't handle this.' I didn't realize. . . . But instincts—I went back and looked again, and I realized it wasn't a girl."

On the nightstand Victoria saw a phone, an assortment of pens, a TWA baggage ticket, and, resting upside down on Bob's appointment book, a pair of wire-frame glasses. The glasses looked like Bob's, she thought; he would not leave them behind because he could not see without them. An expensive French watch was on his wrist. She thought she recognized it. "I looked down," she remembered later, "bent closer to him. Back-forth. Back-forth . . . He was unrecognizable, that's how bad it was."

The violence had been so intense to the man's left temple (the only side Victoria could see) that she could not tell if the hunched figure was Bob Crane or his close friend, John. Though shocked, Victoria was still able to think and observe. Gradually several details began to register with her: a pair of yellow shorts were wadded up on the bed, and there was something around the throat of the man.

It was a rope or cord tied in a neat, tight bow. Victoria realized a black plastic electrical cord had sunk into a groove on the left side of the man's neck. It was tied with a single, right-handed twist knot. The other end of the cord had been cut off cleanly with a knife or some very sharp tool.

The room showed no signs of a struggle. Victoria noticed a large black bag on the bed, sitting open. It was over two feet wide and could be folded in half. Both zippers were undone, one at the top, the other at the side.

"It struck me as very odd," Victoria recalled, "when I thought about it being placed there, and I thought, Gee, even if you're tired, no matter who, you would not leave a big bag on your bed. I know I wouldn't. I had not seen that bag before, but it matched Bob's luggage when I thought about it. He had heaps of luggage. He took his luggage everywhere."

Whatever had been in the bag had disappeared. All that was left now were a few pieces of paper and a couple of old tickets. It appeared the killer or killers had taken whatever secret Bob had kept in his mystery bag.

In a state of disbelief, Victoria began to leave the room, but backward. She crossed the living room, and at the front door she exited. Crying, shaking, she wheeled about looking for help and stopped a woman named Mary Lou Hawkins, who had come to house-sit her son's apartment. "Please help me," said Victoria. "There's a man in the apartment who is dead, and I'm afraid it's Bob."

Hawkins quickly climbed the steps to 237A, dialed the operator, and was connected with the Scottsdale Police Department. It was 2:20 P.M. Officer Paulette Kasieta arrived first, followed by Kord's Ambulance attendants Stu Glenn and Jesse Geddis and RFD (rural metro fire department) men Lieutenant Daniel Waring and Mark Provinzano. Medics rushed in, leaving their first-aid equipment in the hall. "Back there!" said Kasieta. It was quickly evident that nothing could be done, and the rural metro people left. "I made sure they had touched nothing," Kasieta said later.

At 2:30 Scottsdale police captain John Pratt arrived and took charge. Five minutes later he was joined by a flood of cops—Darwin Barrie and Barry Vassall, Chris Bingham, Tom Molloy, and Dave Evans. Kasieta and Evans were posted at the front while identification technicians Ernie Cole and Laura Wheale took photos of the room. By 2:50 officers were going door to door, questioning the neighbors.

"It could be Bob Crane, or his friend, John . . . John . . . I've forgotten his last name," said Victoria.

"Calm down," said Pratt. Victoria's confusion was understandable.

"Oh, I know him," she said, "I just can't think of the name. I'm just blank . . . but John was to have left for L.A. this morning at nine-thirty. I don't know if he completed the trip or not. He's been a very personal friend of Bob's for at least the past fifteen years." Victoria was so confused that she forgot to tell the police to notify Bob Jr. of his father's death. "It was a terribly sick person who did this," she said.

Later Victoria filled out a one-page handwritten statement for the officers. She was so upset that it was practically unreadable:

> *Last seen was after the show with best friend John (Don't know last name) I watched them drive off. I had 2:30 P.M. appointed. I knocked no-answer-door unlocked & I saw body—I think it's Bob Crane. He knows everybody at the Dinner theatre Windmill. 1st wife Ann—divorced. 2nd wife Pattie. She was here 2 days, unwelcome!—going through divorce. 1 son to 2nd marriage, Scottie, I think 2 daughters to 1st marriage. Stage manager Chris, Ed Beck, Bill McCale (can't spell his last name) Faye, publicity—she called while police were here looking for Bob as he had appointment and guest speaker*
>
> *Victoria Ann Berry*

While she was writing, the refrigerator was opened. There was Coors beer inside. "I don't know of anyone in the cast who drinks beer," Victoria said. "John doesn't even drink. He doesn't even have one drink. And I don't know of anyone who drinks beer or Coors beer. That beer wasn't here on Monday when I came."

Then her eyes fell on the half-empty bottle of Old Smuggler's Scotch and a bottle of Booth's gin on the counter next to where she had been writing. "I was staring right at them," she said later. "I had never seen Bob buy *any* alcohol while he was with me. I had never seen them before that day. The only thing Bob would drink was vodka, and *this* was a bottle of Scotch. It was right in front of me."

To one of the policemen she said, "That's funny that he

has alcohol here 'cause this much of the Scotch is gone and Bob does not touch Scotch. From time to time a bottle of beer, but that was all.

"He could not have drunk the Scotch," Victoria insisted.

6
DEAN

Cutoff—Decision made by network not to take up option to have a writer write a script after he has written an outline or treatment.

Lieutenant Ron Dean's phone rang at home at 2:40 P.M.

"When they called," he remembered, "they did not have him identified at that time. I believe I received the call from Johnny Pratt, my immediate supervisor. He was captain of the team."

Ron Dean was both an assistant team commander and a detective. Scottsdale had recently been divided into three geographical team areas, something like precincts, in an experiment known as team policing. Under this arrangement one complete set of uniformed officers was designated to one team area, which they would know thoroughly as jacks-of-all-trades, rather than having to patrol the whole city.

Thus detectives who handled the everyday burglaries and robberies committed in their designated areas were also called upon to handle the one or two murders that occurred annually, since Scottsdale wasn't big enough to have an individual detective squad, much less a central homicide bureau. Pratt was captain of Team III.

Dean climbed into his tan uniform, a color distinctive to Scottsdale, since the bordering towns used the more standard blue. A blurred tattoo of a skull was visible on his right bicep just beneath the short sleeve of his shirt. The lettering beneath was so faded that it was unreadable. What it said was "Death Before Dishonor."

Six feet four, 210 pounds, thirty-three years old, broad-shouldered, tough, and burly, with thick, straight, dark hair, Dean had always known what he wanted to be. "Part of my high school education," he recalled, "was at Our Lady of LaFollette, a Catholic seminary, during my freshman year. For a while I thought I might be a Catholic priest, but after going to public high school I changed vocations. Went on to become a marine and then a cop. I did well for what I wanted to do."

Dean strapped on his .357 side arm with the six-inch barrel and got into his blue Corvette. Because he was off duty he was using his own car to get to the scene.

Married, with three daughters, Dean was the only member of the family without a drawl. He'd come to Arizona from the Midwest, first passing through with his family on the way to visit in California.

Dean credited the Marine Corps with his sense of discipline. As he trained in the different battalions that came through Twenty-nine Palms Marine Base near Joshua Tree National Monument, he was close enough to Scottsdale to visit a relative there, and he came to love the town. "The desert just seemed to be the place," he said.

In 1965, when *Hogan's Heroes* was premiering, Ron Dean was a marine sergeant in Vietnam. He was under fire a number of times in Chu Li and around Da Nang. "Somebody counted the shells," he remembered. "Twenty-seven mortar rounds came into our encampment."

By May of 1966 Dean was back in the States, being transferred from base to base. As he made his way toward Scottsdale, a small box followed him. When he received it,

it contained medals he didn't even know that he had won—
among them two Bronze Stars and a Presidential Unit Ci-
tation from President Johnson for "Operation Starlight,"
one of the major battles of the war.

The following year Dean joined the police force, eventually graduated from Scottsdale Community College, and
was currently seeking a B.A. from Arizona State University
in administration of justice. Three years earlier he had been
named Outstanding Young Law Enforcement Officer of the
year.

As he drove toward the Winfield Apartments, Dean figured he was headed into another of the bizarre cases he'd
investigated in the last couple of years: a harassed man who
found his slaughtered Great Dane lying in his bed in a pool
of blood; a $235,000 theft of Indian jewelry; a million dol-
lar counterfeit check racket; the finding of a five-hundred-
year-old skeleton; the struggle with a suspected child
molester and rapist who kicked out a plate-glass window
and almost put Dean, his partner, and the suspect in the
hospital; the tracking down of the body of a woman who
had died in the desert.

"So I came in to see what all the fuss was about over at
the Winfield Apartments, received the assignment, and
asked for a couple of officers to work with me," Dean said
later. One was Officer Dennis Borkenhagen. Dean knew
that Borkenhagen had the ability to work a homicide case
and was experienced in investigations. Dean had him pulled
from patrol to be his assistant. The other available investigators were new. "They just weren't as ready as Borkenhagen was," said Dean.

Only twenty minutes had elapsed since Dean had gotten
the call and arrived at the Winfield. At one end of the lot
was the red Camelback, at the other was Crane's door.
"Johnny Pratt greeted me," Dean said. "Victoria Berry in
blue hot pants and a tight T-shirt was standing outside. By
that time there was quite a group of people gathering, and
then somehow, some way, newsmen began to gather, too,

adding to the people out there. It quickly became a confined area.

"I brought Victoria back into the apartment for purposes of identification. The first time she saw the body there, I guess she felt someone was dead, but she didn't take the time to see who the person was.

"The air conditioner was going. It was cool in the apartment. Dark. Quite dark. Victoria Berry seemed very upset. She still didn't know for sure who the dead man was."

Dean moved through the homicide scene, silently, almost reverently, keeping his hands in his pockets to avoid disturbing any evidence left by the killer. The curtains were held back, examined; dust settled, frozen momentarily in shafts of lowering light. Dean was struck by the relative orderliness of the death room—considering the violence to the victim, nothing much had been disturbed. Occupants in the adjoining apartments on both sides and above would be interviewed. Even though the walls were thin, Dean predicted that they would have heard nothing—the choice by the murderer of a blunt instrument had, in all likelihood, been determined by how easily sound carried at the Winfield. Naturally a shot would have been heard, but an attack with a club on a sleeping man would be nearly silent.

"Crane didn't give any personal attention to the apartment," Dean said later. "There were no pictures on the walls. It was almost like he was staying in a motel room. There was only the personal camera equipment, Polaroids, and other pictures he'd leave lying around. Otherwise he just pretty much lived out of a suitcase."

Dean remembered something that Paul Theroux had written the year before: "The least dignified thing that can happen to a man is to be murdered. If he dies in his sleep, he gets a respectful obituary and perhaps a smiling portrait; it is how we all want to be remembered. But murder is the great exposer: here is the victim in his torn underwear, facedown on the floor, unpaid bills on his dresser, a meager shopping list, some loose change, and worst of all the fact that he is alone. Investigation reveals what he did that

day—it all matters—his habits are examined, his behavior
scrutinized, his trunks rifled, and a balance sheet is drawn
up at the hospital giving the contents of his stomach. Dying,
the last private act we perform, is made public: the murder
victim has no secrets. . . . Murder is the grimmest, briefest
fame."

"The man's face," Dean noted, "wasn't so much swollen
and bruised when I saw it. Mainly, what sticks in my mind
was the blood. There were a few killings in Scottsdale, but
even so, nothing like this. Bludgeonings and stranglings are
almost unheard of, and I doubt if the city ever had one like
that ever at all. A city like Phoenix never had one, and they
have a lot of homicides."

Inwardly Dean winced. The left side of the victim's head
had been struck twice and caved in with some blunt object,
possibly an iron bar, a pipe, or a lug wrench. There was no
way of knowing at this point. Apparently to make doubly
sure that the man was dead, the assailant had wrapped some
sort of black cord around his neck and tied it.

The detective fought to stay aloof and objective, but he
was shocked by the damage to the victim. It was so severe,
it was difficult to determine the means of death. The cord
was "tied around the neck with a single right-handed twist.
The knot was at the left, the rear of the man's neck," the
official report would read. "The other end of the cord had
been cut off with a knife." The sliced end of the cord
glowed dully in the lamplight. Dean began to scan the room
to locate its source. Eventually he would find that it was
cut from a ball of wires behind the camera equipment in
the other room.

"The cord around his neck was from the VCR machine
area," said Dean, "but I could tell it wasn't the cause of
death because there was so much damage to the head, and
although it was very tight, the way it was around the neck
didn't really look like it could have caused strangulation.

"You sometimes have what we call an 'overkill,' " Dean
said later. "Anybody should have known two blows to the
head were enough. But this person was in such a state of
mind or a frenzy of sorts that he went out and cut that cord
off and tied it around Crane's neck. There were many

things the cord could have been taken from—for instance, the lamp next to the bed or a closer recorder. But he went over and reached very specifically for this camcorder, this plug-in cord, and grabbed that instead of any more convenient cord."

Crane was in a fetal position on the right-hand side of the bed. His right hand was hidden by the pillow, and there was the possibility he might have been clutching the murder weapon because none was in sight. The body, though, could not be moved until the medical examiner arrived. Dean later learned that while living in the Winfield complex, Bob slept on the right side of the bed away from the bedroom window because he was a light sleeper and the morning light would awaken him.

A pool of blood had puddled in the hollow of the pillow and dried on the victim's face and head. Some, however, was still quite moist and even wet in places. Blood ran from the nose. Once Dean became aware that the blood around the body was still damp, he cautioned everyone not to touch it. "We didn't touch it because we didn't want to put our fingerprints on it. Strangely enough, fingerprints can be lifted from blood and even from bodies. People don't commonly hear about those things, but it can be done," Dean said.

"There was no spread on the bed. There was just a sheet, a bottom sheet and a top sheet." The killer had lifted the bottom right corner of the top sheet, "just grabbed a handful of sheet," and wiped the weapon on it, letting the corner drop back.

At the bottom of the sheet was a stain where something had been wiped off. The bloody shape had an eternal feeling about it, as if it could never be washed away. Dean finally realized what the shape reminded him of: "The stain on the sheet," he said, "looked like a sword."

Dean studied the blood spatter pattern. "There were two strikes to the head. The first strike puts an indentation in the skull, and then immediately following that comes the second blow. But by the time the second blow is coming down—even though it probably came down very fast after

the first one, by this time there's a little bit of spatter that
went up.

"But it could have been held back a little bit by the hair.
And then the instrument itself blocked some of the blood,
so there wasn't a real pattern of it. Just a spurt to the wall."

Many times blood spatters answer crucial questions for
investigators: the pattern, the sequence of the blows, the
strength, and often the height of the perpetrator. However,
from the two rapid blows to the victim, Dean could not tell
if the assailant had been right- or left-handed. It was almost
as if the killer had used both hands. Whatever he did,
thought Dean, he did it with great force.

Crane had a mysterious "little black bag," which Victoria
described as "an equipment bag with several zippers." It
lay on the bed beside the body, and it was almost empty.
Through the actress Dean established that it had been kept
hidden in Crane's closet, had contained objects of weight.
It was light now. Obviously the killer had ransacked it.

"It was just a typical overnight black suitcase with standard locks," observed Dean, "and it was sitting open on the
bed. The bag was probably too large for the killer to just
take with him."

On the end table next to the dead man were a magnifying
glass, pens, and a TWA baggage claim ticket. Beneath a
pair of wire-rim glasses was Bob's personal date book,
spattered with blood. Dean opened it a page or two with
the end of his pen.

The actor was supposed to take his friend John Carpenter
to the Sky Harbor Airport at 10:00 A.M. today, June 29,
Dean observed. There were a series of small Xs drawn
through the weeks ahead.

On the bedroom dresser were a few personal notes, sew-
ing kits that Crane had taken from the various Hyatt Hotels
he had stayed at, a tube of Aim toothpaste, a package of
Halls cough drops, and a second pair of eyeglasses and
case. Next to the wastebasket was a pair of brown shoes.
In the closet the investigator found two Polaroid photos in
a sealed envelope. They were of a nude woman.

Dean fought against a sense of urgency. "You can't let yourself feel that way. You've just got to gather up the facts and see what you have. See what begins to pull in from there. Way over ninety percent of homicides are committed by people who know the victim. The first twenty-four to forty-eight hours is a crucial time, and usually within that period you're either going to solve it or you're not.

"Crane kept his camera and recording equipment there," Dean said later. "Just this vast entanglement of wires and cameras.* From what I could learn he seemed always to have this layout at each place he went to. It was set up by his friend John Carpenter because he was the one who knew which wire went where. Almost everyone is using those things nowadays, but at that time they weren't as common."

Just two months before *Hogan's Heroes* had premiered in September 1965, Sony had introduced the first commercial home videotape recorder into the United States. Priced at $995 it was mostly a toy for the rich. Within twenty years, however, over sixty percent of all American homes would have a VCR, and enough cassettes would have been sold so that every man, woman, and child in the country could own one. Crane's Betamax tapes were all in black and white. Color would come later.

Wires and video equipment were in such abundance that they hid the fireplace and blocked the drapes. On top of the Sony Betamax resting on the television set were Bob's editing materials—scissors, black ink, screwdriver, Webcor C-90 cassette, flashlight, cords, jacks, splicing tape, microphone, and wire cutters.

---

*Crane's equipment: a Panasonic videotape recorder, a black-and-silver GBC video-tape recorder, a Sony Betamax, a Panasonic R. F. converter in a black cabinet, a Sony digital timer, a Panasonic cassette tape recorder in a black vinyl case initialed "B.C." on two sides, a Sylvania color television in a simulated wood grain cabinet on a two-shelved chrome TV stand on rollers. On the bottom shelf of the stand were four boxes of Zenith video-cassette L-500 tapes, now empty.

Located on a kitchen chair in the center of the arcadia door was the Sony SL-8200 that Bob had borrowed from Dyna-Tronics. "The camera mounted on a tripod was one of those big old square box ones, not at all like the ones that came later," said Dean, "and it was set up to take pictures. It was very visible, and there could be no doubt Crane's sex partners saw it.

"It was pointed toward a couch, one of those old striped types. Just a typical apartment-style couch. Not very expensive, but not necessarily that cheap, either. He did a lot of screwing on that couch, we found out later.

"A film was in the process of being edited on that equipment, *Saturday Night Fever*. It was the only legitimate film there." Next to the sofa, blocking the way into the master bedroom, under a pair of two-tone blue swimming trunks, was the copy of *Saturday Night Fever*.

By the TV Dean found stacks of black unlabeled Beta cassettes. "You've got to speculate," he said, " 'Jesus, what could be on these tapes? Could the killer be on them?' Things like that." His heart leapt. As soon as possible the tapes had to be reviewed, cataloged, the pictures of the people in the various scenes copied onto still photos and located.

Dean was excited by the prospect, but he returned his focus to the apartment. In the white slacks hanging over the sofa he found Crane's wallet. It was untouched. In the rear pocket was the Visa receipt from Bob's last meal at the Safari. From the beginning, therefore, robbery was ruled out as a motive. On the end table against the south wall among all the magazines was a close-up ring for a Nikon camera and a stack of twenty-four glossy black-and-white pornographic photos. On the road Crane often made copies of the Polaroid shots for friends in black and white using the 35-mm close-up lens.

Earlier Dean had noted the gin and Scotch, and now the detective opened the door to the bathroom, which was just off the master bedroom. There he found a photographic lab on the tank lid of the toilet, including one cassette tape, a Durst M300 photo enlarger, trays, two boxes of Kodak photo paper, photographic chemicals, and several strips of

35-mm black-and-white film. A darkroom lightbulb was balanced precariously on the edge of the toilet lid.

In the enlarger Dean found a strip of negatives and gingerly held them up to the light. They were initially photos of a clothed woman, but as he unwound the strip Dean saw that she was nude farther on and even farther on engaging in sexual intercourse with a man. Because the strip of film had been in the enlarger, it was possible that the killer had overlooked it in his search. Later Victoria told Dean that many glossy black-and-white prints were missing.

Dean wondered how much time the killer might have actually spent in the rooms. He seemed to have moved leisurely, carefully. "The killer probably got there around two-thirty to three A.M., and he would have stayed till maybe four and then left," said Dean. "There was no reason for us to think he might have been sitting around. He would have had blood on his hands, and so on. And there was no trace of it in any room except the front bedroom, where someone had pulled the drape back, probably to see if anybody was outside. When we looked up and under the drape, we saw where somebody had touched it with a bloody finger."

A piece of the lining from the drapes where there were two spots that appeared to be blood was cut off. ID technician Laura Wheale put the fabric into a plastic bag. Although the sliding window on the east wall was unlocked and ajar, both screens were in their proper positions. The northeast bedroom window was slightly open.

"No marks on the windows," said Dean, "to show they were ever forced in any way. Not on any windows or the arcadia door [which was locked] or front door. Also, the reason we know the killer left by the front door—on the front inside door we know there was a drop of blood plus a bit of a smear in between the locks from opening it." Wheale scraped off the spots of blood and put these into another plastic bag. A partial latent fingerprint was lifted from the outside of the front door, and more latents were lifted just above the locks on the front door.

Dean was puzzled by the lack of fireplace equipment in the apartment. There was no poker, no tongs. Had the poker

been the murder weapon? Dean knelt by the brick fireplace
next to the drapes. Here were very fine white ashes and
three strips of charred video magnetic recording tape. Had
anything been taken, erased, or burned by the killer?

"It only took a few minutes to go from room to room,"
Dean said. "At that time I had been on my job long enough
to have walked through quite a number of crime scenes.
You know where the evidence is sitting, and you avoid
stepping on it for sure. We retraced our steps to make sure
of entries and what the person might have done while in
the apartment. By that time we had Victoria sitting on one
of the breakfast bar stools writing out her one-page statement."

The Scottsdale detectives had been handed one of the
most complex and puzzling cases of the decade, and it was
understandable that a series of small blunders were made.

"It was not a situation where they made the mistakes and
knew better," said one Scottsdale reporter much later. "This
was a very big deal for them, and they weren't prepared
for it."

The first real mistake occurred when Victoria Berry,
filled with anguish and nervous energy, began to pace the
rooms. As she wandered, she chain-smoked, contaminating
the crime scene. Dean eventually got her a heavy yellow
ashtray to carry around with her. She crushed her empty
cigarette package and dropped it into the ashtray. Additionally, a throng of policemen themselves roamed in and out,
propping up their radios on the tables.

"The waiting was killing," said Dean. The body itself
could not be touched until Dr. Heinz Karnitschnig (KAR-
nitch-nig), the Maricopa County medical examiner, arrived.

Since 2:50 P.M. Officers Chris Bingham and Barry Vassall
had been going from door to door on Crane's floor in the
motel, but the neighbors either hadn't heard anything or
didn't want to get involved—many were not at home, and
one was deaf.

Another woman told Officer Darwin Barrie, who had
been assigned to the second level of the complex, that she

was certain Crane's car had been driven away at 9:30 A.M.
and returned later. Residents of apartments 232A through
235A were not at home. Sandy Miller, in 229A, told Barrie,
"On Monday evening I saw something that struck me as
unusual. Bob Crane had pulled up in his car and begun
walking to the apartment very fast. A second person was
behind him, a heavyset individual. The person was walking
slowly behind him. At seven this morning I did see Bob's
paper on his front steps."

In Bob's apartment Vassall observed a paper on the Formica kitchen counter—it was dated June 29, 1978. How,
he wondered, had it gotten *inside*? Some of the small mysteries such as this would soon be solved.

Just above Crane's apartment, Officer Barrie spoke with
Louis Billera in 225A. "I've only been at the apartments
since ten forty-five, that's when I arrived to meet the moving men," said Billera, "and we began moving furniture.
I've been in and out all day, but I haven't seen anything
unusual."

Mrs. Billera was "uncooperative, would not answer questions or give the phone number," Barrie wrote in his notebook. "We don't want to get involved," she said. "We're
just moving in and we don't have time for such things."

7
CALLS FOR THE DEAD

Subtext—The meaning below the actual dialogue.

At 11:36 that morning John Carpenter's plane, Continental flight number 57 from Scottsdale, landed at Los Angeles International. He went to his home at 133 W. Lime in Inglewood and picked up his car. John later said that he had trouble with it and drove it to a garage for service and then went on to his place of employment at AKAI. At 2:30 P.M. he called Jenny Brown at the Windmill Theatre in Scottsdale. Brown had heard that there was "some problem at Bob Crane's apartment, that the police were investigating an incident."

"Is Bob there?" Carpenter asked.

"No."

"Do you know where he is?"

"No."

"Will Bob be in this evening?"

"Yes."

"Do you have the telephone number for Victoria Berry?"

"I can't give out that information," Brown said.

"Well, that's not very friendly."

Before he hung up, Brown gave Carpenter the number of Linda Hinshaw in the other theater office.

At 2:45 Hinshaw received a call from Carpenter. "Is Bob around the theater?"

"No," she said. "Can I take a message and have Mr. Crane call you back?"

"No. Just leave a message for him. Tell him I arrived in town okay."

"I'll do so," said Hinshaw.

"What's the matter?" said Carpenter. "You sound sad."

"Nothing's the matter," said Hinshaw, concealing the fact that she knew there was some problem at Bob's, "I guess I'm just overworked."

At 3:00 P.M. Carpenter called Bob Crane, Jr. "What's going on?"

"Nothing. I'm just transcribing an interview."

"I had heard nothing about my dad's death at this point," Bob Jr. recalled later. "Carpenter calls me, and it's rare for him to call me after visiting my father. He may call me before he leaves to visit my father because he needs his phone number or because he's bringing Dad a piece of equipment or a tape or whatever. But afterward, upon returning? It's rare, and I didn't quite understand the phone call. He calls and says, 'What's going on?' 'Nothing, I'm sitting here transcribing an interview,' I told him. 'Well, listen, Bob, I just want you to know I'm back in town and if you need anything, just give me a call.' And I'm kind of sitting there thinking, Yeah, why, why'd you call? I didn't say it, instead I said, 'How was Phoenix?' and he said, 'It was all right. I didn't really make out too well.'

"Since there was no reason for the call, I almost asked him, 'John, *why* are you calling?' The whole conversation I think was a minute and a half, two minutes. My impression of it, after finding out the events that happened, was that at three P.M. he knew something. Looking back on it, he didn't have the nerve to tell me what had happened in terms of my dad." Carpenter talked on for another minute and then hung up; his tone had been normal and matter of fact.

At 3:10 P.M. Victoria looked up from her handwritten statement at the kitchen counter in Bob Crane's apartment; the phone was ringing. Dean turned to ID technician Cole and asked, "Is that phone okay? Is it clear to answer?"

"It's checked," said the fingerprint man.

Dean gestured for Victoria to answer. At this time she was still unsure whether the deceased man was Bob or John. It was John Carpenter on the phone. After a moment Dean took the receiver from her and introduced himself as a policeman with the Scottsdale PD. He said he was investigating an incident but did not describe what type of incident it could be.

"I'm John Carpenter. I was with Bob Crane last night. I called him at one this morning to tell him I was preparing to return to California. He told me he was going to be sleeping late in the morning." Carpenter said he had last talked to Bob at 1:30 A.M.

One minute later Kathy Reid called and Victoria answered. Dean took her number. Bob Jr. called at 3:17. "Hi," he said. "Is Bob Crane there?"

"No," said Victoria, "he's out right now."

"Who's this?" said Bob Jr., and she told him. "Oh, this is Bobby, Bob's son. Tell my dad I called. Nothing important."

Dean took the phone and told him only that some sort of investigation was going on, but he did not elaborate. As Bob Jr. hung up he thought that maybe something was wrong and that this might explain John's odd call to him.

At 3:30 Carpenter called back; Dean asked him a few questions about his relationship with the actor and said he'd call him. Carpenter left a number where he could be reached. At no point did he inquire about the police presence in Crane's apartment.

*   *   *

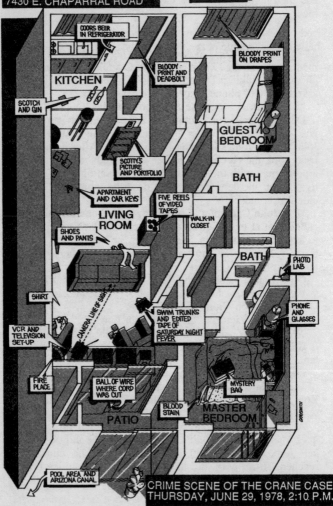

FRONT ENTRANCE TO #132 A
WINFIELD APARTMENTS
7430 E. CHAPARRAL ROAD

OPEN PARKING LOT

COORS BEER IN REFRIGERATOR

BLOODY PRINT ON DRAPES

BLOODY PRINT AND DEADBOLT

KITCHEN

SCOTCH AND GIN

GUEST BEDROOM

BATH

SCOTTY'S PICTURE AND PORTFOLIO

APARTMENT AND CAR KEYS

FIVE REELS OF VIDEO TAPES

LIVING ROOM

WALK-IN CLOSET

SHOES AND PANTS

BATH

PHOTO LAB

SHIRT

CAMERA LINE OF SIGHT

PHONE AND GLASSES

VCR AND TELEVISION SET-UP

SWIM TRUNKS AND EDITED TAPE OF SATURDAY NIGHT FEVER

FIRE PLACE

BALL OF WIRE WHERE CORD WAS CUT

MYSTERY BAG

BLOOD STAIN

MASTER BEDROOM

PATIO

POOL AREA AND ARIZONA CANAL

CRIME SCENE OF THE CRANE CASE
THURSDAY, JUNE 29, 1978, 2:10 P.M.

At 3:48 P.M. Dennis Borkenhagen, Dean's partner, arrived. "I had been up at the Sunburst a little east of the Winfield when I heard they found a body," he said later.

"Once I got the call I was there in two minutes. Everybody knew what was going on because Victoria Berry called a few people at the theater right away." Anyone calling the Windmill heard a recording saying, "Due to the untimely death of Mr. Bob Crane, the run of his show has been canceled."

Borkenhagen had started with the police in 1965 in Des Plaines, a suburb of Chicago, with the same department that had arrested serial killer John Wayne Gacy. He came to Scottsdale in March of 1970, passed the physical and written tests, sold his house, and in less than two months was on patrol for the Scottsdale PD. "I spent about three and one-half years on the road before I joined Dean in detectives," he said later.

"When you started out with detectives you started out with the real minor stuff—bicycle thefts, petty offenses—and then you worked your way into felony thefts, burglaries, and on up the ladder into what we call 'person's crimes'—robberies, rapes, assaults, and homicides. When the department broke up into three teams, we had a central corps of special investigators that handled all the heavy kind of crime. When Dean made sergeant I joined him in that unit."

Borkenhagen took one glance at the messy apartment, all the electronic equipment and sex photos, and pronounced the case "a bucket of worms." His eyes strayed toward the gin and Scotch, and he said to Dean, "It appears he had company last night."

The detective bent to examine the door for marks of forced entry, and finding none, he accompanied the still distraught Victoria into the bedroom. "It just doesn't look like him," she whispered to Borkenhagen. "His face is all bloated."

Chris Roberts, Bruce Hurst, who was house manager of the Windmill, and Ed Beck, VP of the theater, arrived at the door and were ushered into the bedroom, where they stood at the bedside to attempt to identify the victim. All three were uncertain that it was Bob.

Actress Ronni Richards, who had costarred in *Beginner's Luck* until the death of her husband, was in New York when she heard. "My parents were waiting for me in the lobby of my apartment when I got home from a date, and they told me. In fact, my brother was in California and he heard it first and called them. He said, 'You'd better be with Ronni when she hears.' Because to me it was like losing another husband."

In Los Angeles, Bob Jr. was driving his grandmother, Bob's mother, out to Tarzana to his stepfather and mother's house, so it was his stepfather, Chuck Sloan, who first heard the news. "I was waiting for Bobby to arrive," he said, "because he had to pick up his car at VMW in Woodland Hills by five-thirty, and I was watching the clock. So I remember that Bobby walked in at twenty minutes to five. Lloyd Vaughn [Crane's business manager] had called me and told me what had happened, and I like to have died there. I said, 'God, the craziest thing is that Bob's mother and Bobby are on their way over here right now. They are going to walk in that door any minute.' "

Crane's mother reached the house first, and Sloan broke the news to her, but he had no idea how to tell Bob Jr. "Let it out," said Bob's mother, "all hang right out. There's no other way."

Sloan stepped to the door and yelled, "Get the hell in the house!" and Bob Jr. came running in. Sloan told him to call Vaughn.

"There's been some kind of crazy rumor involving your dad. Something about being shot," said Vaughn. "You've got to get over here. I should get to Phoenix immediately."

"I want to go, too."

"That's what I thought. Everything is set."

Bob Jr. got over to Vaughn's office, then drove to Bill Goldstein's home [Goldstein is Bob Jr.'s lawyer], and the three men took the 7:35 P.M. flight to Phoenix.

Goldstein had phoned Patti's attorney, Lee Blackman, at four when he heard the rumor from Vaughn that "something is going on at Bob's apartment." Blackman called Patti at Mrs. Bucks's off the coast of Washington. She was not to be found. He left a message, and it was after 7:30 P.M. when she called back. That was how Patti learned of Bob's death. She returned immediately to Los Angeles.

Less than an hour and a half after she had called Bob and been told by Victoria, "He isn't in now," Kathy Reid learned from a friend that Bob had been killed. She called the apartment once more and spoke with Dean. She was already on his list of suspects. Kathy said that she lived with her boyfriend. "What time does he get off work?" asked Dean.

"One oh-five A.M. But last night I was up with him till four A.M. The whole time."

The wait for the medical examiner continued back at the apartment. Black-and-white photographs, color slides, and videotapes were being made of the kitchen, dining room, living room, the unused guest bedroom, and the window and drapes there. Fifteen color Polaroid photos were taken of the body.

Laura Wheale's job was to dust all the video equipment. She lifted partial latents off the GBC viewfinder and "very faint latents" off the color VTR and the top of the plastic on the Betamax. The inside and outside of the front door were dusted with black powder. Tongs were used to lift and place item after item into individual bags.

Chain-smoking, Victoria continued to wander. (A Merit cork-tip filter cigarette was discovered and sprayed with ninhydrin, but no prints were raised. It was known that neither Bob nor John smoked, and Dean was excited until he found that one of the cops had left it.)

The entire Formica countertop in the kitchen was dusted—no prints; electric stove—smudges; refrigerator—smudges and partial latent ridges. The rough surface of the enameled wall near the entryway into the kitchen was not conducive to producing latents. However, the Booth's gin bottle yielded one latent print and the Scotch two prints. A cocktail glass had three prints, but an empty Perrier bottle found in the trash was too smudged for comparison purposes.

Dr. Karnitschnig, the medical examiner, finally arrived at 4:00 P.M. Now that the coroner was there, the body could be moved and Victoria could make a positive ID. "Up to that time I would not admit it was Bob Crane because he was unrecognizable, that's how bad it was," she said later. Dean now sent her downtown with Detective Chris Bingham to retell her story on tape. Outside, Victoria and Bingham were met by the television and newspaper cameras. She brushed aside a tear.

Dr. Karnitschnig was accompanied by two assistants. One was a pathologist who had been visiting the ME's office when the call about Bob came in. She was observing in place of Assistant Medical Examiner Dr. Tom Jarvis. The other assistant was Eloy Ysasi, a former Phoenix homicide investigator.

"He is a strange, unusual guy," said Dean. "He thought *he* was going to solve the Crane case. He remembers when he was a Phoenix detective." Dean found him patronizing.

The forty-eight-year-old Karnitschnig (or Dr. K, as he was known) was outspoken, controversial, and intelligent. A short, bearlike man, he was a former ski instructor from Austria who studied medicine there and then in Scotland and Virginia. He had been a pathologist for almost twenty years; for the past seven he had been the Maricopa County ME. Karnitschnig was highly argumentative, especially with the police, and his bluntness was equaled only by Ysasi's, possibly the reason they got along so well with each other.

Dr. K decided to do an on-the-scene preautopsy, so the top sheet was pulled off. Bob was clad only in boxer shorts. The ME proceeded to shave a portion of the victim's head so that he could see the shape of the wounds and determine what kind of weapon might have been used. Dean found this an unusual occurrence. Autopsies were rarely begun at the scene. Technician Ernie Cole videotaped Dr. K's preliminary examination; the irony was not lost on Dean.

"The victim is cold, and rigor is well established," said the doctor. Carefully he cut the middle of the black electrical cord from around the victim's neck to preserve the knot. The cord was then taped back together at the point of the cut. Dr. K also cut out the section of sheet where the weapon had been wiped and had it sealed in a plastic bag. (In the confusion of shaving a portion of Bob's head, a single hair that was not Crane's was brushed from his forehead and discarded with the shaven hair. The process was captured on tape by the video recorder. However, it would be a dozen years before anyone realized the existence of the hair.)

Karnitschnig told the men that there were a minimum of two blows to the temple on the left side of Crane's head and that the ligature was applied just prior to or at the time of death. "He must have been murdered in the early morning," said Dr. K, and noted how little the apartment had been damaged. "Mistreatment of the body, however, is considerable," he continued. "The murder was apparently well planned."

Dr. K believed that the killer was a man and not a woman. He based this theory on the lack of blood spots on the ceiling. "The killer's first blow laid open Crane's scalp, covering the weapon with blood. The second blow was delivered with a short arc, slinging only a couple of droplets onto the ceiling and table lamp near the bed." Dr. K felt that if the attacker had been female, she would have had to swing the heavy weapon in a wider arc, which would have flung a trail of blood onto the ceiling.

The wounds were deep, explained the examiner, and the skull was crushed by a very strong man who not only took his time, but knew Crane. The police were unable to find any signs of haste, noting that the assailant had carefully wiped off the murder weapon and methodically tied a cord around Crane's neck. "The person who did this," said Dr. K, "knew that the skull was crushed, that the person was essentially dead."

"Dr. K finished the on-the-scene examination," Borkenhagen said later, "and we get to looking, and there was what appeared to be semen on Crane's left thigh. I think there were a couple of blobs. Number one, we assumed it was *not* Crane's semen. It was our theory that the killer whacked Crane in the head and then beat off over him. 'Here, you son of a bitch, here!' It had all the earmarks of a homosexual murder."

Dr. Karnitschnig studied some flaky, white, dry material in Crane's groin area and felt that this indicated the actor may have had sexual relations just before his death.

Dean briefed his superior, Captain Pratt, who had been one of the first on the scene and who had remained in the apartment after Dean assumed charge. Dean told Pratt that the killer could have been someone Bob knew since there were no signs of a struggle and no sign of forced entry. "There were no defense injuries," he said. "Bob Crane must have been in some state of sleep. Struck while he was asleep. We took some fiber and hair samples. Some blood and other liquids are going to be checked."

In turn Pratt told the press outside, "He was asleep, taken by surprise. He didn't know what hit him. There are no clues. No motive."

Dean made a short statement to the press, purposely not revealing any of the important details of the case. "I understand that Crane did go to the nightclubs and was very personable, giving out autographs and all that. We have no prior reports of burglaries or robberies in the apartment complex, and the neighborhood is not plagued with these kinds of crimes."

Then Dr. K and Ysasi held a press conference outside. Karnitschnig described what had happened in general terms, but Ysasi mentioned the electrical cord found around Crane's neck, the kind of information routinely held back from the public so that when someone confessing to the crime turns up, the investigators will be able to check his story.

"We were all kind of mad at the medical examiner's office," said Borkenhagen, "because they came out and conducted an off-the-cuff press conference right at the murder scene and said a lot of things that probably shouldn't have been released to the public." One cop said bitterly that he thought the preautopsy had been rushed so that the ME would have something to tell the press.

Ysasi, seeing Victoria using the phone and not knowing it had been dusted, later told the county attorney's office, "Oh, they didn't even check that phone, that's how sloppy the investigation was."

"Ysasi's smart-ass remarks," Dean said later, "began the bad blood that developed between the police and the county attorney's office."

Dean and Borkenhagen would have to contact the cast members of *Beginner's Luck* and begin to put together a picture of Crane's activities offstage. Dean went to Crane's bedside. On his back, on his left shoulder, was a single long black hair, which had evidently gone unnoticed before. This was bagged.

Crane's body was placed in a black plastic bag, lifted from the bed, and put on a stretcher that had been laid just outside the bedroom door near the couch. Medics lifted the stretcher onto a cart and carried it out of the apartment. At 5:48 P.M. the body was released to Sinai Mortuary for transportation to the ME's mortuary in Phoenix. Dennis Borkenhagen had filled out the red tag that accompanied the body.

8

THE SEARCH

Subplot—Subordinate plot. In a good teleplay the sub-plot relates causally to the main plot and is introduced to help move the story toward its climax.

The heat fell like showers of rain. "It was extremely hot!" recalled Dean. "I remember a TV crew came over from Los Angeles. They were uncomfortable with their bulky equipment, but then so was I."

Pete Noyes, KNBC-TV newsman, had worked with Bob during his KNX radio days and had brought a camera crew from Los Angeles. "I was there when the cops bagged all the stuff, and we were the ones who took all the television footage inside the room," he said. He had viewed Bob's rise to the top and his subsequent fall.

At 5:00 P.M., the hottest part of the day in the desert, Dean and Borkenhagen walked out to the white Monte Carlo Chevrolet parked in Crane's reserved space. It had been leased for Bob from Lou Grub Chevrolet. Dean noticed that the spare tire was missing in the trunk, but the jack and jack handle were there. Several *Night Life* newspapers were in the glove compartment, along with a piece of paper reading 7220-2nd Street, 7221-1st Avenue, and 10818 North Scottsdale. They would turn out to be the addresses of stationery stores.

Meanwhile Ernie Cole, the ID man, began impounding items from the kitchen area, including a small tripod. Cole moved to the living room, bagging and boxing the videotaping equipment and all the tapes, papers, notes, and photos. He took hundreds of items, even garbage, using tongs to lift everything into individual glassine bags. "We impounded just about everything," said Borkenhagen, "everything in his apartment, not knowing what we were dealing with or what was going to happen."

Bob Jr. arrived with his attorney, Bill Goldstein, and Lloyd Vaughn, Crane's business manager. Dean sensed that Vaughn was nervous, preoccupied; he appeared to be only going through the motions of attending to Crane's final affairs. He could have been merely upset over his client's death, considered the detective.

Still, Dean found Vaughn's behavior strange. "He was sort of nervous, but he's also one of those horse's butts, let's say horse's ass. He was throughout and around everything, being a 'big help.' In some cases you could be helpful by just shutting your mouth. He should have done a little bit of that. Because he was talking so much, he became a suspect, too."

Wheale and technician Ed Halverson placed signs reading "Crime Scene" at the front door and rear arcadia door now that it was passable again. At 8:30 P.M. the impounded items, the shabby relics of a famous man's life, were transported to SPD.

Dean and Borkenhagen drove directly from the Winfield back to the station. The simple alabaster blocks of the building were reflected in the still pool at the front, along with the crowd of media people who had gathered there. The mood was tense, excited, and speculative.

Dean went to his office and sat, pondering. "When working," he said, "I can see Camelback. It is a backdrop to just about everything—you could see it from the Winfield as soon as you pull off onto the street or into the drive. Bob must have seen the sun set behind it from his front door each evening."

Borkenhagen returned home briefly to change from his uniform into civvies. Earlier that morning a large, jet black Labrador retriever had followed his child home. "Somebody'll claim him," Borkenhagen promised as he left for work in the afternoon. But when he got home to change, the dog was still there. "He had come at just about the time Crane had died," Borkenhagen said. "Both had thick black hair, and it was almost as if Bob Crane's spirit had entered that dog." To this day the dog remains at Borkenhagen's.

Around 11:30 P.M. Dean and Borkenhagen were leaving headquarters in their Mercury police cruiser when they got a radio call that a man and a woman at the Pointe in Phoenix had some information for them about Crane's death. "It was one of those wild, tangential trips," said Borkenhagen, "but we had to investigate."

At the Pointe two couples told the officers that a drunken man, with hair "fluffed out on the sides above his ears like Bozo the Clown," had come up to them at a pool party and told them he had been out partying with Bob Crane. "I'm into some heavy dealings," he added. "Don't be surprised if the police come and get me tonight." But Dean and his partner quickly established that the man had nothing to do with the killing. It was the first of what were to be dozens of false leads.

On the way back, Dean remembered he had yet to contact the county attorney's office. Dean located a phone booth and called Larry Turoff, the county attorney's investigator and director of the major felony bureau. Dean came back to the cruiser. "I called Larry," he said, "and I think he was insulted that we notified him this late." The Maricopa County attorney, Charles Hyder, had initiated a program in April 1978 where police who got to a crime scene were to call the county attorney's office so it could send out an observer. Thus the prosecutor's office would be involved from the beginning.

* * *

Friday morning, June 30, at 7:18 John Carpenter, anxious
for information on how the case was proceeding, called the
Scottsdale Police Department.

"Officer Richards here. Can I help you, please?"

"Are you on the case with Dean?" asked Carpenter.

"No, sir. Dean won't be in until about nine A.M."

"My name is Carpenter. I talked to him last night. I was
running over in my mind the statement that I made to Dean
about the last time I talked to Bob. I told him I talked to
Bob about one-thirty in the morning. But then I realized
later that it was probably around two forty-five.

"I asked Officer Dean at the time if there was an alter-
cation. If there was a fight in the room, because, you know,
Bob don't ever fight. And then of course I heard on the
news that he was hit on the head and then strangled with
a lamp cord." Carpenter wondered if Bob had been shot
and was told no. His long message listed all the women
Bob had met and a possible male suspect.

John described the bookcase at Bob's. "On top of it is a
ram or an elephant," he said. "Four or five tiers down . . .
there's a photo of a girl who has a name like it's a band
name, Donna Dean or Deanna Don, or something like that.
Now in there is her portfolio. It gives her name, her address,
her height. She is married to a guy that plays in a band in
town. Now this is the only married woman that I know Bob
knew or associated with during the period of time that I
was there. . . . I called Bobby Jr. right after I talked to Dean
yesterday. I was under the assumption that it was a robbery,
prior to finding out that it was a homicide."

John explained he would be in only until early afternoon
if Dean wanted to talk with him. He was waiting for his
car to be repaired. "Today might be a short day," he said.
"As soon as I get it, I'll be splitting."

At 8:00 A.M. Carpenter called John Ayers at Dyna-Tronics
and told him that Bob Crane had been killed and if they
wanted the Sony videotape recorder they had loaned him,

they should call Lieutenant Ron Dean of the SPD.

An hour later Dean came in galvanized and excited. "This was the first day after the murder and a critical time to start," he said later. He called Carpenter back to arrange a further interview. John said that due to the Fourth of July holiday he would not be available, but he gave Dean his home phone number and business numbers.

After he hung up, the detective considered Carpenter's call. Changing the time he last spoke with Crane was both strange and suspicious. An innocent person doesn't have to worry about trying to be *too* accurate, he thought. Dean knew that John was trying to give him a list of possible suspects, since his first statement over the phone to Dean at Bob's apartment put him with the actor at one-thirty. The time of the murder was three A.M.

"Carpenter was swimming in the pool," said Dean, "and left his trunks in Crane's room. He tells us he last talked to Bob Crane around two-thirty to three in the morning. He said that Bob was editing a tape of *Saturday Night Fever* and that the tape and his trunks should have gone back to California with Carpenter."

This was the first time Dean and Captain Pratt had used a new police technique called "charting," which laid out the investigation minute by minute, hour by hour, through flow charts, graphs, and maps. "It's designed to give you a picture of what is happening," said Pratt, "as opposed to having to read it all in a printed report."

"Phoenix Police Department intelligence was assigned to do charts of the Crane case," Dean said. "Every supplement that we did, they received. Later on in the investigation, when their report goes over to the county attorney's office, some of it turns up missing. It caused us headaches in the months to come and made it difficult to put everything back in perfect order."

Dean had seven detectives and a full squad of officers to assist him. "What I did was put Crane on a clock for twenty-four hours before his death," said Dean, "so we could get a tight schedule on that. I assigned Gary Maschner specifically to do that—to fill in the missing minutes of that twenty-four-hour clock, to re-create Bob Crane's last day. We found it had been pretty much of a routine day for him.

"We talked to the people at the Winfield Apartments. They really didn't know that much about him staying there. Other celebrities had stayed there before. It was the people on the floor above who heard Crane's voice raised in anger on the phone. They lived there before it went condo. It had been relatively quiet around the Winfield prior to the murder, so those people were concerned. However, no unusual persons were seen around the area.

"Crane didn't dress in expensive or bright-colored clothing while he was in Scottsdale. In fact, one of the things he often wore was his *Hogan's Heroes* leather jacket. At least that's what I've been told. We know the last place he ate at was the Safari with John Carpenter. We spoke at length with the two women they were with.

"Crane's life during the three weeks before his death showed no deviations. His time in Scottsdale patterned his behavior in Texas. He would be doing the play there and do his same activities with people he would meet."

Each of Crane's videotapes, at least the ones the killer had not taken, were screened at headquarters, and later a careful record of the contents of each was made, using the tape counter on the VCR to mark the parameters of the different scenes.

There were six numbered reel-to-reel tapes and thirteen videotapes that ran from A through M. D, F, and L were unlabeled by Crane; the others had general titles such as "Road Show." All were in black and white and were taken from a fixed camera on a tripod. Tape four was the version of *Saturday Night Fever* that Bob had finished editing at the time he was killed. Profanity had been excised, and certain questionable scenes had been scissored. Victoria's rehearsals in *Beginner's Luck* were on two videotapes and one reel-to-reel.

In between the X-rated encounters Crane had with various women and couples were taped sitcoms such as *The Dick Van Dyke Show*, soap operas, and a special from Caesar's Palace featuring the big bands the actor had loved so much. There were many episodes of *Hogan's Heroes*.

At 10:00 P.M. four of the boys from the CA's office, still hot under the collar, met with Dean. Borkenhagen attempted to mend feelings during the conference, but the atmosphere remained cold. "We'd try to have a conversation on who we thought the suspects were," Borkenhagen said, "but they decided they were more interested in seeing Crane's sex tapes. In fact, they just watched those and didn't talk to us the rest of the meeting."

" 'Put on the dirty movies!' they said," recalled Dean.

Dean himself didn't have much interest in the tapes. "I saw them every once in a while when someone else would review them. The prosecutor's office, that's the first thing he wanted, a copy of all those tapes. Many of the copies we made were mislaid or vanished as the case progressed."

Dean drove over to the Winfield to meet again with Bob Jr., Lloyd Vaughn, and Bill Goldstein. The rooms were eerily silent, the walls spotted with smudges. A patina of black fingerprint powder remained.

Dean allowed Crane's son to take some items of his father's from the apartment, including a bottle of imported Burgundy wine and the six-pack of Coors from the refrigerator, his dad's underwear, and a pair of drumsticks. Bob Jr. cleaned out two dresser drawers and packed the contents in two brown suede suitcases that had belonged to his father.

Goldstein found two empty packages of cigarettes on the cabinet next to the couch and put them on the coffee table. "I showed them to the police officer who was with us," he said later, "and he said the investigators probably knew about them and took no further notice. They were crushed packages. Nobody bothered to open them up to check the brand name. There were butts in the ashtray."

"That was the yellow ashtray," said Dean, "that Victoria Berry used while we were waiting for Dr. K."

Allowing Bob Jr. to take items from the apartment was a decision that haunted Dean for the next dozen years. It would be only one of the obstacles that Dean would have to overcome in his quest for an indictment. He would be told, "You allowed evidence to be packed up and taken back to California."

"We walked into the apartment the day after the murder and did as we pleased. It was not taped off, and a lot of personal items were still lying around," Vaughn told the press much later.

And why, Dean wondered to himself, did Lloyd Vaughn, Crane's business manager, look so nervous? In his gut Dean knew the man was guilty of *something*. "Vaughn had been sweating. We were all sweating, but his was a cold sweat."

9

THE VAULT

Causal relationship—Cause-and-effect relationship of scenes and characters to each other in a teleplay.

At 8:00 A.M., Friday, June 30, Deputy Medical Examiner Tom Jarvis began his autopsy examination of Bob Crane. He was observed by Dennis Borkenhagen.

First Jarvis noted the copious amounts of dried blood on the face, hair, right arm, and upper chest of the victim. Then he carefully measured the ligature mark around the neck. It was three-eighths of an inch wide.

Twenty-two bones make up the human skull, and of these, eight curved, ragged-edged, continent-like plates form the precious vault that houses and protects the brain. It takes a quarter century for the floating, phantom bones of an embryo to ossify into rigid, locked hard segments. But there is a deadly area of the vault where a blow almost always results in a skull fracture—just above the temple, where the thinnest part of the cranium lies. That was where Crane had been struck.

The two parallel lacerations behind Crane's left ear measured only one and one-half inches long and three-eighths of an inch wide. The wounds were remarkably close together, one-half inch apart, and were rounded at the top. Since the scalp fits snugly over the hard bone of the skull, blunt force creates clean, straight lacerations.

Jarvis knew the real damage lay beneath the skin— Crane's left temporal skull fracture measured four by two and one-half inches in diameter. Here there was a macroscopic bruising to the point of pulpefaction. Fractures of the skull do not cause death unless the brain underneath has been damaged. Crane had deep frontal and temporal contusions of the brain.

The brain, floating in the skull, was compressed on the injury side and then torn away and jarred against the side opposite the point of impact, which explained why the victim also had a hemorrhage of the *right* temporal region.

Jarvis surveyed the legacy of the two blows—a contusion to the left upper eyelid, right lower eyelid, and left lower lip and an abrasion to the left ring finger.

Dr. Jarvis felt that the first blow would have inflicted serious brain damage; the second surely would have brought death to the victim.

The murder weapon was not a pipe, Jarvis knew; wounds caused by an iron pipe often show circular marks created by the ramming end of the pipe, and there were no such marks. If the weapon had been a straight metal bar, it would have caused ragged, broken edges at the ends of the fracture instead of the rounded, unbroken upturns at the upper part of each of the wounds. Therefore the weapon was a heavy metal instrument with a turned-up end, which indicated something bent.

Murder by blunt instrument is the most common form of homicide, but a bludgeoning combined with strangulation is almost unheard of. There were ways for the ME to tell if asphyxia had caused the death or if Crane had been dead when he had been strangled.

If Crane had still been breathing, there would have been minute areas of bleeding due to the rupture of small blood vessels in the skin within the groove left by the strangling cord. The absence of any black-and-blue marks along the edges of the groove confirmed that the victim was dead at the time of the strangling.

Jarvis still had to see if there had been any compression of the windpipe and thyroid gland or fractures of the bones of the larynx and throat, principally the wishbone-shaped hyoid bone, usually broken only in manual strangulation. He found the hyoid bone intact. The lack of water in the victim's lungs and high content of oxygen in Crane's arterial blood were further confirmation that he had been dead before the cord was tied around his neck.

Perhaps the single thing that makes a bludgeoning so horrifying is the actual destruction of the brain and personality, memory, self. This was more than a murder, this was a blotting out.

Eloy Ysasi told Borkenhagen after the autopsy, "As for the cord, it didn't strangle him. The cord was put on after he was dead, but it was put on tight."

The medical examiners thought the murder weapon might be a lug wrench, crowbar, fireplace poker, or automobile jack, but Dean had his doubts. A tire iron in particular didn't make much sense to him, especially the regular type of tire iron. "There's not enough leverage," he said. The killer had been able to bring the weapon down in such a short arc that the blood spatter to the ceiling was minimal and only a few droplets of blood pelleted the bedside table lamp. Powerful, controlled blows, delivered in poor light, precisely side by side, would have been difficult with a tire iron.

Whatever the weapon, Dean doubted that it had already been in Crane's apartment. "Crane don't fight," his closest friend, John Carpenter, had told Officer Richards, and it was true that cast members and backstage employees at the Windmill had heard Bob mention his strong distaste for weapons.

As for the bodily fluid, or jelly (a jar of K-Y jelly was nearby), found in Crane's groin area, Dean said, "The white flaky powder, it was never tested. To this day I don't know why. It isn't a difficult test."

Borkenhagen concurred. "When I went down to the autopsy," he said, "I asked Eloy Ysasi to collect that bodily fluid, what we thought was semen, and he said, 'What's that going to tell you? That he had a piece of ass.' And that was the end of it. It wasn't collected." All that Dean had heard about Bob's nonuse of alcohol and drugs was borne out by the toxicologist's findings.*

The search for the murder weapon went on. Pratt ordered the Arizona Canal dragged. Since the canal cut through the Winfield complex, the killer might have discarded the weapon there.

In the days ahead, the Maricopa County Sheriff's Department diving team would search the canal seventy-five yards north of the Winfield and proceed seventy-five yards south of the Chaparral Bridge. Pat Hintz and the other members of the team† would do this four times from 10:30 A.M. until 1:30 P.M. All they found were three golf clubs.

The Scottsdale Youth Patrol searched diligently along Chaparral Road to Miller and to Scottsdale Road, and they too were unsuccessful.

The lid to the sewer drain northeast of Crane's apartment was found partially open, but the only thing discovered inside was a long, wooden-handled shovel. Possible weapons continued to be recovered in the early days of the case—a four-way wrench and a tire iron found on a

---

*Chief Toxicologist Ramon A. Morano's analysis showed *negative* for alcohol, fluorocarbons, volatiles, barbiturates, methaqualone, diazepam, chlordiazepoxide, propoxyphene, phenothiazines, salicylate, meperidine, amphetamine, methamphetamine, methadone, and cocaine.
†Lee Fultz, Fritz Holly, Brenda Sorauf, Chris Sorauf, and Dave Hendeshott.

highway in Phoenix, another tire iron discovered in Mesa, and a third found in a Scottsdale self-service car wash. "People were finding them in Dumpsters," said Borkenhagen, "and all over. Each one we got we submitted for any kind of blood trace."

None was found.

At the same time Dr. Jarvis was beginning his examination, a twelve-year-old girl named Sue* approached the police at the Winfield Apartments with information about something she had seen the morning Bob had died. "I play tennis nearly every morning at the Chaparral Tennis Club [located between Crane's apartment and the Sunburst, where John had been staying]. Yesterday morning, around six, I saw a motorcycle pull into the second drive of the Winfield Apartments on the west side [Crane's apartment drive]. The motorcycle pulled into the last parking space on the right side toward the back of the apartments.

"I didn't think anything about it, but about five minutes later, the motorcycle drove back out. It seemed strange to me because I've never seen a motorcycle in the complex before. There was only one person on the motorcycle. It was big like a police motorcycle [but] it didn't have any saddlebags like a police motorcycle."

The twelve-year-old pointed out to an officer the tracks left by the cycle, but at the time her information was not considered important. The girl's mother thought differently and followed up with a call to Darwin Barrie at SPD. Barrie took a page and a half of notes, and again the tip was consigned to the files. That is, until the following night, when the phone rang.

"I'm the one," said an unknown male voice, "the one who was riding a motorcycle on June 29 at six-thirty in the morning near Crane's apartment. At that time I saw a white female with blond hair about five feet four, one hundred and twenty pounds, with a small child. She was carrying

---

*This name has been altered.

an object wrapped in butcher paper about twenty inches long. She left the exact apartment on the lower level that Crane was staying in. I can't give you any more information, but I'll call you again." The connection was broken.

Police, still in search of the odd weapon that had left such unusual marks on Bob's temple, realized that Japanese motorcycles have specialty tire irons. These were a different shape and size from car tools. Could one of them have caused the odd wounds? Because of Sue's information, the police didn't consider the anonymous caller a crank—the girl's sighting placed a cyclist at Crane's apartment at the same time the caller claimed to have seen a woman and child exiting. This was only hours before the actor's body was discovered. If the motorcyclist was telling the truth about when he was there, then he could be speaking the truth about seeing a blond woman with a package leaving 132A. This left two questions—who was the caller, and whom did he see?

Dean realized that the motorcyclist's description of the woman and child matched the photos of Patti and Scotty Crane found in the apartment, but they had been in Scottsdale only on June 18 and 19. The description also matched Brenda Broyles, who had a seven-year-old son.

In an effort to enhance Sue's memory, Detective Fred Fiore, an expert in the art of hypnotism, and county attorney's investigator Dave Arellanes met with mother and daughter on the third floor of the CA's complex in mid-morning.

"Now it's all your show, Sue," said Fiore. "There's a couple of ways we can do this. Why don't you just lay your hand out flat there. . . ."

Sue began to giggle. "Uh-huh."

"I want you to go to sleep," said Fiore. "One, two, three, relax, going deeper and deeper and deeper. . . . That's fine. Just relax. Feeling so comfortable. As I count to three, Sue, you'll find you can become even more relaxed and go even deeper. One, two, three . . .

"Sue, in your mind's eye, if you would, I'd like you to

imagine that you're at the top of a flight of stairs, and there's going to be ten stairs on that flight of stairs, and if you would, I'd like you to do me a favor. Imagine you're going to start down those stairs. As you start down and take each step, I'd like you to tell me what number and take a nice big breath and exhale and then step down and tell me the other number. . . ."

"Nine," said Sue, "eight . . ."

"Going deeper, going slower, and relax."

"Seven, six . . ."

"And relax, with each step you'll find you're getting deeper. . . ."

"Five . . . four . . ."

"Getting so relaxed as you go even deeper. . . ."

"Three, two . . . one."

"At the bottom of those stairs you might find a small lobby, and imagine that on the other side of that lobby is a pretty red door, and as you open that red door and step inside, it can be your own favorite room. And in that room you may even find a nice soft easy chair. Just imagine that you're sitting in that easy chair, feeling so comfortable and so relaxed and going even deeper and deeper."

Sue was now in a light trance state. Fiore told the young girl that she would see a television set and that she could control what she wanted to see on that set and replay it at will.

"You're going to see that event just like you saw at six o'clock in the morning. Feel more comfortable while I turn the television on, and while it's warming up you may even see a calendar, a big calendar, and the calendar is going to have the date of July 20. As each page comes off you'll go even deeper. Twenty is gone, you can see nineteen. . . . Going deeper . . . three, two, one . . . That's fine, now one is gone and it's June 30 and the 30 is gone, it's 29. It's back on June 29 and it's early in the morning, and you may even see yourself on a tennis court. . . ."

"I'm playing doubles," said Sue, "with Andy and Jeff and Scott." She went on to describe her partners and the game.

"Okay," said Fiore, "let's just run the camera a little bit faster."

"Well, I was looking for a ball. I looked through the fence and mesh and the citrus trees, and I saw a motorcycle."

"Can you see that motorcycle now?"

"Yes, and then it turns a corner into the apartments."

"What color is that motorcycle?"

"Black."

"Is it all black? Can you see any other colors on it?"

"White."

"White. Where is the white at?"

"At the very front."

"What else do you see on that motorcycle?"

"A person."

"Okay, what is that person wearing?"

"Levi's, I think."

"Okay, let's look at him. Stop it right there. Just kind of zoom in. Now look at him. What's he wearing? Can you see his shoes?"

"No."

"Can you see any other clothing he's wearing?"

"A white shirt. Not a T-shirt, a golf or tennis shirt."

"Okay, let's look up now past his shirt. Can you see his head?"

"Not really."

"Why not?"

"Because," said Sue, "he has a helmet on . . . all white."

"Can you see the front of that helmet?"

"Just at an angle. . . ." Sue could only see a bit of his face.

"Let's stop the TV there and just zoom in on his face. . . ."

"All I can see is that he's tanned and maybe he has glasses on, I'm not sure. . . ." Sue could not see his nose or mouth. She could make out that the rider was sitting on a black seat but could not see the license plate because of the angle.

"What is the motorcycle doing now?"

"It's turning into a cul-de-sac . . . parking."

"Can you see the guy? Do you watch him as he gets off?"

"No . . . I'm playing tennis."

Fiore had Sue go back to where the rider parked. "Can you describe him as he's standing there by the motorcycle?"

"It seems like he would be, umm, between the ages of thirty-five and twenty, around in there."

"Would you say he was a fat guy, a skinny guy, a tall guy?"

"Not really fat . . . a slim guy."

"Okay, let's run that tape a little bit faster until the next time you hear the motorcycle."

"The guy's coming out of the cul-de-sac about five minutes later and driving off on his motorcycle pretty fast . . . onto Chaparral. I think he turns east, maybe. . . ."

"Why do you say 'maybe'?"

"Because the tree's in the way."

"Let's back it up just before, when you have a good clear shot. Let me know when you can see the motorcycle pretty clearly. . . . Now look at the bike pretty close . . . is the whole thing black?"

"The front isn't . . . it's black with the white reflector or the white bug shield or whatever it is, and it has a high windshield. The front wheel has a funny shape . . . the tread has got cubelike things that eject from it. . . . It looks more like a dirt bike, but it's not dirty. It looks kind of old, kind of used."

"Can you see his face?"

"No."

"Why not?"

"Because he still has the helmet on. It's on his head and he has his shield down and it comes around." Sue recalled long, light brown hair sticking out from under the helmet.

"When you look at him and you see that shirt, does the shirt have buttons on it?"

"No," concluded Sue, "it's just kind of like my shirt, and it's just a golf shirt."

"That's fine, that's fine," said Fiore, and he began to bring her out. "I'd like you to take two nice deep breaths and exhale and completely relax.... All right, Sue, all these things that we discussed here, you'll find at a later date you'll be able to see and recall them just as vividly. Okay, Sue, in just a moment I'm going to awaken you as I count from A to D. When I reach the count of D you'll find you'll be alert and clear-headed. A going on B. B going on C. C going on D. D, and your eyes are open."

Police now searched for the motorcycle Sue had seen. Officer Chris Bingham was given a suspicious vehicle log listing three motorcycles observed by Officer Dave Evans in the area of 7430 and 7436 East Chaparral around the time of Bob's death.

The first was a red Suzuki that Evans had stopped. Rider and passenger both expressed no knowledge of the call and knew of none of their biker friends who might have made it.

The second vehicle was parked under an awning and covered with a sheet in front of apartment 146A at the Winfield. Sue said that it was not the bike.

The third cycle was discovered on the east side of 7436 East Chaparral and had a chrome gas tank. It was registered to Doug Effron. A check by Bingham showed Effron and his mother had lived at Winfield in apartment 206A until June 2 and then moved away. Bingham asked Effron, "Are you still the owner of a 1974 Suzuki 550?"

"No," said Effron, "I sold it to Pete Wessell, a guy in 148B."

"Could you describe it?"

"Sure, silver with a chrome gasoline tank, equipped with a smoke-colored ferret." Effron denied making the call, as did Wessell.

The identity of the phantom motorcyclist would remain one of the unsolved mysteries of the Crane case. But if the information provided by the caller was true, it appeared either Brenda or Patti could have been in Crane's rooms near or at the time of Bob's death.

*   *   *

Forced out of his office by the unceasing attention of the
media, Dean took his men to "team placing"—a secret,
black-doored office in a small depot in the center of Rail-
road Park. "By the time you tell a hundred different people
what's going on," said Dean, "you don't have time to do
anything."

Still in the first-forty-eight hours of the case, Dean and
Borkenhagen began to trim away the overgrowth of clues.
For example, the Scotch and gin were present in Bob's
apartment not because the killer had been drinking them,
but because they were a complimentary gift for Crane from
the Windmill Theatre management, a common practice.
"The comp drinks were routine," said Borkenhagen. "Any
visiting star who stayed in that room got them as part of
an agreement between the theater and the apartment." On
the other hand, in the weeks before Bob's death, no one
had ever noticed drinks there before.

The June 29, 1978, morning paper that the killer might
have brought into 132A was explained by Victoria, who
now recalled absentmindedly bringing it inside with her.
She also provided an answer to what the "mystery bag"
may have contained: an album of pornographic stills, "very
graphic," she said. Apparently the killer had taken them.

As noted, there was a fireplace hidden behind the curtains
and Bob's videotaping equipment, but there was no poker.
The manager of the complex informed Dean that there
never had been any fireplace utensils in the apartment. Dean
had also wondered if the killer had burned something in
the fireplace, since white ashes had been discovered. However, the previous occupant of the apartment, JoAnne Worley, who had been there with her husband, Roger Perry,
recalled that she had seen ashes in the fireplace while she
was there.

It was the big questions—who? how? why?—that perplexed the officers. Aloud, they wrestled with the riddles.
Crane had had sex with two or three women at a time,
sometimes with couples. In some cases it appeared the
women on the tapes were not aware they were being filmed.
The motive could be retaliation by a special lover, a crime
of passion by a jealous husband, a blackmailer after the

pictures, or someone interested in covering up what was recorded.

"A jealous boyfriend would go in there and whack him right in the bean," said one investigator.

"Unless," said another, "there was a girl who let a guy in."

"If it's the husband of some woman whom Crane had jumped, is he going to come in there and take one video when there's twenty or thirty lying around all either unmarked or with generalized titles?" said Borkenhagen. "How would the killer know which one to take?"

"And the killer," added Dean, "missed all those glossy black-and-white photos lying around on the table, the negatives in the bathroom. If you're an irate boyfriend or husband or something like that, you're not going to take just one album."

Crane produced an album for every city he visited during the *Beginner's Luck* tour—albums from Hawaii, Texas, and Cincinnati were presently in the home he had shared with Patti in Los Angeles.

Both Dean and Borkenhagen thought that the sex photos had been taken to lead the police astray. "We surmised the album was a red herring, so to speak," said Borkenhagen. "Somebody took it to say, 'This is what I want you to look for.'"

During the next few days, as Dean wondered about the tapes left behind and puzzled over what might have been taken or erased by the killer (no one knew how many tapes there had been to begin with), the videotapes were re-screened. "They were black Beta cassettes with no labels. You pretty much had to play them to find out what was on them," said Dean. "I assigned one detective to do it—Mark Salem—he just had to sit there and do a report. It took quite a while.

"Later in the case I sent Officer Salem to Texas to connect the two areas because some of the same names were coming up. It was hard to put names with the faces on the tape. We told him, 'Every time you see a shot of one—stop the tape and get a picture. Let's see who these people are.' We made hard copies. They turned out grainy because we were taking a picture off a TV. But we were still able to print them."

Dean eliminated some suspects within a fairly short time after the murder—two of Crane's lovers, for example, had been working at the French Connection Massage Parlor between 6:00 P.M. and 3:00 A.M.

Dean had zeroed in on one of Bob's lovers first. "Kathy Reid fucking on tape," he said. "I saw her on the videotape, and then I saw her picture on publicity photos in Phoenix."

Almost immediately after Bob's death, Kathy had received an unusual telephone call. "This is John," said a voice on the phone. The caller sounded young.

"John who?" Kathy asked.

"Guess," he said, and then remained silent.

"I don't have time for silly people!" Kathy snapped, and hung up. The next day she received a second call, though this caller did not sound like the first man. "Do you like oral sex in the morning?" he asked. Kathy slammed down the phone.

Borkenhagen interviewed her. She had called Bob's apartment at the Winfield early in the afternoon just after Victoria had discovered the body. She'd left her number. "I wanted to see if Bob was home so that I could drop off a tape recording of myself for promotional purposes," she said.

Kathy coolly explained that Bob had taken some Polaroid pictures of her in the nude, and although she didn't care that Crane had them, now that they were in police custody she wanted them back.

Borkenhagen was puzzled. "No Polaroid pictures of you were ever recovered from the apartment," he said, "none at all." At the realization that the killer had taken the pictures of her, Kathy had to fight to regain her composure.

During his call to Officer Richards, John Carpenter had proposed the theory that Kathy's boyfriend, who was a drummer like Bob, had discovered her affair and killed Crane. "*That* was impossible," said Dean. "*She* didn't know she was on tape because Crane had done it secretly. She only knew about the snapshots." Kathy's boyfriend lived with her and got off work at 1:05 P.M., a couple of hours before Bob's death. "I was up with him till four A.M. The whole time," said Kathy.

When other women learned that they had been secretly filmed by Crane's cameras, they were at first stunned, then hurt, then furious. "Frankly, I wasn't sorry he was dead," one said much later. "When you deceive people it's going to come back on you—I don't condone anybody being killed, but I'm not sorry he got what he got. I'm not the only one. I'm sure there are a lot of other people out there."

In Dallas, Bob had fought with another cast member: Jack DeMave. "He was one of the actors in the play in Dallas," said Borkenhagen. "Everyone tells me they didn't get along. Crane was a very good actor and just did his thing as a professional and expected those around him, like DeMave, to come up to the same standards." Since DeMave was away on vacation with his wife, his whereabouts were unknown and it would be some time before he could be located and questioned.

Ernie Braun, a friend of Crane's for several years, spoke with Dean. "I was driving Bob to the airport last May 28 after *Beginner's Luck* closed in Dallas," he said, "when he told me, 'I've had a problem with someone connected with *Beginner's Luck*. We had an argument, a heated one, and he threatened to cut my throat.' " Mistakenly, Ernie thought Crane meant Norman Barasch, coauthor of the play, and for a time it led detectives astray until Bob's son set them straight.

"To my knowledge he got along great with Barasch," said Bob Jr. "From everything I've heard from my father and a couple of meetings on my own, Barasch seems like a real nice, ordinary, concerned, loving-type guy. I think my father and Barasch had utmost professional respect for one another."

On their ride to the airport Bob told Braun of another problem. "The last time I was in Phoenix," he said, "I became involved with a married woman, and I had some trouble with her husband. He had me followed, and I'm worried about any contact with either of them in Scottsdale. Her husband has some big connections in the Phoenix area.

"I'm scared to go to Phoenix."

Dean turned to the motive of financial gain. "What about Crane's will, his business agreements, his insurance policies?" he asked Borkenhagen. "Who benefited financially?" It would take a little time to find the answers.

As they pondered the various avenues of inquiry, Dean and Borkenhagen began to get more tips than they could handle. Some were quite bizarre. "The people were trying to help," Dean said later. " 'I think the Nazis did it,' we got a lot of letters like that."

Dean was contacted by one witness who swore she saw Colonel Klink and Sergeant Schultz of *Hogan's Heroes* sneaking out of the room after having killed their former prisoner. Borkenhagen was philosophical—"Schultz is dead. [John Banner, who had played the part, had died.] We could clear this whole thing up—pin it on him. The perp is dead."

Raeburn Martin, a small-time hood who had previously informed against organized crime figures in Arkansas, called his control agent at the Louisiana out-of-state crime unit. "I know who killed Bob Crane," he said. "I want to talk to you about it as soon as possible, but not over the phone." Two days later Martin was found hanged in a Scottsdale City cell after an arrest for drunkenness. A million-dollar contract had been placed on Martin's life by the underworld, and his control was suspicious of the "suicide"—there had been a number of abrasions on his body.

County Attorney Chuck Hyder asked Chief Nemetz to look into Martin's allegations. "It appears quite important," he said.

However, Martin's widow said, "He was probably drunk. He talked strange and said things that were untrue when he was drunk."

A short time before Bob's murder, a woman received an angry letter from her estranged husband in which he threatened the lives of Crane and her agent. On July 11, 1978, he sent her a second letter in which he claimed to have taken care of Crane and stated that his wife's agent was next. On July 13 the agent died. But no one connected the husband to any crime.

In a series of letters to the police and to two judges, a man in prison confessed that he was the killer. Borkenhagen knew that some cons confess just to break routine or get cigarettes. Still, he made the trip over to the prison at the request of one of the judges.

"So he bums a cigarette and tells us the story," said Borkenhagen. "Says he broke out of jail the day before. He took one of the prison trucks and drove around, came out to Scottsdale. Bob Crane flagged him down and said, 'I'm having a little game over at my house. There'll be some women, some booze.'

"As he spoke, he smoked that cigarette down to nothing. His fingers are all burned, burned *black*, and on his last drag there was nothing left of that cigarette but a burning ember. He tells us he figured 'What the hell,' so he went over to the house with him. 'We had a lot to drink, and I got pretty smashed. We got in an argument over cards. I had three aces and he had two kings. He started on me first, started pushing me around, so I picked up a gun and shot him. I did it.' "

Dean knew that Crane habitually locked, even double-locked, the front door, but if there was another key to 132A beyond those accounted for, it would not be remarkable. Over the years countless guests had stayed in the room, and all had been given keys. Not all had returned them. The killer could have had a duplicate.

Another possibility was that Crane had a visitor, who had unlatched a window or gimmicked the front door in some way so that it would not lock behind him. Once Bob was asleep anything could have happened. But Bob Jr. reminded Dean that his dad was a light sleeper.

"If somebody used a key even," Bob Jr. said later, "he would hear. I know for a fact that he positively dead-bolted the front door every time. Assuming that the sliding doors were locked, even a person with a key turning the dead bolt, that would wake my father up. So I assume the person was somebody he was comfortable with."

Had Crane let his own murderer in? Felt so at home with the assailant that he fell asleep in front of him or her? Dean was convinced that Crane knew his attacker.

"There were no signs of forced entry," said Borkenhagen, "and no signs of struggle. On the surface it looked like the killer was someone who knew him or knew how to get inside his apartment."

No one could envision Crane falling asleep in front of a jealous husband.

Since Bob had no weapons in his apartment, it meant that the killer might have brought one in with him. It could have been concealed inside a package, a gift, a large purse, or even a businessman's briefcase.

As far as Dean was concerned, the weapon was most likely not a tire iron, but for the time being that was what the detectives were searching for. They considered how that particular weapon could have been obtained and disposed of.

A local man could have taken it from his own garage and then replaced it, blood wiped away. If the man were from out of town, he could have brought it in the trunk of his own car, used it on Bob, replaced it in the trunk, and driven away. Most likely the weapon would have been discarded in the desert, tossed from a fleeing car or, worse yet, buried.

The detectives discussed the cord around Bob's neck. "It would take some strength to tie that cord," Dean said. "Because now this was a dead body, pretty heavy. You'd have to be strong to go around and knot it that tightly."

"Right," said one cop. "But then there was no struggle. Why eliminate a woman? I think it's very possible. The question is, was there one person there or two people?"

"If it was a woman," said Borkenhagen, "it would have to be a pretty healthy woman." If the killer were a woman, she might not have thought herself strong enough to deliver a death-dealing blow. The cord might have been used to make certain the victim could not survive.

Bob was found in his shorts, but when he was with a

woman he always slept nude. He had "bodily fluid" on his groin, most likely semen, but at all times after intercourse he would wash up carefully. Such anomalies bothered the detectives.

The cord around the victim's neck might have been more than insurance; it may have been window dressing, a ritual, a sly message, or a dig from the killer. The significance of the electrical cord haunted and eluded the detectives—was there a message implicit in the fact that the cord had once been connected to a video recorder, a VCR? Could the choice of the cord point to someone who was actually in the taped sex scenes? Crane's friend John Carpenter serviced VCRs. Was the cut cord a symbol of a severed bond of friendship?

"The cord was cut very efficiently," Dean said to his men. "Look at the photos. See how the camera equipment was laid out. To go for that part of the cord in a darkened room took some doing. The killer's already whacked Crane in the head, and now he's got to go into the other room past a lot of cords—the lamp cord next to the body, the phone cord outside the bedroom door, to get the one he wants and cut it off. . . ."

"Then sort through a ball of hot wires," said Borkenhagen.

"The cord was cut with a real sharp instrument."

"Yeah, the lab guys say a pocketknife or cutter," said Borkenhagen. "You take a cord like that, double it up, and cut through it. If your knife isn't real sharp, it'll pull some of those copper wires; some would be more extended than others."

"The instrument could have been Crane's," said Dean. "He was doing editing."

"Right. The killer must have used clippers," Borkenhagen said, "most likely the pair that Bob had on the TV. But again—why go for that *particular* cord?

"I've seen people who've been dead for an hour—all of a sudden, snorf! They give a little spasm of the diaphragm. I've seen that many times. I kinda thought this was a possibility. The killer could have been in there dickin' around with that bag, looking for the photo album, and Crane, who's dead, gives a little reflex action. 'Holy shit!' goes the murderer. 'I better . . .' "

"This sends him scrambling," said Dean. "He scrambled in a pretty good way, getting back in there behind the TV. This was somebody quite familiar with the room."

Finally, the door to the ground-level apartment was left unlocked by the murderer. Was this to facilitate the finding of the body? And why? To be certain that the exact time of death could be determined?

The first day after the murder, Dean, Borkenhagen, and the other detectives broke up by 11:00 P.M. Dean was anxious to go on, but it was too late to do much more. "When you're fresh on a case," he said, "you don't feel tired. You just want to keep on accomplishing things, and we were accomplishing a lot."

He stopped at the Safari on the way home. It was the last place Bob was seen alive. Tonight there were few people in the brightly lit restaurant. Dean tried to visualize Bob, John, and their dates at their booth, but no one could help him with information about Crane's activities that fateful night.

Dean slept well, ate little the next morning, and by seven was at the office cashing out some reports. Wind swept in from the sands. Thunder boomed across the flats. A few fat drops of rain pelted against his office window. July was here. The clouds traveled on, and Scottsdale was caught in an all-pervasive warm, olive light. The sky had taken on the color of grass above the grassless desert.

The police were unsure of anything during these first forty-eight hours, but they believed the killer was someone Crane had known and trusted. They had no weapon, no witnesses, and no clear-cut motive.

For Dean to find out what had brought Crane to this end and to uncover the elusive "who," the even more undefinable "how," and the mysterious "why," he had to go back to the beginning—Crane's roots. If Bob had known his killer, then the answers lay in the past. Everyone had said how Bob had changed from his early years, and Dean needed to know what had altered him and whom he had met on his way.

PART TWO

The Second Prison: The Stalag

HOGAN: Look. Orders from London are to hide you until the krauts stop looking for you, then we'll smuggle you to London.

SPARROW: Four men? Is it possible?

HOGAN: No, but we'll do it anyway. The first thing is to get you into Stalag 13.

SPARROW: You'd hide us in a prisoner-of-war camp?

HOGAN: We're the only motel for miles around.

10
THE GLASS FURNACE

Protagonist—Main character in a teleplay.

Waterbury, Connecticut, the hub of the U.S. brass industry, rests in the valleys of two serpentine rivers. Great outcroppings of granite thrust like fists through gray-as-granite hillsides denuded of all but the lowliest saplings, stripped to provide "muffle wood" for the annealing of brass. The remaining trees give a speckled, uncertain, startled look to the gray hills that the Indians had long before called Mattatuck, "the badly wooded region." Brown hills rise without warning along the banks of the Mad River and the Naugatuck, but in spite of this, tracks trace and delineate each curve of the waters, faltering only to break off into numerous spurs like the ribs of a lady's fan.

Bob Crane was born here on July 13, 1928, and soon must have sensed the relentless pulse of the original Yankee industrial town. Saffron-colored clouds pumped from the yellow firebrick stacks over the casting shops or billowed with a greenish tint from the chimneys above the rolling hills. An endless river of brass—buttons, clocks, wire, pins, and cartridges—flowed from Waterbury; millions of blank disks for American nickels emerged from the mills.

From the beginning Bob was musical, with a remarkable sense of tempo, drumming ceaselessly on picket fences near the shaded central green along West Main.

By the time he was eleven he was already performing in skits and playing with his own musical group. "I never settled for second best. It always had to be the best band," he said later, "and I always strove to be the best drummer." People were naturally drawn to the handsome boy, and Bob began to crave this attention. He dreaded criticism, and he dreaded being alone.

Bob attended high school in Stamford, another manufacturing town. He was a good Catholic boy, but his grades were mediocre. The New York State line is only eleven miles away from Stamford, and it was in New York City that the boy felt his future lay.

When Bob was fifteen he was determined to become a musician; it was the swing era, and percussion was his passion. His favorite drummer was Gene Krupa. Bob loved his ear, his control, his sensitivity and intensity. Krupa, it was said, "did everything but skate on the ceiling," and Crane, as part of his rocking, foot-stomping audience, heard him whenever he could.

A favorite and recurrent dream of Crane's was instant success. "I wanted to be a drummer," he said, "like Gene Krupa. . . ." His eyes would grow wistful as he continued, "I would have this fantasy. I would be at the Paramount Theatre in New York in Times Square, and Louis Prima's drummer would fall sick.

"The theater managers asked, 'Is there a drummer in the house?' I would run up on the stage and play—instant fame!" He sighed. "I never made it, though I never stopped practicing on the skins."

Bob dropped out of high school; he would feel insecure about it for the rest of his life. "I can't tell Puccini from a pizza," he would say, lamenting his lack of education, "or Sartre from a samba."

At sixteen Bob started his career as a drummer with the Connecticut Symphony Orchestra, but his comic flair and sense of humor often got him in trouble. After only two years he was fired for clowning around during a Bach fugue. Soon he would travel for a while with several East Coast bands.

Since he was only seventeen in 1945, Bob had no opportunity to serve in World War II. However, he spent some time in the National Guard. "I was a Remington Raider—the typewriter, that is," he joked.

Bob had dated his high school sweetheart, Anne Terzian, since he was fourteen and she was twelve. They were married in May of 1949 and for a time they lived with her parents while Crane played in dance bands at night and worked in a jewelry store by day. The couple would have three children together: Robert David, Deborah Ann, and Karen Leslie. Throughout the early years of the marriage, Crane continued to practice on the old, battered drums he had kept since school, his "lucky set."

It was 1950 when Bob got his first big break. The good-luck drums came along. Tiny WLEA in Hornell, New York, had advertised for an announcer, and forty-one applicants, all with New York experience in radio, showed up. Crane was at the end of the line, but he was the one who got the job—at $37.50 a week. For a while he endured terrible hours, living at the YMCA in Hornell while Anne remained in Stamford, until he signed on with WBIS in Briston, Connecticut. He next moved to WICC in Bridgeport, his salary now $500 a week, where he remained for six years. Legend has it that Bob got the Bridgeport position because of all the applicants he was the only one who didn't drink.

When Boston's WEEI offered Crane a job at $700 a week, he turned them down. "I'm afraid I was too ambitious for Boston by then," he said. "I was auditioning for a New York station at the time, but I wound up in Hollywood. I got there as a direct result of a magazine article that mentioned the Bridgeport show and WEEI offer. So I'm grateful to Boston."

Ralph Storey, who had the top-rated morning show on the CBS-owned station KNX in Los Angeles, quit in 1956 to host *The $64,000 Challenge*.

"An executive on WCBS in New York recommended me," said Bob, "because the Connecticut radio show was cutting into WCBS's local ratings, and they wanted me far away. I picked up the phone in Bridgeport and was told, 'This is Bob Sutton of KNX Los Angeles. How'd you like to do our morning drive-time show?' " Crane accepted and brought Anne and his kids—Bobby, fourteen, Debby, six, and Karen, five—along with the lucky drums, to Los Angeles.

Bob's quick wit, brashness, and the fact that he was a threat to WCBS's ratings weren't the only reasons he won the West Coast slot. In another of the good breaks that seemed to typify his early career, Crane's audition tape was played at the wrong speed for one CBS executive, giving his voice a resonance it lacked in reality.

There was a precedent at KNX to the type of show that Crane was offered: Steve Allen had done a late night talk show back in 1948 packed with ad-libs, craziness, and interviews, the "spiritual precursor" to the *Tonight* show that Allen was to originate years later. Crane's provocative program had much of Allen's wildness, timing, fast talk, and off-the-cuff brilliance; nevertheless his first month's ratings were tame. Crane was up against the growing popularity of Dick Whittinghill at KMPC down the street, so he hit the L.A. banquet circuit, making 256 personal appearances in a single year. As he made contacts, he began to receive offers for acting jobs.

Gradually Crane put his signature on the morning show, a mile-a-minute collection of ad-libs and gentle put-downs. He became known as "King of the L.A. Airwaves," and as his ratings spiraled so did his income, until he was earning almost $100,000 annually.

Crane could be testy, barking at his engineer when commercials cut into his interviews, and when he did play the spots he ribbed the sponsors unmercifully—for example, laying in the sound of coughing over a cigarette commercial. Sponsors rarely complained. With his lampooning, Bob usually tripled the amount of air time they had paid for.

Southern Californians still remember tuning in KNX to hear Crane sing, "I've got a rose between my toes from walking through the hothouse to you, pretty baby."

KNX was right next door to KNT, channel two, and the stations shared some of the same reporters. Pete Noyes, now with KNBC, was one of them. "Bob was around all the time," he recalled. "He would come over to the cafeteria, actually a bunch of machines where everyone sat down and had coffee. Crane was very affable. He didn't seem to have an inflated ego or anything. In those days DJs and news anchors were just ordinary people, not overly impressed with themselves."

However, Bob, who rarely played records, would sometimes caution, "Don't call me a disc jockey. A disc jockey gives nothing of his real self to what he does, and that's not my approach at all. I'm a radio personality. My sights were always on the comedy acting end of the business. When people asked me why I was doing little bits in television, guest roles, I would always tell them, 'I gotta prove I can act.' I can keep 'em laughing at the rush hour, five to nine, on a crowded L.A. freeway, six days a week, and that ain't easy. People say to me, 'Aw, you're just naturally funny. You don't have to work at it.' I don't care if that's what they think. But, man, I *do* work at it. I work *hard*."

Crane didn't smoke or drink. "He's not only a square," said one friend, "he's an insecure square." Bob once said on the air that the movie *Tom Jones* was so shocking that he would never take his mother to see it.

Gary Owens, a longtime colleague, top disc jockey, and the announcer on *Laugh-In*, summed up the young man: "He got a big name for himself in radio on the West Coast. He used to interview stars and producers like Frank Sinatra and Otto Preminger. He was truly a talented man, and he also was a fine actor and drummer. He always wanted to be an actor as much as he wanted to be in radio. I remember a comment he made to me one day when we were having lunch sometime in the early 1960s. He said, 'I want to be the next Jack Lemmon.' "

Lemmon was on record as saying, "I want to play every part better than any other actor could ever play it." Bob had the same kind of drive, but it was not as easy for him. "I had the damnedest time getting people convinced," he said. "They had me typed. I'd beg for jobs, and they'd give me bits, a few lines."

Bob subbed for Johnny Carson on *Who Do You Trust?* and at one point could have succeeded Carson as host. "I had gone as far in radio as I wanted to go, but I didn't want TV game shows or an emcee type of assignment. The public can change its mind on emcees rather suddenly, and I was looking ahead five years."

Crane was on *Alfred Hitchcock Presents, The Lawrence Welk Show, Your First Impression,* and *The Jack Benny Show*; he played his drums on *The Ed Sullivan Show* and the *Tonight* show. He persuaded Carl Reiner to give him a shot on *The Dick Van Dyke Show*, and it was here that Donna Reed saw him and decided to use him as a one-shot character. His character, Dr. Dave Kelsey, the Stones' personable suburban next-door neighbor, was a hit. "Bob, we've been looking five years for you," Reed told him.

"And I ran," said Bob. "I was so sure she was going to say, 'And now that we've found you—good-bye,' or something like that." Crane feared compliments because he was certain they would eventually turn into criticism.

For the next two years, while maintaining his morning show, Crane began working for Reed. She played prim Donna Stone, a woman so flawless it was joked that her program should be called *The Madonna Reed Show*, and Carl Betz played her equally perfect doctor husband, Alex. Shelley Fabares played their daughter, Paul Peterson their son, and in 1963, the same year Crane joined the cast as a regular, Patty Peterson, Paul's real-life sister, joined the show as an orphan taken in by the Stones.

The Kelsey role added another $50,000 to $75,000 a year to Bob's income, but it required a backbreaking schedule. Crane was up by 4:00 A.M., behind the wheel of his Thunderbird, and speeding away from Tarzana, his home in the

San Fernando Valley (named after Edgar Rice Burroughs's creation, Tarzan the Ape Man).

By 10:30 A.M. Bob had finished his program at KNX in Hollywood and literally had to dash the two blocks to Screen Gems Studios to act on the Reed show under the hotter lights and heavier makeup of those days. His day's acting completed by 7:00 P.M., he sped back to Anne and the kids.

One of Crane's reasons for moving to Tarzana was that "my old barber from Bridgeport had opened a shop there, and I wanted to be close to him." Soon afterward, Donna Reed's husband, Tony Owen, the producer of her show, talked Crane into abandoning his old barber and going to a stylist. "Ten dollars a cut!" said the flabbergasted and economical Crane. In one article about Bob, Tarzana was described as "a nice, hardly fashionable town." The remark so stung Crane that he mentioned it in subsequent interviews.

Generally glib, cocky, and disarmingly open, Bob could also be an anxious man who could take the merest fragment of criticism between his teeth and, mongrel-like, fret and worry it. He was virtually the only bit of spice on the sugary Reed sitcom, and his agent, Leonard Cohen, felt that his client was entitled to more money. He approached Tony Owen, who said, "He ain't worth it. We hadn't been looking for Crane at all. We gave him a one-shot, then signed him for a regular. But ask me what Crane added to the show and I'll say nothin'."

When Bob heard of Owen's feelings, he was hurt. "I decided to pull out," he said. "I thought Tony was my friend—he was like a father to me. When I called him up about the things he told me, 'That's the business. You'll have to get used to it.'

"I left after two years," said Bob. "I thought I'd proved in the show that I could handle comedy. What's good for Donna Reed may not necessarily be good for me. I knew that show wasn't the end-all of my career. Frankly, I never felt comfortable in the role. It's a nice little show, but it's not watched by the trade. What I always wanted to do was be a con man—a flip, hip character."

Bob Crane left the Reed show with a quip: "At least Tony Owen introduced me to a good hairstylist." But he felt more insecure than ever. At age thirty-six and in spite of national exposure and high ratings on his radio show, he was still not the "top banana" he wanted to be.

After Crane left the Reed show in 1964 he appeared on ABC's *Channing*, a dramatic show. Crane had played serious parts before—three years earlier in *Return to Peyton Place*, under the direction of José Ferrer, and *Man-Trap*, directed by Edmond O'Brien, a picture packed with "adultery, robbery, and disaster"—but it was not the kind of acting he preferred.

In 1964 he had the opportunity to appear onstage with his idol, Jack Benny. However, the audience so excited Crane that he managed to offend the easygoing Benny. "You know," Bob said sadly after the show, "when it was all over, Benny never said a word to me, not even good night."

Since 1960, Bernard Fein, a former comic actor who had appeared as Private Gomez in the *Sergeant Bilko* shows of the 1950s, had been trying to sell what he thought was a hot idea: placing a Bilko-type character in a federal penitentiary. Bilko was a con man who continually outwitted his straitlaced, befuddled commander on a Kansas army base during peacetime.

Meeting with no luck, Fein vowed to get out of show business forever and boarded a plane for New York. "Sitting next to me," he recalled, "was a guy reading *Von Ryan's Express*, about a group of POWs who hijack a trainload of art stolen by the Germans. The minute I saw it, I said to myself, That's it! I didn't even leave the airport when I got to New York. I bought a ticket back to Hollywood."

Time was of the essence. The author of *Von Ryan's Express*, David Westheimer, had written a sit-com for NBC, *Campo 44*, which was set in an Italian POW camp. It was a matter of who would get their show on first. Fein and Ruddy contacted the head of Bing Crosby Productions,

Basil Grillo, who in turn called Edward H. Feldman, a vice-president at Desilu. Feldman was a producer who had been successful in radio and advertising, but had not yet scored in television although he had done the first dozen *Gomer Pyle* shows.

In four days, Ruddy and Fein had a deal ($80,000 for their script, "substantial royalties," and Feldman as producer), attributing their tremendous opportunity to a combination of ignorance and luck. Fein, in the time he was associate producer, attempted to cast a friend, actor Robert Hogan, in the series lead role. He had named Colonel Robert Hogan after him. He was unsuccessful, and briefly Van Johnson and Walter Matthau were considered for the part.

Aspects of *Stalag 17,* which had been a 1950s Broadway hit and an Academy Award–winning movie, intrigued Feldman, especially the bits of black comedy that the POWs in the prison camp used to maintain their sanity. Strong elements of the play would be worked into *Hogan's Heroes* and eventually would cause Feldman serious legal problems.

In the early stages of development, Hogan was supposed to be a captured enlisted man. Richard Dawson, the English comic, most famous for his marriage to glamour queen Diana Dors, was tested for the Hogan part and corpulent John Banner for the pompous commandant, Colonel Wilhelm Klink. Feldman felt the mix was wrong and kept looking.

For some time CBS, owner of KNX, had been searching for a vehicle for their popular morning star, Bob Crane, and negotiations were begun between Feldman, CBS, and Bing Crosby Productions, which would package the series and provide studio space.

"A comedy about a POW camp?" asked Crane, trying to visualize "Nazis with a laugh track." "But then Eddie Feldman explained the plot to me . . . so I thought, Why not?" When Bob signed for the lead role of Colonel Robert E. Hogan, he knew that "fun and frolic in a German POW camp" could by the nature of its appalling and bizarre concept spell either stardom or widespread condemnation and the end of his television career.

"I did research on prison camps to make sure the idea

wasn't too farfetched," said Feldman. "One camp housed twenty-five thousand prisoners,* and in one so many escape tunnels were built they caved in on one another. It wasn't very funny then, but in retrospect there was humor." Later Feldman admitted using William L. Shirer's *Rise and Fall of the Third Reich* as source material for plots.

Bob was concerned about offending any former POWs. After the series was running, he said, "I was being made up for an appearance on the *Hollywood Palace* when I heard that the makeup man had been a POW, and I thought, Oh, boy! This is going to be trouble. But he told me they actually did have all kinds of deceptions they put over on the Germans."

Development of the pilot was begun; it would cost almost $250,000 to produce.

Richard M. Powell was chosen to write the pilot for *Hogan's Heroes*. "I worked on a number of series in television," he said. "The year before *Hogan's Heroes* I had done a special for Bob Hope and Lucille Ball. And I met Eddie Feldman while he was working on two series—one was *The Andy Griffith Show*, the other was *Gomer Pyle*.

"The pilot was originally written by Al Ruddy, who later became a producer of some note, and Bernie Fein. They weren't really writers. They had this idea for the show and it was purchased by CBS, and they hired Ed Feldman to produce it, and he saw that the script was really not shootable and he got me to do a pretty complete rewrite.

"Well, what happened was CBS had a deal with Bing Crosby Enterprises, and they had commissioned the pilot to be filmed. When they looked at it, I don't think anybody had any great hopes for it, but at least they knew it was an excellent job of producing and directing.

"The pilot was called 'The Informer,' and the idea was

---

*In 1944 the SS was in charge of the prison camps with gestapo chief Heinrich Himmler as supreme prison commandant. Captured fliers were handed over to the SS, interrogated, and often executed. Sadistic commandants murdered stragglers and whipped, starved, shot, and poisoned POWs. Prisoner massacres began near the war's end.

that a spy had been planted in the ranks of the prisoners, somebody who was actually a German but was posing as a captured flier, and he was supposed to investigate what the prisoners were doing. Naturally, he's found out."

Hogan and his international band use their secret tunnels and hidden radios to run an intelligence and sabotage operation, assisting the underground and helping Allied fugitives to escape. As the true masters of Stalag 13, they perpetuate the myth that the prison is escape-proof so they can continue to operate unimpeded.

Comparisons were made to *Sergeant Bilko* and *Stalag 17,* but Crane admitted that the character he played was based on one portrayed by James Garner in John Sturges's 1963 film, *The Great Escape*. Bob said, "He was a military guy who didn't start out as a Jack Armstrong. Also, instead of being a straight down-the-line comic, like Bilko, mine's a more rounded character. There's more longevity that way."

"I did read *The Great Escape*," said Powell, "but I didn't read or see *Stalag 17,* and Sergeant Schultz was a character I invented. I took the name from the Jack Benny film *To Be or Not to Be*. There was a general in there, I think he was played by Sig Ruman. He kept saying, 'You haff your orders, Schultz.' The Schultz character was important to the sitcom because I felt some sort of go-between was necessary between the prisoners and Klink. Somebody who was in both camps.

"I invented the character of Kinchloe. We needed a character of some stability. Ivan Dixon was not a comedy actor, but he was wonderful as Kinchloe. I had met him through a project I was heading up in the Writers Guild, the Negro Writers' Workshop—the word *Negro* tells how long ago this was. I wrote in a black character and asked Ivan if he'd like to do it, and he did.

"Ed Feldman wanted Werner Klemperer, and he wanted John Banner when casting was being done. He was uncertain at the start which one would play which character, and I put in a strong vote for Banner to play Schultz and Werner to play Klink. Eddie probably would have come to that conclusion anyway.

"Crane was signed early on. He was with the project right from the start."

11
THE SURVIVORS

Development—Elaboration of an idea or concept by working out the characters and plot structure and sequence of a TV play.

Ironically Robert Clary, Werner Klemperer, and John Banner, three men who had been victims of the Nazis during the 1930s—interned in camps, driven from their homeland, or witness to the exterminations of their families—ended up playing Nazi officers and prisoners of the Third Reich on a television comedy show.

Robert Clary was born as Robert Max Widerman on March 1, 1926, and had been acting, singing, and dancing since the age of twelve. His family came from Poland, arriving in Paris about four years before Robert was born and taking up residence on an island in the Seine, in a low-cost apartment complex built for Jews. His father, Maurice, a tailor, had sired five children by his first wife, and Robert was the seventh son by his second wife, Berthe, the youngest of the twelve children.

In the fall of 1940, after the Germans had entered Paris, all Jews over the age of six were compelled to wear a yellow cloth Star of David on their coats. The first morning Robert, the only Jew in his advertising art class, wore the star, all his classmates strode in solidarity alongside him to school.

"When the Germans occupied a country," Clary said later, "they first arrested the foreign Jews, the ones who were not citizens." Forty-three deportation trains would leave France in 1942, the peak year for incarceration of Jews during the war; of the almost 42,000 taken that year, only 6,500 were French born. Throughout the German occupation a total of 80,000 Jews would be deported from France to the camps and of these only 2,000 returned alive.

On September 22, 1942, the SS began poring over the census files to locate any foreign-born Jews in Paris. They plucked out almost 24,000 index cards listing the names and addresses, grouped them by arrondissement, organized 9,000 especially recruited French police into 1,632 arrest teams, and began gathering up the families.

"Usually they would arrest Jews early in the morning—before they went to work," Clary said. "We had a curfew. We could not be seen on the streets between eight P.M. and eight A.M. The police would usually come before eight A.M. But we were arrested [September 23] at nine-thirty at night. It was a complete surprise."

Some of Clary's brothers and sisters had joined the underground and thus lived. "But of those of us in my family who were deported," he said, "I was the only one to survive." On September 26 an engine pulled ten boxcars out of Drancy, north of Paris, about seventy people to each car, including Robert and his family.

For three days the train sped on, roaring past every station, and inside the sweltering cars there was scant food and no sanitation facilities. Only two buckets of water per car had been provided for the entire journey. Finally, the train stopped and the doors were rolled back to reveal SS troops with machine guns and fierce German shepherds straining at their leashes.

"Do whatever they tell you to do. Don't fight it," Robert's mother told him.

Because he was sixteen and fit for hard work, Robert was separated from his parents and interned over the next three years in camps in Upper Silesia on the border of Czechoslovakia and Poland. "These camps [Ottmuth, Blechhamer near the river Oder, Gross-Rosen, and Buchenwald] were satellites of Auschwitz, and they were concentration camps, not extermination camps," he said. "I was lucky to have been there to work, and I worked very, very hard."

Throughout his imprisonment he was dressed in a baggy zebra-striped uniform and matching beret. On the back and front of his tunic and on his pants was a yellow star. Finally, on his left upper forearm was tattooed "A-5714."

Wind whistled in off the flat Silesian plain, the watchtowers were crowned with hillocks of snow, barbed wire beaded with pearls of ice. Too cold to sleep on the straw mattress on the three-tiered bunk or to sit to drink his thin, barely warm potato soup and eat his nightly chunk of bread, Clary stood. "We hung on to life by pure guts," he said.

Even though the windows of their barracks were barred, the door bolted with a heavy padlock and transverse iron bar, the fences electrified and guarded, the prisoners were repeatedly awakened and counted throughout the nights.

"I worked in a factory [Obersliese Hydrier Werke] that made synthetic fuel from coal—and, yes, the Allied bombers would come over every morning at eleven and bomb the factory. Yes, and we could not go to the shelters." Hours were from 3:00 A.M. until dark.

"We'd come back exhausted from hard labor—we were building an elevator and installing pipes on it," recalled Clary. "The SS guards would line us up at attention for three hours to witness the hanging of some poor wretch who maybe stole a piece of garbage to eat."

On January 18, 1945, as the Russians advanced, the SS ordered the camp evacuated, and the European death marches began in subzero temperatures. Clary was one of the marchers. Columns of 2,500 sick, starved prisoners stretched westward in an agonizing crawl toward the cities of Silesia. Both concentration camp survivors and German refugees packed the roads, shoulder to shoulder, and fought for the same meager rations and the same shelter.

Exhausted, fearful, Clary stumbled on, his hands bleeding and cracked, held under his armpits to keep warm. He slipped often; his greatest fear was that he would be unable to regain his feet. Guards crushed the skulls of anyone who did not rise immediately. After fifteen days only 1,200 still lived.

Somewhere around the eighteenth day, Clary was transferred to a train bound for Buchenwald. He had heard rumors, and when he was sent to the bathhouse by the SS, Clary fully expected gas to come from the showerheads. But it was only a place for the prisoners to sleep and again he was spared.

Clary made two friends at Buchenwald. One was Yves Darriet, the orchestra leader of the camp band. The other was his bass player, Jiri Zac, a Czechoslovakian Communist. "He had a secretarial post at the administration," said Clary. "The camp was run by inmates. They were responsible for seeing that the camp ran smoothly for the Nazis." Zac hid Clary in his barracks as the Jews were being readied for another death march. It saved his life.

On April 11, 1945, Weimar gestapo phoned the Buchenwald administration building with orders to blow up the camp and all the remaining inmates. However, the Nazi administrators had already fled. "The camp has already been blown up," announced the prisoners in control of the office.

Clary, in his hiding place, realized that it had grown still. The SS, the guards, and even the dogs had vanished. At 4:00 P.M. the G.I.s of the U.S. Third Army arrived at the gates.

Jubilant, some of the prisoners put on a jazz concert for their liberators and Clary sang a song in English that he had learned phonetically—"A Tisket, A Tasket."

Returning to Paris, Clary had no sooner put his foot in the door of a hotel set up for survivors when the first person he saw was one of his sisters. She was a nurse taking care of people returning from deportation.

"The emotion was just unbelievable," he said. "I thought they were all dead, and then she told me I still had brothers and sisters. The reunion was not to be believed. How can I describe it? It was . . . tears came from my whole body!

"The whole experience was a complete nightmare, the way they treated us, what we had to do to survive. We were less than animals. Sometimes I dream about those days. I wake up in a sweat terrified for fear I'm about to be sent away to a concentration camp. But I don't hold a grudge because that's a great waste of time. Yes, there's something dark in the human soul. For the most part human beings are not very nice. That's why when you find those who are, you cherish them."

In 1948, after a hit record, Clary came to America and was a success in clubs and on Broadway. On Christmas of 1964 he went to Hollywood to see his agent there and met an enthusiastic Eddie Feldman, casting for the romantic, feisty, bantamweight French gourmet chef on *Hogan's Heroes*, Louis LeBeau. "I know you," Feldman told Clary. "I used to see you at the Cafe Gala when you were singing in the fifties. The part is yours."

"Getting the part was *luck*," Clary said. "I was there at the right minute, and I never even had to read for it."

Werner Klemperer, born in Cologne, March 22, 1929, grew up in Berlin, the son of Otto Klemperer, one of the great orchestra conductors, and Johanna Geissler, an ex-opera singer. As he matured, young Werner was rigorously trained in his father's "iron regimen of music."

The public perception of the six-foot-five-inch Otto was that of a tall, gaunt, unsmiling giant who "enters a room as if he were carrying the podium," while his reputation among musicians was as "a tyrant with a fearsome temper." Yet the stern, introverted conductor made efforts to reveal himself to his sensitive son. Each morning while Otto bathed, Werner was welcomed to talk until the water had grown cold. "He wanted to relate to me on a human level," said Werner, "something he never did when company was around."

In 1931 Klemperer's association with Berlin's Kroll Opera (many called it "Klemperer's Kroll") ended as anxiety over the growth of national socialism rose and the hall was closed. In February of 1933 Otto was awarded the Goethe Medal by Hitler, who was present in a box seat at the Linden Opera for a performance of *Tannhäuser*. There, Otto suffered a fall from the podium (possibly rigged by the fascists), injuring the left side of his head. He would develop a cerebral tumor, in all probability brought on by the fall, and a later operation would leave him seriously disabled on the right side.

Two months later Otto, who was born Jewish but had embraced Catholicism, was branded as harmful to German society. "My goodness," he wrote on April 3, "it is time to leave." Werner, his mother, and his sister, Lotte, followed Otto first to Zurich, then to Vienna, where they lived until 1935. "We left for America on the Cunard liner the *Majestic*, the largest ship afloat at the time. My father, who had been a guest conductor with the Los Angeles Philharmonic for several seasons before that, had arranged a permanent post with them. It was a wonderful way to come to a new world," said Klemperer.

"In 1964, just prior to *Hogan's Heroes*," he went on, "I was trying to work steadily as an actor, doing lots of guest shots in TV films in which I played a variety of foreign-born villains, all heavies."

Eddie Feldman and his closest friend, actor Richard Crenna, were leafing through the *Player's Directory*, looking for an actor for the second lead in *Hogan's Heroes*, Colonel Wilhelm Klink. They came across Klemperer's picture, and Crenna said, "That's Klink!"

"You're crazy," said Feldman. "I know the chap. He's a nice actor, but he plays serious. He's not a comedian. He plays heavies." Crenna insisted, and Werner was called in.

"I met Feldman, Ruddy, and Fein, and they told me this was a comedy, and I really thought they had lost their minds," said Klemperer. "My model for the character was Crown Prince Wilhelm, a notorious, pompous, not terribly bright, stuffy, womanizing pain in the ass. And all of these things intrigued me for Klink. I used the riding crop because I felt he needed something to squeeze to cover up his insecurity. The monocle came from my historical knowledge of what it meant to the Prussian aristocracy. The first day I couldn't hold that bloody thing—they glued it in."

As a military policeman of the Thirty-third Infantry in Hawaii, Werner had picked up a military bearing that would serve him in good stead as Klink.

In May of 1965 Werner flew to Stockholm with some consternation to tell his seventy-nine-year-old father of his good luck. A year earlier in London at the Mermaid Theater Otto had taken his cane to actors in an ironic Brecht play with comic Nazis. Tears streaming down his face, he'd lashed out, shouting, "It was not like that, you fools! You make jokes of these things you know nothing about."

When Werner told him he had a TV series, Otto boomed, "Who's the author?" There was an awkward pause as Werner thought, How do you explain? "Then he asked me to send him a script. I didn't *dare*."

Of Feldman's carefully chosen actors for *Hogan's Heroes*, few would become more beloved than John Banner, who took on the role of Klink's maladroit chief aide, the roly-poly, perplexed Sergeant Hans Schultz, a soldier who had been coopted through a series of small bribes until he was able to be blackmailed by the POWs. He was a reluctant accomplice because of his fear of being sent to the Russian front.

Banner, too, was Jewish. By 1938, when he was twenty-eight, the Nazis had gained power in Austria, and his entire family was liquidated in an extermination camp. John fled to Zurich, where he played romantic leads. In those days he weighed 180 pounds.

When the parts dried up in 1939, he came to New York as a refugee. He spoke no English but was cast as the MC

of *From Vienna*, a musical revue. He memorized each word
of his part phonetically, the same way Clary made his hit
record. As far back as 1942, Banner had, like Klemperer
who had played Adolf Eichmann in *Operation Eichmann*,
played a number of Nazis. "Who can play Nazis better than
us Jews?" he said.

By the time he got the part of Schultz, Banner weighed
about 280 pounds, but with the gourmet cooking of his
wife, Christine, and his love of fine restaurants and veal
kidneys flambé, he would continue to gain weight throughout the life of the show.

Though he admitted he would rather have gotten mail
from "beautiful blondes," Banner loved the bags of fan mail
from children asking for pictures of him or wanting to know
how he got so fat. He thought of himself as a "good uncle,"
but Crane's own kids thought Schultz was "Santy Claus."

The rest of the cast was quickly chosen: a cockney En-
glishman, RAF Corporal Peter Newkirk (Richard Dawson);
an American black, Sergeant James Kinchloe (Ivan Dixon);
and a stereotypical "dim farmboy who can fix anything,"
Sergeant Andrew Carter (Larry Hovis).*

In the beginning the overworked Crane sometimes didn't
know his lines, but none of the other actors seemed to be
concerned. "You hear about these shows where they're
having trouble," said John Banner, "but it's not like that
here."

"One peculiar thing about Bob Crane," Richard Powell
said. "He came across on radio as a very 'with it' man. But
on the show he had a lot of difficulty understanding the

---

*Characters who were almost regulars on the show were bellowing
gestapo Major Hochstetter (Howard Caine); rotund, dueling-scarred
General Burkhalter (Leon Askin); Hogan's Allied nemesis, Colonel
Crittendon, senior officer at nearby Stalag 16 (Bernard Fox). Appear-
ing often were Tiger (Arlene Martel), the French underground agent
Marya (Nita Talbot), the Russian spy Berlin Betty (Antoinette Bower),
and Olga (Ruta Lee).

plots. Sometimes he would come in and say, 'Well, I've read it three times and I still can't understand it. But it's all right, I don't have to.' And these were fairly simple things. I never quite understood that part of his personality."

Through Feldman, Bob kept in touch with each step of the production of the pilot. One day Feldman carefully explained to Crane what his theories about the character of Colonel Hogan were.

"Hogan's believability," he said, "is a major key to the series, since Hogan subtly sets the moral tone of his followers and consequently of the total show. I want to make it clear to you that you absolutely must not play Hogan as a buffoon. I want you to play him seriously, as a hero, as a leader who can inspire other men to keep fighting, even when behind bars."

This entreaty appealed to Bob. He loved heroes. "That to me is the ideal," he said, "a good man, a brave man. What I would want to be."

Just as Feldman had promised, there would be heroics in abundance on the show. "The manner in which we play the comedy is tricky," said Crane. "We make our fun *out* of the characters. The grimness is still there. We're no *McHale's Navy* in that we never go too far without an element of danger.

"The lines have to mean something. Then if there's any romance, it's believable. I'm not Joe Buffoon, but I was always the nut in the neighborhood—the wise guy. That's Colonel Hogan.

"I originally tried to make the character funny," said Crane. "Eddie convinced me to change. 'You have to be a hero,' he said. I asked myself, 'What the hell is a hero?' Then one day I had a line—just a simple line, a kind of understated acceptance of a challenge. I said it in a certain way—almost in a dead-flat, guttural tone. Three guys whirled around and yelled, 'That's it! John Wayne!' That's the story. If you want to be a hero—think John Wayne. He'll rescue you every time!"

"It was a delightful cast to work with," Powell said later. "The funny thing—they were all liberals aside from Crane, who was a conservative. He wasn't an obnoxious-type conservative, but he was basically conservative, and the rest of them used to kid him about it all the time. I forget what politics were going on then, but Crane was definitely a Republican."

Crane admitted, "I'm the Ronald Reagan of the *Hogan* set. I believe in independence, individualism, courage, patriotism—the traditional American values. People call me a flag-waver."

"But," said Powell, "Bob was still kind of an odd man out. Kind of a square. At least we always regarded him that way. I think it was that Bob Crane wasn't primarily an actor. I think he just happened to fit in. The other characters were carrying so much of the comedy load that everything kind of bounced off him."

Most of the ideas for network TV series were born on the West Coast, as many as eight hundred proposals annually. They would come from major motion picture companies, independent producers, experienced writers, directors, and even a member of the network staff. Four years earlier, in 1960, the shift in power over who determined what was aired had gone from the sponsors to the networks, who now not only chose programs, but determined scheduling. And CBS was the most powerful of the networks.

With urban riots, student protests, racial tensions, and marines beginning to arrive in Vietnam, Americans seemed to be welcoming the most implausible, escapist programming imaginable.

Of the myriad series ideas discussed, "spitballed," firmed up, and pitched, from March through May, only a scant fifty ever made it to New York for serious consideration. *Hogan's Heroes* was one of them.

After a second story conference in the fall of 1964, a refined treatment of *Hogan's Heroes* was sent on to CBS's West Coast office. A teleplay was ordered, which was then revised, rewritten, and polished by the show's writer, Richard Powell. It was this teleplay that was submitted to New York; a twenty-six-minute black-and-white pilot was ordered to be cast and filmed. Only about fifteen scripts at each network ever reached this point.

Crane told interviewers that he thought he was walking into a gold mine. "If the show's a hit, it could run several years and I could become a millionaire. If it's not, I'm out of work, that's all. The nice part of this is I have a piece of the show—that is, after what Crosby takes off for his golf clubs."

Klemperer agreed with Bob. "I saw rushes when we were shooting the pilot before it was sold. I think that everybody on that sound stage felt we had something. It was not the first time I had worked with Bob. I had met him once before when he was a disc jockey at KNX. I think there was a kind of natural chemistry. That's why I got the job. We worked together just perfectly . . . we were such goddamn opposites in every way." Where Bob was fretful, Werner was sunny; while Crane was into jazz, Werner loved classical music. Bob often kidded him by saying in a German accent, "You are *soooo* competitive."

Throughout the fall the ordering of pilots continued, each finished pilot pretested before a cross section of viewers. *Hogan's Heroes* was screened for an audience selected at random off the New York streets. They showed green flags on the program analyzer, a graph that tracked their interest. Green meant go; the sample audience was intrigued.

CBS president James Aubrey, a physically impressive, boyishly handsome six-footer, entered the new forty-story CBS headquarters, a rough-textured black granite and cold Polaroid glass building known as "Black Rock." Aubrey worked out often and could stand on his head longer than just about anyone else. He did so many sit-ups that he had a washboard-flat stomach. When they were just starting the *Hogan's* pilot, Bob Crane came wheeling around the corner and ran smack into him. "It was so hard," remembered Crane, "that I almost upset him. I said, 'Oh, my God!' and he said back, 'You better believe it.' "

The patrician Aubrey never wasted time with preliminaries and was known to make his decisions with lightning

speed. He heard proposals, screened pilots, watched half a
dozen movies on weekends, and flashed through scripts. He
had been the one to okay Crane's pilot.

Aubrey was known in the industry as the "Smiling Co-
bra." He had doubled CBS's profits since assuming the
presidency in 1959 at the age of forty-one; a million dollars
a night poured into the "Tiffany Network."

For more than a decade CBS had not had a losing season;
at one point in 1962 it had eighteen of the top twenty prime-
time TV shows and all of the daytime top ten. By 1963,
under Aubrey, the network had taken a rural bent and
showed one hayseed comedy after another. An industry
joke was that the letters CBS actually stood for "Country
Broadcasting System." And in 1964, for the first time,
CBS's invincible position was threatened.

NBC was called 30 Rock; CBS, Black Rock; and ABC
was now being called Hard Rock, because during the 1964
fall season ABC had staked out an early lead by showing
all their new programs, while the other two networks were
still becalmed in summer reruns. Even though the lead had
evaporated by Thanksgiving, Aubrey was forced to do
something he had never done before—conduct a drastic
overhaul during midseason. With only *Gomer Pyle,
U.S.M.C.*, and *Gilligan's Island* as clear winners the year
before, he was hungry for a hit sitcom.

It was now just a few days before Washington's birthday
1965, and William S. Paley, sixty-four, the CBS chairman
of the board, made his way from his green-carpeted offices
on the thirty-fifth floor of CBS headquarters to the conference room on the floor below, where the final full programming meeting that would decide the fate of *Hogan's
Heroes*—indeed, of the whole fall schedule—was being
held.

In this room stood two magnetized, rectangular boards
holding the existing schedules for NBC, CBS, and ABC.
Red, blue, and tan cards held the names of all shows, new
and old. CBS programmer Fred Silverman later recalled a
scene that had taken place in the room before Paley arrived.
One executive, some said Aubrey, had decided to rearrange
the whole schedule. "By the time he finished with it," said

Silverman, "Tuesday night was playing on Sunday and Sunday was on Wednesday. Paley walked into the room and took one look at the board, then glared at the offending executive and said, as if he were talking to a child—'Put it back!' Programming at CBS was almost a religious experience. You didn't move a show lightly."

Programming, Paley felt, was the most important part of network success and writers, along with producers, the most crucial elements to a series. "Consistently good writers," he maintained, "ones who can handle their material over the long haul . . . are as scarce as precious stones, and their prices are not dissimilar."

Gathered at the most important meeting of the year were James Aubrey, Robert Wood, Bobby Wussler, Jack Schneider, Fred Silverman, and Mike Dann, CBS's top programmer. A self-proclaimed cynic, nicknamed "the Weathervane," Dann derived scant enjoyment from viewing what he called in his high-pitched voice "the same crap as last year."

Paley recalled, "It was a typical final programming meeting, filled with fierce battles. Like all such meetings, this one was long, agonizing, painful, ego-bruising, and extremely stimulating. Lunch was brought in. Telephone calls were held. Each pilot was taken up in turn, presented by its advocate, and criticized by some, condemned by some, and praised by others.

"The more we narrowed the field down, the more intense the debate, but it was understood that the pilots, the projects, and a man's opinions were wide open to criticism, not the man himself." As the owner of 1.7 million shares of CBS stock, Paley knew he would have the final word, but he relished the "tension, rubbing of raw nerves, and interplay of strong minds." One programming meeting had gone on for five days.

Paley felt he had a special sense of what the masses wanted and that he had to appeal to a broad spectrum of tastes even if he didn't like the program himself. "I think," Paley said, "I was born with a sense of what was important to the American public."

As the pilots were projected on a large screen in the

conference room, Paley took notes about the casting, writing, acting, and directing. Assistants raced over to apprehensive producers carrying last-minute suggestions; cards were shuffled over and over.

Nibbling on his favorite sandwich or a pickle as he paced, or favoring his bad back on the couch, Paley would talk through a poor pilot or leave the room if the pilot was hopeless. The subject matter of *Hogan's Heroes* didn't faze him. "The execution rather than the idea itself is often what makes a show successful," he believed, and he thought Bob's show had legs. "Good job," he said of *Hogan's Heroes*. With these words, the show was accepted.

Friday nights at 8:30, right after the hour-long *Wild, Wild West* (in 1965 prime-time ran from 7:30 until 11:00 P.M.) and just before *Gomer Pyle, U.S.M.C.*, would be the slot for *Hogan's Heroes*.

With Crane's show locked into the schedule, Aubrey personally called Eddie Feldman with congratulations, and an order for thirteen scripts and an extra three or four went out. Aubrey's last official gesture was this order. He was fired at the end of February after the new shows were chosen.

Feldman got Bob on the phone and relayed the good news: "They're picking it up. They're doing it!" Feldman, whose own heart was racing, heard a stunned silence at the other end of the line. Bob was overcome with emotion. He had traveled far and worked hard to reach this point.

"It was after he left KNX and *Hogan's Heroes* came along that Bob became more interested in exotic dancers and nightclubs," said KNBC newsman Pete Noyes. "Don't you think it's a case of a guy getting away from his roots and all of a sudden being turned loose in that Hollywood culture? I remember when I first met him he seemed like a typical midwesterner. I know he was very faithful to his first wife, but Bob started hanging out at topless places. I could see over the ten years a sort of personality change. Nobody could quite explain this—he was from a very strong Catholic family. He was a good Catholic boy."

12

THE SELLING OF *HOGAN'S HEROES*

*Blind spot—Something important that the protagonist of
a drama is unaware of in his struggle toward a goal, but
which is removed in the climax.*

Once the fall schedule had been announced, launching an
eight-week frenzy of selling and promoting, major advertisers and their agencies rushed to presentation screenings
of the winning pilots. The shows were bait for the true
fare—the ads. During the summer of 1965 the network
brought all the managers of the affiliate stations to Hollywood and Palm Springs to be pampered, fed, and cajoled.
Of the nine new CBS shows they saw, *Hogan's Heroes*
was their favorite.

Feldman made arrangements for Crane, Klemperer,
Clary, and the rest of the cast to be present as greeters at
a *Hogan's Heroes* party in Palm Springs.

As a publicity stunt, CBS transformed the Ocotillo Lodge,
where the party was held, into a replica of a POW camp.
Black-shirted "guards" strutted to the sound of German mil-

itary marches; a "drunken" Hitler impersonator arrived.

"The party was unbelievable," Klemperer said. "They fixed this whole hotel up, and they invited the international press and the national press. They were all there. And they had things in every room. When you opened your toilet seat they had a picture of Colonel Klink there. I mean real crazy stuff. They had a World War One plane fly over the swimming pool, dropping leaflets."

Daily Variety had pegged Crane's show as "one of the sleepers of the next semester," and the word from coast to coast, from Vine Street to Madison Avenue, was of a hit to equal *The Beverly Hillbillies*. There was intense anticipation for the show billed as "World War II with a laugh track."

But Eddie Feldman was cautious. He had been burned before with a show called *Fair Exchange*. "Everybody predicted it would be a hit," he recalled. "When it went on the air, the reviews were all raves—I still have them. Even today people tell me how great it was. They just didn't watch it."

From the beginning, CBS, Bing Crosby Productions, and Feldman went to great lengths to ensure that *Hogan's Heroes* would be in good taste. Not everybody believed they would succeed.

On his first day as the new president of CBS, Jack Schneider had his chief graphic designer, Leo Dorfsman, hire CBS radio satirist Stan Freberg to prepare a radio script for a *Hogan's Heroes* preseason commercial.

Freberg flew back to Hollywood to work with Crane thinking, A situation comedy set—I still can't believe it—in a Nazi prisoner-of-war camp. As a satirist, he couldn't help lampooning the whole idea.

The taping began:

"Where does the show take place?" Freberg asked Crane.

"In a Nazi prisoner-of-war camp in Germany."

"Always a good situation comedy locale. What are some of the amusing ingredients?"

"Oh, German police dogs . . . machine guns . . . the Gestapo . . ."

"Just a few of the laugh-provoking elements to be seen

this fall on *Hogan's Heroes*, Friday nights on CBS. Shall we say, 'If you liked World War Two, you'll love *Hogan's Heroes*'?"

"No, let's not say that, no."

There was a flood of adverse publicity, and the announcement was pulled by the network.

The first few shows of the season were critical for the success Crane dreamed of. Formerly prime-time programs were given a longer chance to prove themselves, but now a second premiere season was waiting in January to replace the shows that faltered. If *Hogan's Heroes* didn't click with the 1,200 Nielsen families, Bob's chances of ever getting a second pilot were remote.

Things were equally exhausting for Feldman. Producing a weekly sitcom was like being on a treadmill; as fast as he ran, he still gained little ground. Feldman did, however, take advantage of the months before the actual September air date to get as many shows finished as possible.

Caught between the production company that employed him and the network, Feldman had to determine the budget; negotiate the salaries; hire the writers, crew, staff, stars, and supporting cast; develop new scripts; and choose directors, and when he'd finished that, he had to order the sets; have costumes made; rent or buy equipment; and draw up the schedule for preproduction, rehearsals, and the shooting of the interiors and exteriors. He had to deal with unions, the censors at Standards and Practices, and the Nielsen ratings, and he was responsible for overseeing postproduction—the editing, dubbing, adding of sound effects, and scoring of each episode.

"I must tell you," Clary said, "Ed Feldman really held the reins, and he did it beautifully. The reason the show was a success was because of him. He hired everybody. He supervised everything."

CBS print ads continued right up to *Hogan's Heroes'* opening night on Friday, September 17. Nine new shows were debuting that same evening out of the entire lineup of thirty-five new programs that would run over eight consecutive nights. Crane felt his competition on the other two networks was weak—*The Addams Family* on ABC and the first part of the hour-long *Convoy* on NBC. To an ambitious man like Crane, being second was the same as being last. His competitive flame burned with equal parts of self-doubt and self-criticism, fueled by a lack of satisfaction with everything he did.

The credits for the first show began rolling—spirited military drums rose on the sound track, and, flags flying, a German Mercedes touring car rushed through the barbed-wire-enclosed Stalag 13, a prison from which no one had ever escaped.

It was night. Snow was on the ground. Each of the men dressed in Wehrmacht green in the watchtowers had machine guns. Other guards were armed with Mauser rifles. Powerful searchlights beamed forth from the towers, while night patrols scoured the woods.

The screen filled with a close-up of a tough German guard, bright emblems on his collar, strap pulled uncomfortably under his square helmet. Prisoners raced from their barracks to line up for inspection. And the show proper began.

The overnight Arbitrons that provided instant rating tabulation gave *Hogan's Heroes* a high rating. But Bob would still have to wait for the networks' bible, the national A. C. Nielsens, which provided both mechanical and detailed demographic information, to learn whether his show was a hit. The data had to be transferred to punch cards and tallied at the Chicago home office. The results would not be known until Tuesday. A biweekly Tele-Index was published then, containing Nielsen data broken into fifteen-minute segments.

In a field of ninety-eight prime-time programs, *Hogan's Heroes*—astonishingly—came in at number five! (Of all the new shows, *Hogan's Heroes* was number one.) The show was a sensation!

The *Los Angeles Times* wrote that *Hogan's Heroes* "offers the premise that life in a German POW camp can be beautiful." Crane was dubbed "pixie-ish." "With comedy this season all but moribund, it comes as a surprise to find it popping up in, of all places, a German P.O.W. camp," said *Time* magazine. "*Natürlich*, the World War Teutons are *Dummkopfs*, and the prisoners run rings around their captors, blackmailing them into submission with dark hints that if anything goes wrong at the camp, Hitler will send them all marching off to the Russian front. So they allow the captives to print money, smoke their cigars—to do everything, in short, but escape. It's slapstick *Stalag 17*."

The second *Hogan's Heroes*, "Tiger Tank," ran on September 24 in color (the first episode had been in black and white, but with a million and a half color sets being sold a year, CBS was already at fifty percent color). It had actually been filmed in April. On the third show, Klink was exultant when he had word from Berlin that Stalag 13 was among the top ten prison camps in Germany. On the October 3 episode, Hogan and his band are horrified when they learn that Klink is about to be transferred to Berlin. In other episodes that first season, a hoard of gold was swiped and buried for use after the war and a German baroness defected and wanted Hogan to help her escape.

Over the weekends, special messengers delivered each new script to Bob and the cast. Bob was almost always pleased with the lines. "They didn't seem too jokey," he said.

Powell, whose early scripts defined the entire series, told Crane, "I very, very seldom make changes because *Hogan's Heroes* is a gang comedy with well-established characters. I think in this type of program you've got to keep moving and you've got to keep three balls in the air at all times." This was the same principle Bob had used at KNX.

From April to August 1965, Bob had labored at two back-breaking jobs. Rising before dawn, he shaved and left the house by 5:00 A.M. in order to arrive at KNX by 6:00 A.M. and tape a two-hour morning show for release at 8:00. At 8:15 A.M. he arrived at Desilu Studios, where two huge sound stages and permanent sets (Klink's office, the POW barracks, and the prisoners' secret tunnels) were set up for the new show.

The cast rarely finished before 7:00 P.M., and after a lonely dinner in town at 8:00 P.M. Bob would speed home to Tarzana, where he would study his script for the next day until he dropped off to sleep.

Having given up his radio work after the premiere of

Hogan's Heroes, Bob began showing up at Desilu earlier and earlier, usually around 6:00 A.M. "He's the first one on the set in the morning," said Feldman, "and the last to leave. He goes into everything with enthusiasm."

Laboring at his normal career, plus the amount of time and work that had gone into the filming of the pilot, had been far more emotionally draining on Bob than his two-year stint on *Donna Reed* as a supporting actor—this time Crane carried both the thrust of the plot and the bulk of the dialogue.

Crane's wife, Anne, used to the life of a suburban Connecticut housewife, felt out of place in the Hollywood glitz. She had weathered the long hours and dedication that Bob had devoted to his career—from the early morning DJ jobs back east and in Los Angeles, to the MC circuit and his television work on Donna Reed's show and the *Hogan's Heroes* pilot. But Crane's newfound fame had begun to affect his marriage.

Bob's growing addiction to pornography and the important part this material was playing in his lifestyle was no secret. "I was totally aware," said Werner, "that he collected pornographic material." For Crane pornography acted as a release from the tremendous weight of his workload. Sex became a constant preoccupation and a goal.

Every Monday morning Bob would be on the different sound stages, walking through the action, script in hand, with the principal cast members. The scenes would be blocked out by the director so that by five in the afternoon Feldman and Powell could come down and watch while the cast gave them a run-through.

On Tuesdays and Wednesdays interior filming would be done. By 7:00 A.M., while Klemperer was in the makeup chair desperately going through his lines, Crane was already out of makeup and dressed in his flier's cap and black leather USAF 504th Bomber Group jacket.

Klemperer was enormously pleased and relieved not to be playing villains. By 6:00 A.M. each morning he was out the door of his smart, Danish-modern-furnished home, downing a cup of coffee as he drove the twenty minutes from the Westwood area to the studio in Hollywood.

Crane and Powell both noticed that Klemperer had a bit of Klink in his own makeup. "He had no difficulty playing the stuffy character," said Powell. "Banner would try to upstage Klemperer by holding back at readings and coming on strong once the cameras started rolling." Banner would say, laughing, "They can't upstage me. It's a physical impossibility."

In the beginning Crane was exhilarated by the work, but the grind was draining. *Hogan's Heroes* was filmed like a motion picture on 35-mm film, with a large crew and a single camera. "But much, much faster time," said Clary. "We did a half-hour show in four days." Sitcom directors had to possess raw animal energy to prepare a show, shoot, edit, and dub it, and then move on to another program, going from episode to episode for a full season.

Exteriors were filmed on Thursdays. "We'd go out unless the weather was rainy," said Robert Clary, "but most of the time here it's very beautiful." Clary had the advantage of living midway between the interior stages and the exterior lot, about twenty-five minutes each way. Exteriors were done at Forty Acres in Culver City, where they had filmed the burning of Atlanta in *Gone With the Wind*. "Sometimes we'd not even film a full day of exteriors," said Klemperer, "because we had a duplication of exteriors inside for close-up work." Sets were as important to a series as the actors.

Fridays at 11:00 A.M. Bob and his costars gathered around the table with director Powell, producers Feldman and Bernie Fein, and the guest stars to read the next script through a couple of times.

In the early days of the series the cast would call each other up after the show. "Every Friday night our phones were busy," Klemperer recalled. "Robert calls John. John calls me. Everybody says everyone else is great. We were that kind of company. We all liked each other very well."

While Klemperer and Crane had a good working relationship, they weren't really friends on a social level. In December of 1965 Bob began what would be an annual event for the life of *Hogan's Heroes*—his Christmas party for the cast and the crew and their wives. On December 25, 1965, the entire cast of the show made what would be their only public appearance together on the *Bing Crosby Show*, hosted by the man whose production company owned *Hogan's Heroes*.

As a teenager, Bob Jr. was on the *Hogan's Heroes* set as much as he could be, and he became aware after a while that there was friction between his father and Richard Dawson, who played British corporal Peter Newkirk. "I saw the relationship," he said, "and it was cool at best. Dawson and my dad didn't get along because of competitive factors, jealousy on Dawson's part, due to the fact that my dad was the star of his show and Dawson was not. Dawson had tried out for the role of Hogan and had not gotten it, but they needed an English guy in the show and they felt Dawson was funny and a good enough actor, so they hired him.

"But it was that continual 'I lost the starring role' type of ego attitude on Dawson's part that was the basis for a couple of verbal arguments. All these disagreements were confined to the set, offstage, or in the dressing-room areas."

Bob Jr. never saw any heated exchanges or physical blows traded between his dad and Dawson, but the arguments were so intense that Crane mentioned them to his son at home. Whenever Crane muffed a line, Dawson would say, "Well, you really fucked up again." That kind of chiding was typical between the two men.

Dawson, born in Gosport, Hampshire, England, on November 20, 1934, had his education interrupted by the war as he and his brother were evacuated. Unlike Crane, who was sensitive about his lack of schooling throughout his life, Dawson educated himself by reading an entire book a day. At age twenty Dawson conned a London theatrical agency by passing himself off as a vacationing Canadian comedian and snagged a six-week contract with a Plymouth music hall. "I didn't even have an act," he recalled. "I got together a few jokes, bought a stock arrangement of 'Georgia on My Mind,' and reported for work."

Ninety-year-old comic Billy Bennett provided him with a routine and helped him polish his material. Soon Dawson was playing the London Palladium. By 1959 he was married to Diana Dors. When they divorced, Richard quipped, "She didn't renew my option." His dreams of success easily equaled Crane's.

Like Bob, Richard needed only a few hours of sleep each night, and he, too, was a high-energy man—his day included filming *Hogan's*, drinking thirty cups of coffee, wolfing down a big steak for dinner, and tape-recording an hour or so of routines or short stories to be transcribed by a secretary. He even worked on a *Hogan's Heroes* script.

Dawson also spent a lot of time playing with high-tech video equipment with a new friend: John Carpenter.

Feldman had his share of problems with the fledgling show. A lawsuit was brought by Donald Beven and Edmund Trycinski, the authors of the play *Stalag 17*, and by Paramount, which had released Billy Wilder's Oscarwinning film version. Plagiarism was claimed. The final legal settlement was kept secret, but Klemperer said, "They went away successful. It was settled out of court, so they got something, at least."

Then there was the hate mail—Jews, Germans, and the American Nazi party were united in their dislike of the program. Jews found the show particularly offensive and soft on Nazis. Germans resented the portrayal of emotionless, sadistic, madly efficient jackbooted officers. The Nazi party thought they were being lampooned. Crane even got some neo-Nazi threats.

"There was all kinds of bullshit in the beginning," said Klemperer, "but it all died away. The show was a big hit." To many who were still astonished by "funny Nazis," the ratings of the show must have been bewildering.

It would take over a year for the criticism to taper off. One critic wrote, "*Hogan's Heroes* depicts Hitler's 'master race' as harmless—hopeless oafs, easygoing simps." There were complaints of "the depiction of Nazis as silly old buffoons . . . having more in common with Desilu than Hitler." Another chided, "Germans, conquerors of a continent, are played as lazy, doltish, cuddly, lovable, and cute." Others believed that the show's ultimate tastelessness rested in the

Bob's apartment at
the Winfield, #132A

At the upper right of the photo is the morning paper discovered in Bob's apartment, which had been published *after* his death. On the cluttered table are *Key, Where, Down-Beat,* and *La Parada* magazines, a pink note with "Dawn" on it, personal letters from Dallas, a video library catalog, a manila envelope labeled "I.C.M." and a news clipping titled "Hogan, From Radio to Residuals." Also found were tickets to *Beginner's Luck,* a Continental Airlines ticket, the front half of a Nikon camera case, a Dymo-Label maker, a receipt from Bobby McGee's, a 9-volt battery, two rolls of Tri-X 35mm film, a Kodachrome 40-minute film cassette, Breath Fresh Spray, a lime squeezer, a red key, and a blue key. At the lower left is the box to the SL-8200 Bob and John borrowed from DynaTronics. (Exclusive, unpublished police photo)

**All photos, unless otherwise noted,
are from the author's collection.**

In the foreground on the living room coffee table: two *T.V. Guides*, three *Down-Beat* magazines, copies of *Esquire*, *Cosmopolitan*, and *New West*, a blue address book, a script of "Crash," memos for days of June 21 and June 23, a health spa credit card, two Polaroid SX-70 film covers, a Beta video-cassette marked "Cindy," the original videotape for *Saturday Night Fever*, a Polaroid camera with strobe flash unit, an aspirin box, and two black ash-trays.

In the background against the curtains is Bob's equipment: a 19-inch Sylvania color T.V., Panasonic VTR, a GBC videotape camera on a black and silver tripod, a Sony Betamax video recorder, a Sony digital timer, and a Panasonic cassette tape recorder. Crane's editing materials are on top of the Sony video machine on the T.V. (Exclusive, unpublished crime scene photo)

Detective Lieutenant Ron Dean examining a jimmied door lock. (Photo courtesy of *Scottsdale Progress*/Ray Wong)

Lieutenant Ron Dean today

The stars of *Hogan's Heroes*, Bob Crane, John Banner, and Werner Klemperer, at the time of the show's greatest popularity, 1965–1966.

Photo of entire cast of *Hogan's Heroes* on the Desilu Culver City lot in 1967. Reading clockwise from John Banner on the motorcycle: Werner Klemperer, Bob Crane, Patti, a director, Richard Dawson, Robert Clary, Ivan Dixon, and Larry Hovis. (Insurance company photograph taken for insuring production company. Used with permission.)

Richard Dawson

Robert Clary

Detective
Dennis Borkenhagen

Maricopa County Attorney
Richard "Rick" Romley

Jack DeMave

Bob and Patti (Sigrid Valdis) during their happiest time

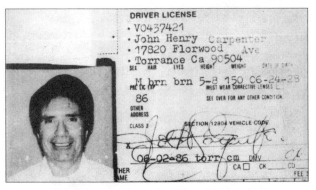

John Henry Carpenter as he appeared in the 1980s

John Henry Carpenter
as he appeared in the summer of 1978

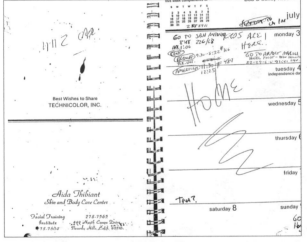

Bob's open datebook was to his right on the phone table, beneath his eyeglasses. The page for June 29, 1978, is spattered with blood. The next page, shown above right, poignantly mentions "Home" and "Go home." Other notations in the appointment journal mention Scotty's birthday, "Karen's Grad!," "Call Carpenter," and "Brenda called."

John Carpenter in
Los Angeles Municipal Court,
Monday, June 1, 1992
(*Los Angeles Times* photo/Lori Shepler)

Investigator Chris Bingham escorts Victoria Berry, who discovered Crane's body when she went to see why he didn't keep an appointment, from Apartment #132A to Scottsdale Police Headquarters so she can give a more detailed, taped statement. (UPI)

On July 5, 1978, a casket containing the body of the slain actor is carried down the steps of St. Paul the Apostle church in Westwood, California, following services. Among the pallbearers are Crane's son, Robert Crane Jr. (in dark glasses at the right), as well as two other members of the *Hogan's Heroes* cast, Robert Clary (left) and Larry Hovis (in center just behind Clary). (UPI/Bob Flora)

fact that it portrayed a world without villains, with comic Nazis who were "only following orders," who were a "barking, *heil*ing, goose-stepping batch of uniformed robots, boot lickers, toadies, cowards, and dupes."

"There is no such thing as a cuddly Nazi," said Banner. "Maybe Goering was cuddly to his wife. He wasn't cuddly to the city of Rotterdam. Schultz is not a Nazi. I see Schultz as the representative of some kind of goodness in any generation."

Klemperer said, "I am an actor by profession. If you can play Richard the Third, you can play a Nazi."

"Ex-POWs are our greatest boosters," Crane pointed out. "The ex-POWs in Albuquerque, New Mexico, have an association. They had a convention and invited me. A lot of POWs are hooked on *Hogan's Heroes*. They're our biggest rooters—along with New York Jewish delicatessen owners!" He summed up the program's theme as "Look how clever the Allies are."

In spite of the outcry, Crane's show was the ninth most popular program of the season, with a 24.9 share, according to A. C. Nielsen, and the sixth most popular on the CBS network.

Crane usually ate lunch alone in his dressing room, where his music and drums were set up. "When a scene was ready to be shot," Clary recalled, "usually you have to go and look for the star. Not so with Bob. We could *hear* where he was." Jerry Lewis once had a musical duel with Crane on his beloved drums. The overzealous comedian destroyed them, but trucked around a replacement set first thing the next morning. Naturally, they were top of the line. Music was everywhere on the set. Clary and Hovis sang Kern and Gershwin between takes while Klemperer played the Strauss symphonic poem, "Till Eulenspiegel's Merry Pranks," to get himself into a kooky mood.

It was through music that Clary found a wife. Natalie Cantor, one of Eddie Cantor's daughters, was a fan of Robert's 1948 hit record, "Put Your Shoes On, Lucy," which had sold 250,000 copies in the United States. She so loved the record that she begged her famous father to bring Clary over from France for his radio show, but Robert was singing at the Place Pigalle in Paris and couldn't come.

Finally, through Merv Griffin, Clary met Natalie in 1950, and for fifteen years they were the closest of friends. After the first dozen or so *Hogan's Heroes* he proposed and they married. "I adore the Cantor family and they love me, I guess," Robert said. "It's been a great relationship."

"Eddie Cantor once told me," said Crane, "likability is ninety percent of the battle, and he was right."

Bob was nominated for an Emmy for his first season, Outstanding Continued Performance by an Actor in a Comedy Series. He wasn't confident about winning, but Klemperer was. He had been nominated, too, also for the first time. At the award cocktail party people pumped his hand. "My God," they said, "have you got a cinch here." "I was so cocksure I would win, it wasn't even funny," said Werner.

Crane's trepidation was justified: he lost out to his hero, Dick Van Dyke. Werner lost as well. "Don Knotts beat me to it," he recalled, "and that gave me a good lesson in humbleness." Klemperer did better in 1967 and 1968. "Then," he said, "I won back to back."

Crane lost again, the next time to Don Adams. "I think probably Crane didn't win an award," said Powell, "because everybody considered it a bit of a natural part for him. He seemed to be playing himself, though he actually wasn't, of course. It didn't seem like he was doing, quote, acting, unquote."

Bob was a shrewd man who knew his limitations and he religiously began to attend the screenings of the dailies with Feldman. From certain angles Crane did not look his best and he was there to be certain that only the most photogenic shots of himself were used. He had never been an athlete as a child, choosing instead to practice his music, and the image of Colonel Hogan had to be heroic. The show was going to be to his satisfaction, he had decided, or else. This drive for perfection would only grow as his career progressed.

"You have to remember," said Werner, "that Bob Crane was basically not an actor. He became an actor. He had a sort of likable American naive quality that was just right for the part."

13

PATTI, RICHARD, AND JOHN

Sitcom—Situation comedy, a comedy series usually a half hour long with continuing characters.

Crane's West Coast publicity tour was in March, and by June filming had already begun on *Hogan's Heroes'* second season—the 1966 fall season. The first episode had Hogan and his men tricking their German captors into blowing up one of their own oil refineries. *Hogan's Heroes* had some real competition this time—butting up against the first half of NBC's smash tongue-in-cheek superspy show, *The Man from U.N.C.L.E.*

During the 1965 season Klink's secretary, Helga, had been played by actress Cynthia Lynn. "Helga may be the only girl in the regular cast, but we live by the Bob Cummings TV formula—keep those girls moving in and out," said Crane. Lynn was moved out at Bob's suggestion to Feldman, said one cast member, and replaced by a pigtailed blonde named Sigrid Valdis. Bob was attracted to her immediately.

For the duration of *Hogan's Heroes'* run, Sigrid would play a character similar to Helga but named Hilda, the commandant's "blond strudel." (The rule in sitcoms is that actors do not replace other actors—characters supersede other characters.) Sigrid's real name was Patti Olsen.

"I had decided to change my name even before I decided to be an actress," she told *TV Guide*. "Sigrid can make it but Pat never could."

The long dry spell at a Park Avenue car dealership ended when Patti walked in off the street and galvanized sales to such an extent that after three months she was made manager. Patti told *TV Guide* in a featured article that after another three months she had salted enough money away to quit and further pursue her acting career. Her expertise was so missed that within half a year the auto salesroom went out of business.

Patti was able to enroll in Stella Adler's acting class and in 1963, separated but not divorced from her New York businessman husband, George Ateyeh, Patti returned with her daughter, Melissa, to Los Angeles, where she had been born.

While filling the role of mother *and* father, Patti was determined to knock Hollywood on its ear. First she located a two-story Westwood apartment with cavernous rooms and high beamed ceilings and set out to transform it into a showcase. She not only succeeded but made it cozy and homelike for her daughter.

Now Patti's agent took a long look at this young hopeful dressed in boots and form-fitting capri pants and with hair that fell as far as her hips. He suggested that she next remake herself.

Patti was already an attractive, delicate featured, intelligent woman with a striking figure, but reluctantly she had her teeth capped, her hair cut and bleached, and was outfitted in new clothes. An agent also suggested that she forget about being a character actress for the time being. "There's no such thing as a young character actress," he advised.

Patti submitted to the alterations and was pleasantly surprised by the immediate effect.

She got work right away in a Frank Sinatra and Dean Martin film, *Marriage on the Rocks*, then in *Our Man Flint* and *The Venetian Affair*. On *The Steve Allen Show*, Patti was "Miss Leek"; she was "Miss Peacemeal" on *The Wild, Wild West* and "Bubbles Broadbent" on an unsold Sid Caesar pilot.

She knew her role on *Hogan's* was an attention getter. "Here's a bunch of guys in POW fatigues and there's a blond girl in a low-cut peasant blouse—who is the audience going to watch? My big line is always *'Herr Kommandant*, Colonel Hogan to see you.' "

Bob told Eddie Feldman that he "had never felt an energy like this before." In fact, the other women Crane flirted with and occasionally saw began to take on a specific look—they all resembled Patti.

Always embarrassingly open, Bob boasted to friends that he and Patti were lovers and hinted that it had happened early in their relationship: "She's the most gorgeous woman I've ever laid eyes on. She's like my other half. I never felt complete until now." The affair caused the actor sleepless nights and anxiety because it was a betrayal—of Anne, his religious upbringing, and his own code of ethics. Since there seemed to be no way out, Bob gave himself over to his passion and began to arrive home later and later, sharing quiet suppers after filming with Patti or roving the clubs.

"We loved to have visitors," said Klemperer toward the end of filming for the show's second season. "Our set was wide open." There were so many visitors to the set that no one was surprised when Richard Dawson brought a friend. Crane noticed him right away.

The stranger had a husky build and a mane of straight, long black hair. His face was pockmarked and his complexion so dark he was often taken for Latin, Mexican, or Italian. He was, in fact, a Native American.

Dawson introduced Bob to the visitor, John Henry Carpenter.

At first Crane dismissed Carpenter as yet another hanger-on, but it developed that all three men had a mutual interest in video and very young women. Soon Crane bought some video equipment from Carpenter.

During the two visits that Bob Jr. made to Dawson's with his father, he had seen Richard's wide range of video equipment, but never any of the homemade videos. Carpenter told him they "were things involving women." Bob Crane told his son that Dawson and Carpenter were in them.

This Beta equipment was expensive and bulky; the setups were very complicated. All the tapes were in black and white. Carpenter had worked for Superscope and was now at Sony. It might be good to know this guy, Crane thought. He could set up my new equipment for me.

Dawson knew that Carpenter had a wife named Diane, and he was aware of a young girlfriend named Rita. On several occasions Dawson visited John's home, but it was Carpenter who more frequently visited Dawson's, where the comic lived with his two sons (the "rats," as he called them), Mark and Gary, a nanny, and a Great Dane. Carpenter often house-sat when Dawson and his boys went on vacation.

The coolness between Crane and Dawson must have put Carpenter in a difficult position. One member of the show recalled: "Of course, Carpenter would be what you call a hanger-on to Crane and Dawson, to get the residue of what there was in the way of attention and glory and extra women. He was the extra male, and the women were attracted by fame. I think he really wanted to be in show business. He used to play Crane and Dawson against each other to his benefit. But he could never tell either one of them he was still associating with the other because of the antipathy that existed between the two actors."

At the end of the 1966–67 season, *Hogan's Heroes* finished its second season as the seventeenth most popular show in America. By April of 1967 shooting for the third season had already begun. *Hogan's Heroes* was moved to 9:00 P.M. on Saturday. "We lost points in the ratings, but

CBS says it's the best they've done in the Saturday night spot, so I guess we're hooked," Crane said in September.

In 1968 Crane made *The Wicked Dreams of Paula Schultz*, a film costarring Elke Sommer and two of the *Hogan's* stars—Klemperer and Banner. "I prefer not even to talk about that," said Klemperer. "It was really quite dreadful. Just because you're in a hit show they think they don't have to come up with good material. I mean, if you think the idea of an East German girl pole-vaulting over the wall is a good one, then you'll like anything. Please don't see it."

Crane was just as unhappy with his choice of film parts. "I was offered a role in an important picture and turned it down because I sincerely did not believe I was right for the part. So I went to see the finished picture, and the actor who got it was no better suited to it than I was. But he came out with a Best Supporting Actor nomination. I'm learning to correct the bad habit of complete honesty in myself."

Bob was excited by a work he had taped in March 1969 that was aired a month later—an ABC television production of *Arsenic and Old Lace*. "It was really thrilling for me to do it like a play on stage with three weeks of rehearsal," he said. "If someone had said to me before it happened, 'Would you like to work with Helen Hayes and Lillian Gish?' I'd have said they were joking." Crane was playing the Cary Grant role and compared it to the experience of being Liz Taylor's next husband: "I knew what I was supposed to do," he said. "The problem was how to make it interesting."

Bob did six weeks in Warren, Ohio, in *Cactus Flower*, having previously performed *Send Me No Flowers* for ten weeks in Chicago. He also subbed for Carson on the *Tonight* show. "These shows are fun," said Crane. "I can be myself, whatever that is."

During the 1969 fall season *Hogan's Heroes* was returned to the slot where it had been the most successful—Friday nights at 8:30. But it was debatable that Bob could curb his ambition in order to ride the show out to its natural dissolution. In April of 1970 Crane's contract with CBS would be up, and the network was already discussing his future with them.

Bob knew a lot of jobs depended on his remaining until the program had run its course. He was perfectly willing to stay. "Every time I drive a new expensive sports car and look at the way I live and am able to keep my family, I'm even more willing." Crane told the network he'd like a total of seven years for the series, but the long periods between seasons bothered him. "I'd go crazy doing nothing," he said, "so I'll do a play or a special. . . . It isn't just the money. I've always had a drive to get ahead. After three days' vacation I want to start working again."

As he reached forty, Bob found his normal insecurities intensified. He hadn't yet forgiven Tony Owen and brought up his firing from *The Donna Reed Show* in several interviews. He considered betrayal by a friend a cardinal sin.

John Austin, who covered the entertainment world for several publications, noted that during the several times he had interviewed Bob over the years, a bitterness seemed to have overtaken the actor. "Behind the scenes," wrote Austin, "they said there was a complex, difficult-to-understand, and often bitter personality. He hid his heartbreak with a smile—like all clowns—and Bob Crane was, in reality, a clown, always seeking a laugh with a wisecrack, a bon mot, a smile, a wink."

Dissatisfaction began to pervade the sitcom. "A lot of times," complained Clary, "all I got to say was, 'Are we going to do that?' or 'Schultz is coming.' And if I had nothing to do, Ivan Dixon had even less. After the fifth year of *Hogan's Heroes* he'd had it. Once in a while they threw him a crumb. Gave him a good scene. Ivan's a good actor. The last year he was saying, 'What am I doing here?' "

In 1970 Dixon left the show to become a director and was replaced by Kenneth Washington in the role of Corporal Richard Baker. Larry Hovis, whose lines were limited to "Sure thing" and "Oh, boy," felt he had become the invisible hero, and when he signed with NBC for the first thirteen weeks of *Laugh-In*, no one at CBS cared.

Hogan's Heroes was grinding down; it seemed as if the

writers had put the zany band through every plot variation imaginable: they had robbed Goering's private train, plotted to kill Hitler, smuggled bulletproof vests to the underground, destroyed a radio tower, immobilized an entire SS division, found the location of a German A-bomb research center, broken an enemy counterfeiting plot, infiltrated an SS meeting to steal a Nazi code book, pulled off a "peace" hoax, gotten Nazi air defenses moved, eliminated a German scientist, blown up an enemy munitions train, saved Schultz from the Russian front, and conned Klink into sending arms to the underground.

Perhaps there were no plots left.

From a faithful marriage, Bob had gone from a few casual affairs to a continuing search for and overwhelming preoccupation with sex. But his religious upbringing caused him periods of despair and shame. He seemed determined to "maximize" his number of sexual conquests, but the more he pursued this, the more intense were his periods of loneliness and depression. Such a destructive pattern of behavior, he must have known, could cause damage to his goal of stardom.

Crane loved Anne, but he was leaving her. She had filed for divorce, charging mental cruelty on May 13, 1969, one week before their twentieth wedding anniversary. He loved Patti, but he was drawn to great numbers of other women. He read a teleplay that echoed his own predicament—a young priest has fallen in love, wants to marry, but is in agony over separating from his church. Crane wanted desperately to play this part.

"I am a Catholic," he said, "and I know what this struggle can mean. In a different way it happened to me when I went through the pain of my wife and me breaking up our marriage after twenty years. There's no conveying the agony of breaks from convictions like these for a priest— or for a husband."

His long marriage was over; he wanted out of his hit show; his son, Bob Jr., was eighteen and out of the home;

he was in love with Patti. By the end of 1969 Crane was making one great escape after another.

When Patti was interviewed by *TV Guide* in 1967 in an article called "Hunting for the Brass Ring," she said, "I'm going to ask the next man who proposes to me if he'll buy me a merry-go-round of my own. If he says yes, then I'll know he's my kind of man. I want my own merry-go-round more than anything else." Bob didn't buy her a merry-go-round, but in 1970, almost five months after his divorce from Anne was finalized, he married Patti.

Bob and Patti's wedding ceremony was conducted on the set of *Hogan's Heroes* on October 16, 1970, with the cast in attendance. Municipal judge James Harvey Brown married the two; the usually unflappable Crane had to ask him to repeat the line "In token and in pledge."

Bob's home with Anne had been middle class, hidden out in San Fernando Valley. His new house with Patti was in Brentwood and more ostentatious. In 1971 Patti and Bob had a son, Scott.

Ironically, it was *Hogan's Heroes* that kept Patti from getting other and better roles. To do Bob's show she had gone from guest star to bit player. "By the time you get anyplace in this town," she once said, "you're too old. In a few years they'll be looking for a young Sigrid Valdis."

By mid-March 1970, when William Paley went down to the thirty-fourth floor for the program meeting, CBS had become a "network for the aging." Profits were down, ads were being sold at half price, and Congress had just banned all TV cigarette advertising—a tremendous loss of revenue for the network. Robert Wood, who had been network president for a year, audaciously called for an overhaul of the prime-time schedule.

Demographics had played a decisive part in his thinking. Although the network's strategy of yokel comedy and escapist fare had captured a mass audience, it was an audience comprised of older, rural viewers, many with lower incomes. Now advertisers were interested not in the size of

the audience, but in their age (ideally between eighteen and thirty-four) and their buying power.

Wood mapped out a strategy at the meeting—they would claim the lucrative "now" generation of purchasers and present relevant dramatic series "based on socially significant adventures and variety shows with youthful irreverence." Realism would replace fantasy, rural settings would be exchanged for urban ones. Wood reasoned that the longer a show stayed on top, the older CBS's audience and the more expensive the program became (*Hogan's Heroes* now cost over $80,000 per episode), with annual increases in the stars' salaries.

As Paley was persuaded by Wood to "get the wrinkles out of the face of the network without losing popularity," a man from the research department began to cry. "You don't know what you're doing," he said. "You're throwing away millions and millions of viewers. If you do this, a year from today you'll all be sitting around here scratching your heads and wondering why in hell you were such goddamned fools." Word spread in the halls of Black Rock: "Bob Wood is canceling every show with a tree in it!"

At the end of the 1970–71 season, Wood canceled *Hogan's Heroes* after six years and axed seven other winning shows on CBS.* Money had been saved, and CBS was on its way to urbanization.

Hogan's Heroes left the network after 168 episodes on July 4, 1971, but eventually proved to be one of the most successful syndicated shows of all time. By 1972 it was running in every major city in the United States, as well as approximately seventy-five countries, though not in West Germany.

Because they were unaware of the hard-line decisions

---

*Put out to pasture: *The Ed Sullivan Show* (after twenty-three seasons), *Lassie* (after seventeen seasons), *Mayberry R.F.D.* (after eleven years), *The Beverly Hillbillies* (after nine seasons), *The Jim Nabors Hour* (after five), *Hee-Haw* (after two), and *Green Acres* (after six). Urban sitcoms such as *All in the Family* and *The Mary Tyler Moore Show* replaced them.

made in the boardrooms of Black Rock, the cast of *Hogan's* was bewildered and bitter. "I know a show can end in mid-sentence," said Crane, "but we were still a hit, still at the top. I just don't understand."

Klemperer said later, "We were all a little pissed off."

Clary said, "I think they were wrong to cut us off. We could have worked at least two more years."

Richard Dawson, who was headed for greater success on *Laugh-In, The New Dick Van Dyke Show*, and (as the highest-paid performer on daytime television) *Family Feud*, cut his ties with the *Hogan's Heroes* cast.* As the kissing host of *Feud* it was estimated he kissed twenty thousand women on three thousand half-hour shows. "People feel they know me and can touch me," he said. "It's magic."

"I live very close to Richard Dawson, and I *never* see him," said Clary.

"Success," said Klemperer, "did not become Mr. Dawson well."

However, Dawson maintained his close relationship with John Carpenter, and Carpenter secretly continued his friendship with Bob Crane.

---

*Eddie Feldman and John Banner hoped lightning would strike twice with their new sitcoms. Both shows failed. Robert Clary found work on *Days of Our Lives* for nearly a decade, and Klemperer became so busy that he was bicoastal: Broadway musicals, films, and classical music soloist (narrator). At the end of January 1973, John and Christine Banner returned to his native Vienna. While they were waiting in the cool evening air for their new furniture to arrive, John suffered an abdominal hemorrhage and died just before midnight on his sixty-third birthday.

CAMELBACK MOUNTAIN

14

"DIS-MISSED, HOGAN!"

Preparation—Anticipating, making ready beforehand, motivating a scene in a teleplay, showing an audience what is about to happen.

After the death of his show, Crane began to drift. A few jobs opened up, and there was money enough. Bob had been smart—in lieu of a raise each year, he had gotten a percentage of the profits and a higher rate of royalties (the other cast members were paid residuals only for the first ten reruns). However, he was told each year that *Hogan's Heroes* was still not a financial success, and it was not until the fall of 1974 that he got his first check. "And that was very small," said Bob. "It's what happens in the bookkeeping that determines whether or not a show makes a profit." By 1976, though, Bob's royalties were sometimes as high as six figures. He had a twenty-five percent share of the show's profits and at this writing the total earnings of *Hogan's Heroes* have been estimated at almost ninety million dollars.

Bob sought to revive his career. He had used his suave,

wisecracking personality to achieve television stardom, and now he was inseparable from that typecasting image Werner Klemperer, for instance, had avoided. "For the first few years after the show went off the air," he said, "I was often asked to do things close to the character of Klink, but I steadfastly refused because I wasn't a hungry actor, and after a few years the problem just went away like the plague."

Had Bob been more like his idol, Jack Lemmon, he might have been more successful. Lemmon not only avoided being typecast, he astutely avoided the suffocation of a sitcom. The public expected Crane to behave, sound, and look like Colonel Robert E. Hogan.

The versatile Dick Van Dyke, far more gifted than Bob, attempted to launch himself from the small screen to movie stardom, failed, and returned to TV in *The New Dick Van Dyke Show*, but he could not succeed a second time. As many faded TV stars had done, Van Dyke began to tour in midwest summer stock musicals and make the occasional television movie and sporadic guest appearances. These shots were so remunerative that Bob began to follow in Van Dyke's path.

He starred in *Send Me No Flowers*, a comedy about a man who mistakenly thinks he's going to die, and was delighted to find that his series exposure had also made him a top box office draw at the theater. On the other hand, he often had to argue with directors to prove his intuitive judgments correct, and this created an industrywide image of Crane as pushy and difficult to work with.

Bob hid his worries beneath a wisecracking exterior, but he was finding it hard to get work on TV, and going back to KNX radio was out of the question; the station's format had changed to all-news programming. In both 1972 and 1973, Crane did briefly return to radio, doing big band and Frank Sinatra specials.

Bob hosted local shows, was MC at some top beauty pageants, attended a POW convention in New Zealand (he had done many previously), taped radio spots, took part in sports events and more stage work, and in March of 1972 even played a villain, Charlie Taggart, on the pilot for the suspense spy series *The Delphi Bureau*. His image remained the same—he was still just a charming comic. None of the pilots he made for other TV series succeeded, and he was getting some bad press for his off-screen activities.

Photographer and Chicago columnist Bob Ellison recalled how whenever he dropped into Los Angeles, Bob would take him along to the strip clubs. One series of photographs taken by Ellison showed Crane playing drums alongside stripper Angel Carter at the Casual Cat, a topless and bottomless club, and later nuzzling the dancers in their dressing room. Ellison's last photos of the evening showed Bob kissing Patti outside the club, where she had been waiting alone.

"Yeah, yeah," he said after reporters saw the pictures, "I read about that, too. But nobody at the studio really said anything. I mean, not officially. They didn't know about my hobby of playing the drums in topless-bottomless bars around town! But what was wrong about that? I loved sitting in with small groups to play the drums, and naturally I like to look at naked ladies.

"I'm a normal, red-blooded guy, and I was only looking at those ladies, I wasn't doing anything with them. It happened that they were at the places where I could play drums." Crane's periods of enforced idleness began to affect his new marriage. But from his point of view it was Patti who was changing. John Carpenter, too, noticed that their marriage was having problems.

"The first three years were great," said Carpenter, "then all of a sudden she just started to change. Most of their marital problems had to do with family. His family and her family. Nothing to do with outside activities at all. All of their arguments were about Bob's two daughters from his first marriage [Deborah and Karen] coming over to the house when Patti wasn't there, and there was a big, big blowup. I mean really hostile. Just screams."

Bob Jr. verifies this. The fights, he said, were about his grandmother and his sisters. He considered his dad to be a "slave" in the marriage. "I called him a 'nigger' in terms of his own marriage," Bob Jr. said later. "And I mean that exactly the way it sounds. In terms of slave versus the plantation owner, Patti was running the ship. She claimed that she was holding the boat together. Since the beginning of their marriage I've been hearing this. But she did not work after *Hogan's Heroes*. She hated my grandmother, my dad's mom. She hated my two sisters."

When Bob Jr., in order to explain the pressures in his father's life, spoke with county attorney's investigators years later he attempted to show the series of misunderstandings on both sides that fueled the bickering between Patti, Bob Jr., his two sisters, and his grandmother. It seemed to be the case that *all* these people loved Bob Crane very much.

Like many successful actresses, Patti may have felt that she was due a certain amount of the spotlight and this carried over into her personal relationships. Prior to meeting Crane she had dated the director Jack Donahue and her difficulties with his two grown daughters may have been a rehearsal for the dynamics of her future relationship with Bob's family.

"Patti is insanely jealous of other females, particularly of the daughters or family of the guy she's in love with," said Bob Jr. "This was true of my two sisters. So the jealousy thing with the daughters carries on to her marriage with my father. My stepmother blamed my grandmother for accusing her that Scotty, my half brother, was not my dad's because of a vasectomy that my dad had had before his marriage with her. She held that against my grandmother, but my grandmother claims she did *not* say it, and from everything I've heard she didn't."

"There's always been speculation as to whether Scotty is his and Patti's. I don't know the exact medical terminology, but a sperm count thing was done on my father around this time. The way I gathered it, there was never any doubt in his mind that Scotty was his child. But he never said anything about it."

While there had never been the slightest doubt in Crane's own mind that Scotty was his son, Bob Jr. presented this scenario to detectives later to show how the misunderstandings in the family had done more damage than the actions of the participants. No one can doubt that the grown-up Scotty of the present is the spitting image of the handsome Bob Crane.

At no time did Bob suggest to Patti that the boy "was not his kid," Bob Jr. said. "Anyway, on my side of the family there were these members who were hated by Patti for all those accusations and jealousies. From everything I read she pretty much wanted my dad to herself. It's okay if her mom's around or her stepdaughter's around or Scotty's around, but any people from my dad's previous marriage, including his daughters or myself, she couldn't take. We got along very well early on. It soured because when you disagree with Patti, you don't get far. She accused me of lying. Scotty soon called me a liar after that. What I'm trying to say is the members of his previous marriage, kids, etc., were on Patti's hate list."

John Carpenter recalled, "When they first got married the routine was they could fuck around out of town, but not in town. And she accepted this with Bob." Carpenter felt that if Bob went to an orgy, it meant little to Patti since no real relationship was involved. She was threatened by one-to-one affairs, however.

In early 1976 Bob and Patti's relationship was still strong, and Patti could sublimate her dislike of Carpenter and allow him to accompany her and Bob to the clubs. Once, they went to the Pink Pussycat on Sunset Boulevard to watch the strip show, but when Patti became ill she went home alone. Bob and John headed for the dressing rooms to ogle the dancers, who in turn tried to hustle the men: "Hey! We're working girls. . . ." Bob said all he'd ever pay for was breakfast.

As a rule, however, Patti would try to be away from home when John dropped by to see Bob. "When I was there," she said later, "Bob and John would go to another part of the house for their business or socializing." Patti based her distaste for Carpenter on the "weird things" John was into. She suspected sadism and masochism and believed that "he was performing sexual acts with girls in their early teens," of which she strongly disapproved.

When queried about his feeling toward Patti, John said, "I got along with her. I just didn't see her that often. I mean, talk to her that much. I'd go over to the house and automatically go right down to Bob's video room. We'd see what his problems were with the video equipment and try to correct them.

"In all the time I knew them, I had dinner only once at the house," Carpenter said. "We'd go out to dinner at the Imperial Gardens on Sunset and places like that, but nothing else. But our relationship was good."

Crane turned to the theater circuit once more. He bought the rights to a two-act romantic comedy, *Beginner's Luck*, and took it to Chicago's Drury Lane Theatre. Bob Jr. said, "My dad was in effect the captain of the team. He directed and starred in the play. He had the most lines and was able to make it flow. If someone else in the play put in his own lines, the timing of the comedy would be upset and my dad might talk to that cast member and tell him to cut it out."

Crane could be hard when it came to his craft. His brash, wisecracking demeanor and his self-confidence put some people off, and his play would customarily go through many leading ladies; the cast was in constant flux. Often after an engagement of *Beginner's Luck*, Bob and the play's coauthor, Norman Barasch, would have a minor skirmish. Norman thought a line should be left in because he wrote it. Crane would say, "Norman, it doesn't work. We've got to cut it out."

Beginner's Luck was the story of an average guy, married for fifteen years, who has a fling with a secretary. When his wife finds out she kicks him out, and they eventually get divorced. The remainder of the play deals with the hero trying to win his wife back from the other male character in the play.

When Bob took his play on the dinner club circuit for the first time in 1973, Scottsdale was on the schedule. Bob got his cast together: Pam Hayes, her husband, John Thomson, and Wendy Warner, who played the small role of Monica, the girlfriend.

Crane hadn't even gotten through rehearsals before he replaced Warner with Pearl Braaten. But the public loved him, women in particular. When Bob walked the streets people waved at him, and he would go out of his way to make the public happy—"Autograph? You betcha! Whatever you want."

"He was a really happy guy," said one Windmill Theatre employee, "a real nightlife type. He'd go out at night and people would mob him. Because he was an outgoing guy, when Bob Crane came to town he immediately had one thousand friends."

He saw Camelback for the first time, dotted with resorts and spas. Without pause adobe-style buildings strode up the slopes of Mummy Mountain. Out toward Carefree he saw substance being created from the insubstantial. A twisting shaft of dust began to grow. The funnel was quickly joined by a series of smaller tornadoes alongside. These were children of the summer—dust devils. They were, he was told, symbols of bad luck.

Opening night in Scottsdale was June 26 (*Beginner's Luck* would run until August 5). At the cast party at Ivanhoe's in Phoenix, Bob met a nineteen-year-old blue-eyed blonde named Brenda Sue Broyles, who was in the midst of a divorce. "I'm modeling," she said when Bob asked what she did.

Crane took Brenda out to the Biltmore (once it had been eight miles from the center of Phoenix, but the city had grown out and around it), where they danced in the Grand Ballroom under the deep plum ceiling and in front of velvet draperies and walls of mirrors and leather. Some days later they had sex, and Crane took Polaroid pictures of her.

At this time Crane had an unpleasant encounter with a woman whom he thought was emotionally disturbed. Whether the woman he spoke of was Brenda or not will probably never be known, but five years later, as we've seen, she was still on his mind. Bob would never mention her name other than to call her a "sickie." Moreover, he thought that the woman had underworld connections. But he once said he thought "most of Phoenix was owned by the Mafia."

Crane was constantly looking over his shoulder. He feared he was being followed by detectives hired by the jealous husband of a woman he knew. Patti knew her, too. Bob had lied just before the Scottsdale trip by telling his wife that this woman and her husband were no longer in the Phoenix area. The husband was rich and powerful, and the situation was so nerve-racking that when Bob was about to return to Scottsdale five years later, he would express extreme apprehension about the visit.

It was also in 1973 that Bob did his first Disney film: *Superdad*. Portions of the film, a generation-gap comedy about a father who competes with his daughter's fiancé, were filmed in San Francisco and Sausalito, and stories began to circulate in the Bay Area about Crane's sexual appetite and his participation in the vast world of alternative sex. "He would pick up two to three girls at a time in bars," Pete Noyes said, "and take them out because they were so enamored of this guy who was a star. He was engaging in all sorts of weird sex."

The articles in the newspapers about Crane's fixation on topless dancers paled before several very specific and persistent rumors that swept Hollywood and San Francisco at this time. While no paper trail existed to support Bob's interest in the underground, his exploits were common knowledge in L.A. and the Bay Area.

Crane made many contacts in San Francisco's sexual underground. Among them was Tiffany Moonlight. "Tiffany Moonlight used to strip at some club on Sunset," Hollywood writer Tony Castro recalled. "She used to be a dominatrix at a place called the Castle, in the mid-seventies. She was Bob Crane's dominatrix, his main heavy squeeze at the time. She used the name Tiffany Moonlight in films with Nina Hartley.

"Crane would take out ads across the country on swingers' club mailing lists for people who were into S and M. If he liked a particular response, he would catch the first flight and meet those people, taking with him all the goodies of the S and M lifestyle. Most of his partners were people of means, though perhaps not as high as his. He would pay for the construction of dungeons in their homes. He would spend literally thousands of dollars, especially here in Los Angeles.

"He had carpenter buddies who would, after a while, start giving him discount rates on the construction of these dungeons. An extra bedroom could be converted into a dungeon or a cell.

"He was known to have people place the ads for him," Tony continued, "since he himself couldn't for obvious reasons. Tiffany Moonlight was among them—a lot of times she suggested connections between Bob and other clients of hers. Crane was so into the sex bondage underground that he had post office boxes all over town. Obviously he couldn't give out his home address and phone."

Writer and film producer Jim Delasandro could talk for hours about the seamy backside of life in Hollywood. "I did this story once about the bondage underground in Los Angeles. There's also a big one in San Francisco. These people go to these parties. They tie each other up, whip each other's fannies.

"From what I understand, Crane was an active participant in all this stuff. He used to go to the A-Frame in Los Angeles occasionally, a place where all those parties used to take place. They said that Crane would fly to San Francisco and participate in those swinging parties.

"Yes, Bob had dungeons built. I hear he built some of them himself. I heard he had one in Los Angeles at a place called the Chateau, which was on Woodland Avenue right off Laurel Canyon. This place was there for many years. A bondage place. It was a big, big house. From what I understand, Crane used to go there often. He evidently put a girl up in a house and paid to keep her there. She was with other guys, but Crane got his for free because he financed the house and this dungeon. Essentially he underwrote the show.

"Crane used to hang out with these S and M freaks, bikers, topless dancers, and so on in Arizona. He was very seriously into kinky sex and rituals. He knew people in Arizona who were very wealthy and very much into the scene. They flew in girls and guys from all over the United States and from all over the world to participate in this stuff. Crane spent a lot of time and a lot of money. I mean he had paraphernalia and costumes, things like that. That's what I was told by a reliable source."

*   *   *

Superdad was released in January of 1974 and flopped. Bob realized what he had heard was true—for TV stars the transition to films is difficult, if not impossible. He continued to work in television, although he would have preferred the big screen. Among his TV work were such dramas as *Channing, Make Mine Red, White and Blue, Ellery Queen*, and *Mitzi and a Hundred Guys*. Bob appeared on *Dinah and Her New Best Friends* and did a segment of *Love, American Style*.

Crane was still a viable television personality, yet he complained that the various scripts and concepts he was offered for a new series were too similar to shows already done by Bob Cummings, Bob Denver, and Andy Griffith. One plot had him serving as the head of a stewardess training agency, while another had him as a bachelor who runs a baby-sitting service.

In April 1974 Crane's "TVQ" rating was still remarkably high, and the networks were anxious to profit by this popularity index. So in June, reluctantly, Bob attempted to return to series television. He won over Grant Tinker of MTM. Bob's pilot, *Second Start*, was sold in May, and NBC made plans to launch it in the fall along with *We'll Get By*, created by Alan Alda. They would fill the time recovered by the network from a previous decision by the FCC to give more time to the local stations. At the last minute the FCC gave an hour back to the locals, and, temporarily, six new shows were shelved, two from each network. Crane's show, now called *Second Chance*, was one of these.

Bob was pleased with the breathing space but also concerned about the time the show would finally go on the air. As the pilot was filmed, he had acquiesced to the network on many elements and now wanted to use the extra time to get back to the original concept. He thought the results too soft.

"I was ready to quit the show after the pilot," he said. "It operated in a one-joke arena about Daddy and the kids. When we were bumped off the schedule, I went to Grant Tinker and said the reason I came here was to do the kind of hard comedy three-camera show in front of an audience that you do with *Mary Tyler Moore* and *Bob Newhart* and

Rhoda. I want to do the kind of show that I watch—with belly laughs."

Tinker got NBC to agree to scrap the pilot and rethink the show's concept. "We flushed the pilot down into the Los Angeles River," said Bob, "and started over."

Crane dreamed of doing a sophisticated sitcom with adult themes, something he would have done well. But the FCC ruled that the first hour of prime time, 8:00 P.M. through 9:00 P.M., should be the "family hour." Crane was furious. "We're trying to do sophisticated comedy and they throw this 'family hour' at us," he said. "They tell us the kind of things we do you can't do until nine P.M. unless you're *All in the Family*. The idea was to do a nice, warm human comedy about a middle-aged guy who throws away a successful business career to go back to med school to be a doctor. I didn't like it. It sounded like *Donna Reed* all over again, but that's what NBC wanted."

In January of 1975, Bob's program, retitled *The Bob Crane Show*, was postponed again. Crane called a press conference.

"Look!" he said. "I know you're not going to believe this, but *The Bob Crane Show* is going on at last! You know I've always said I'd never do another Mom-Dad-and-the-kids series since way back after I finished *The Donna Reed Show*. But I did it anyway because I knew, financially speaking, if I didn't get a pilot that has a chance of getting on the air this year, I was going to be in deep trouble.

"First NBC delayed us from September to January—then they delayed us again until March. I said *March!* No one starts a series *then!* The only thing you do in March is change anchormen on the noon news. We'll never get this damn thing on the air. I was beginning to feel like Wilbur saying to Orville, 'Will it ever fly?' "

Bob's sitcom went on the air on March 6, 1975, with one of what Crane considered the mildest, weakest episodes of the series against the second half of *The Waltons*. *The Bob Crane Show* lasted only three months; the last of the filmed thirteen episodes ran on June 19.

After the demise of his show, Bob was interviewed by entertainment journalist John Austin. "It was a fun show," he told Austin over lunch, "and I liked the character I played. But I was apprehensive about the changes they kept making in it. . . . But there you are—that's all the network wanted, and they were proven wrong. I did all I could to have the changes canceled, and if we had, I really believe we had a chance of making it a success. . . . But it was over, practically before it had begun. I felt good doing it. I felt good about it and getting back to a regular series.

"I thought at the time I could do both—make films and do TV, and everything seemed to be going along fine. Then the balloon burst and it ended. What keeps us moving back? Is it habit or money or what? Well, for some of us it's just that we get kinda homesick for the sets, the smell of the sound stages, the orders 'Cut!' and 'Action!' by a director. Of course, the money is another reason. I'm not that rich, so I can do with whatever money I can get."

In 1975 Patti and Bob purchased a house in Beverly Hills, and in 1976 Bob's second Disney film, *Gus*, the story of a football-kicking mule who leads a losing team to victory, was released. The following year, because of their marital problems, Bob and Patti went to Newport to try to resolve their difficulties. But Patti, Bob later related, wanted something else first. Although he might have offered first, Crane's re-creation of the event went as follows:

"I won't even talk to you," she said, "until you sign this piece of paper."

"A quit-claim deed?" asked Bob. But he signed the paper, handed it back to her, and they talked. In the handwritten document he granted to her all interest in specific properties and said that he would never challenge the paper. Later when he realized the extent of what he had ceded, he was horrified.

Carpenter saw Patti and Bob's relationship at the end of the marriage as "very hostile, very, very hostile. Screaming matches. The whole thing. I felt sorry for him. Everybody else did, but of course Bob told everybody that he knew about his marital problems. He would not hold back that he was cheating on her."

"My dad has told me she hit him with coffee cups," Bob Jr. said. "Glasses, I mean, glasses that you drink out of, and she threw a videotape box at him, hitting him in the lip and cutting him. This was in 1976, I believe, in New Orleans. It didn't leave a scar, but there was a cut, and he in fact did bleed, and he had to go on stage that night. It was that kind of thing." Bob Jr. also spoke of a furious argument Patti had had with his grandmother.

Victoria Berry knew of the violent fights of the two lovers and Ronni Richards later told police that Patti had thrown something at Bob's face during the time *Beginner's Luck* was on the road. "He had to have stitches," she said. "The lip was all blown up."

Patti in her divorce decree claimed that Bob "had harassed and slapped her and had screamed obscenities at her. He threw open the windows of their West Los Angeles home and yelled that she was crazy. She charged that he refused to take their son, Scott, to the hospital after he had broken his arm when he was six and that he had frequently tried to show the boy 'adult films.' " "He started showing Scott kinky films when he was only two," she said. She alleged Crane owned a "large collection of pornographic films, including one with [her] in it."

"My older sister," said Bob Jr., "is now nineteen. Patti accused my older sister of streetwalking in Westwood, which is a heavily populated teenage area. She held my younger sister, Karen, who is seventeen, directly responsible for Scotty, my half brother, breaking his arm. The accusations and the blame put upon Karen never stopped after that incident. Patti also accused Karen of sleeping with my father.

"I heard from my dad that when Patti told a psychiatrist that Karen slept with my father, the psychiatrist said, 'What do you mean by "slept with"? Do you mean that she fucked him, he fucked her, what?' 'Well, no, not necessarily,' says Patti, 'but you know he slept with her.' That was all blown out of proportion because in reality two beds were in that bedroom." The two sisters later denied every aspect of Patti's emotional allegations.

In mid-November of 1977 *Beginner's Luck* began a

month-long engagement in Cincinnati. John Carpenter, as was his custom, made plans to link up with his friend. "Everywhere we've ever gone, if there was a two-bedroom apartment, John always stayed with Bob. Always," said Ronni Richards. "He always came down to Florida, to Dallas, where we played before, to Houston, to New Orleans. Every place."

In Cincinnati, because of a death in the family, Ronni Richards had to leave the cast. She was replaced by Victoria Berry, who felt a special obligation to Bob because he had helped her from the moment she had come to the United States in 1973.

When John Carpenter joined Bob in Cincinnati, the two friends went cruising for women. They came upon "a good-looking lady" at a disco, on her way to Florida to escape the cold.

"How about a party with us?" asked Carpenter.

"Fine," she said, and the two men brought her back to Bob's suite.

"We both balled her," said Carpenter. Crane began by taking Polaroid photos.

"Bob was very good with a Polaroid," said John, "flashing it down when they were giving him head."

Bob got John on videotape and then himself. John's tattoo, a small square scroll, was plainly visible. On tape, though, it was obvious that Bob was the dominant personality and Carpenter only a minor player. "Yeah," said an observer of the film sometime later, "there was one woman Crane and Carpenter were working on—it was a typical stag film kind of thing. One guy is screwing her, the other guy is getting a blow job. I think Crane just left his position, pushed John away, and did what he wanted to do. Captured on tape, it was obvious that Bob was not enjoying himself. It took him forever to come."

On December 19, 1977, Bob and Victoria Berry, his co-star, returned from Cincinnati. As Crane came down the airline ramp, he was served with divorce papers. "It tore him all to pieces," said Victoria. "It blew his mind."

Patti charged him with negligence toward their son and,

among other serious accusations, claimed he had forced her to make the sex video for him.

In Crane's memo book he wrote down one word to describe the days of December 19 through 22: "Nightmare." Bob Jr. said later, "Dad gets home, gets hit with divorce papers, doesn't know where to go, is kicked out of his own house. I think he stayed at my grandmother's house down the street for a couple of nights and then moved into my apartment on Midvale [in West Los Angeles]."

In earlier days Patti had toured with Bob, and recently Bob Jr. had gone on the road with him. The two were quite close, and Bob would often take his son to clubs to see performers such as Buddy Rich. Often Crane would be asked to sit in with the band.

Bob Jr. said later, "It's not even enough to say we were best of friends. We were, I feel, as close as two men can be without engaging in homosexual activity. That's how close I feel to my father and I think he felt to me."

In January 1978 Bob was in New York as the featured guest on the first installment of a half-hour syndicated series from Canada called *Celebrity Cooks*, in which host Bruno Gerussi helped the star prepare his favorite dish. Throughout the taping Bob kept up a manic barrage of tasteless jokes about women and sex. Too, there were "bizarre ramblings" about premonitions of his own death. Whether or not they realized it, the audience was being given a peek at Bob's off-screen life.

As Crane prepared his dish, a chicken recipe that Patti had given him, he began to discuss his deteriorating marriage, and tears appeared in his eyes. "There was something eerie about the show," said the WCBS press manager, Jeff Erdel. "I don't know which there was more of—jokes about death or jokes about sex. Bob was obviously very distraught about the breakup of his marriage."

The program, set to run on July 10, 1978, was never aired.

Throughout the rest of January and into March, Bob, still crushed by Patti's accusations, was argumentative with almost everyone. On April Fool's Day he and John Carpenter went to the studio premiere on Wilshire Boulevard of the

X-rated film *Little Girls Blue*. There they saw promoter Don Haley to find out about producing adult films. For some time Crane had wanted to make a high-class, big-budget adult film and had gone as far as drawing up contracts.

On May 1, 1978, Bob traveled to Dallas to begin the month-long run of *Beginner's Luck*. He was met by the owner of the Dallas Windmill Theatre, who loaned the actor his own Mercedes and booked him room 2101 at the Bend Apartment Complex on Aimsbury Road. The Bend's manager, Sharlmayne Clark, noticed Bob happily floating in the pool, his radio blaring jazz and his eyes scanning the bathers for possible female company.

"He was very open," said cast member Joy Claussen, "and he liked to joke and kid about his social life—nude scenes, picking girls up." Crane would often tell his friends with a shrug, "Well, I didn't score last night." He was equally open about his videotapes and the women he had captured on tape. Contrary to the stories about him that swept Hollywood, there were no signs of bondage in the films and no props that carried over from one tape to the other.

Joy was swimming in the pool one day when Bob called out to her from his room, "Come on up. I want to show you a tape of mine."

"I'm not into this," she said. "I've heard about your tapes."

However, she went up and watched anyway. It was a tape of nude dancers in a nightclub. "That's something, Bob," she said. "See you at the theater tonight. Good-bye." That was all she ever saw of his videos or wanted to see.

Victoria said later that it was not unusual for Crane to masturbate while watching the pornographic tapes he and his sex partner had just made.

Jack DeMave, mid-forties, six feet three inches, with short brown hair and a slim build, was new to the cast of *Beginner's Luck*, but it was the second time he had worked with Crane. The first time had been an episode of the ill-fated *Bob Crane Show*. It was during the May 1978 Dallas engagement that DeMave called Crane "old chap" onstage one night. The line was out of character, and the two actors had a blowup in the dressing room in front of Victoria and Peggy Walton, the two women in the cast.

"Your part doesn't call for that!" Bob snapped. "You're changing the character."

"You're always throwing in extra lines," DeMave countered. "*You* can do it, I'm going to do it, too." He took offense at Crane's being the "so-called director." "Who the hell do you think you're directing?" he shouted. "You can't direct worth shit. You can't act worth shit!"

Victoria saw the confrontation as a competition between two giant egos. "It sounded violent," she said later. "Just before I went on. It affected me. To affect me that much, it *was* violent."

Crane went into his dressing room, saying, "Apparently I have a big ego, but yours is bigger than mine."

"And it just went hellfire," said Victoria. "I mean everyone out in the theater could hear it. DeMave and Bob Crane came very close to a fistfight."

The next blowup came when Crane wasn't present, at the cast party. DeMave had suddenly leaped up, thrown a lawn chair into the pool, and yelled, "Fuck Bob Crane. I hate that man!"

"He just bumped the chair," said Victoria. "Threw it in the pool and swore and stormed into the hotel room. He went into his apartment and put his fist through the wall." She went to comfort him, but her boyfriend, Alan, made her leave because he was worried about what might happen next. "We really went out of our way for Jack," said Victoria. "Alan and I sat and listened to him night after night, moaning and groaning. Jack just carried on and on and on and on."

The third day Crane was in Dallas he was invited to a swingers' group called the Seeker's Club. Crane's invitation was like all the others—written on the back of a business card with directions to the house. Bob had been there on a trip to Dallas years before. But he stayed only a few

•

minutes, signed autographs, and left. "Sorry, I can't stay very long," he said, "I've got another party to go to."

At an acquaintance's house the partying began in earnest. Bob saw eleven people in the living room and knew most of them were married couples. A married pair took him into the bedroom. The husband wanted to do a triple, and all three agreed. However, the husband merely perched on the edge of the bed and made encouraging remarks while Crane made love to his wife. Bob became more and more furious until he leaped up, dressed, and stormed out of the party alone.

Phillip and Bonny, two friends of Bob's from New Orleans, came into town on May 8, and Bob put them up at his place. Bonny came on to him with her husband's encouragement. "I don't want to make love to her," said Bob, and palmed them off on a couple from the Seeker's Club.

On May 9 Crane made another video with a man and two women. On it all four are seen kissing, hugging, nibbling, fondling, and calling each other by name: Sid, Joan, Polly, Bob.

Someone photographed one of Bob's group sex romps, showing the star looking bloated and dissipated. One still showed Crane lying nude atop a fully made bed while a brunette woman performed oral sex on him. A bearded man and a blonde in black bra and panties, rings on every finger, joined them. As Crane moved around behind the blonde, the photo showed a fully-dressed partygoer in a plaid shirt watching dispassionately from the sidelines and drinking a beer. No one appeared to be having much fun.

Crane sometimes took still photos of himself and his partner in a mirror. A black-and-white photo showed him standing, wearing a black T-shirt, and performing "doggy-style" behind a busty blonde dressed only in heels. Her elbows are resting on the back of a counter, but there is a big smile on her face. Unlike many of Bob's partners she was obviously aware she was being photographed.

Gloria, the tenant who lived directly above Bob in Dallas, noticed that of all the people who visited the actor, it was a red-haired woman who came the most often. "Crane had many late night parties," Gloria recalled, "but never with more than four to six people. He played the music loud, but not loud enough to complain about. It was hard to tell if a man stayed there with him, because there were so many people coming and leaving at all hours of the night." Bob convinced Gloria to introduce him to Pepper, a nineteen-year-old whom he had seen at the pool. They became friends. "I think of you as a daughter," he said.

When Bob hit on the waitress at an ice-cream shop, she said, "I'm engaged. I have a fiancé."

"I don't care if you don't care," said Bob.

"I do care, and it would be highly unlikely that we would go out," she said, but she was impressed by how gentlemanly Crane was and how he did not seem the least bit unhappy about the rebuff.

At the Key Note, a frequent hangout of Crane's, Karen, a divorced mother of three, had lunch with the actor on May 16. It soon became obvious that he was smitten with her. "You're the one," he told Karen later. "You're the one I'll never leave. You know I'll never leave you."

"I wasn't that serious about him," she said, but allowed Bob to videotape their lovemaking.

The name of the red-haired woman was Paula. She noticed that Crane's phone rang constantly and that many of the calls were from his estranged wife, Patti. She wanted to come to Dallas, but Bob was against this. He told Paula: "My son has been writing 'Fuck Daddy' on the wall at my house in L.A. Patti said I showed dirty movies to him. Once I filmed Patti having sex, but since she filed for divorçe she's been saying that I forced her to do this film. That wasn't true, Patti did it because I asked her to and she knew I would enjoy watching and filming it."

Bob's close friend Edith "Kippy" Lewis knew of a film with Patti and Patti herself had acknowledged a pornographic film with herself in it in her divorce petition.

On May 19 Bob's mood was brighter. He picked up Carpenter at the airport and drove him to the La Quinta Hotel on the North Central Expressway, where he had gotten John a room. On Monday, May 22, the two men flew down to Houston for a little partying and playing around. Bob promised his friend a "large sex orgy" because he knew a lot of people in Houston from previous tours. He liked it better than Dallas as a swinging town.

At their Houston House suite Bob was dismayed to learn that the orgy had been canceled. The friends went to lunch at a small restaurant and came back with a woman of Bob's long-standing acquaintance, a twenty-four-year-old named Penny. Crane took sex photos of John and her on a couch. One snap showed Carpenter sitting behind the woman while she was getting dressed. "We had just gotten through balling her," he said later.

The next day they returned to Dallas, where a club owner friend of Bob's set up an orgy. "It was at this place way out in the boondocks someplace," said John. "It was raining heavily. There were four women at the party along with Bill, the club manager, and one of Bob's old friends.

"It was a swing party," John said later. "People went around balling each other, and that was it." Crane didn't participate. "I've known all these girls before," he explained. "So Bob sat around and rapped I don't know what about. I was busy—you know, a bunch of chicks and everything. I did my own thing and played around."

Ernie Braun had been trying to set up a date with Bob and a friend. "Ernie was into scamming around too in terms of women and nightclubs," Carpenter said. "We met with him at one of the clubs, and Bob tried to stay away from him a little bit because although Ernie knew a lot of chicks, he wasn't too good at picking up a chick for socializing."

"Bob stayed at my house a couple of nights and had many dinners," said Ernie. "All the time he was here he had a lot of calls from Patti long-distance. He told me more than one time that Patti was in great pain, and he was worried about what she might do if he didn't come back to her."

On May 27 Bob noted in his appointment book that Karen was to see his play and bring along her friend Jean. Afterward they went to Bob's place, where he took straight photos of them. After Jean went home, Karen and Crane had sex, which was filmed. She was wearing dark-rimmed glasses and a white top held up with strings over the shoulders. It was obvious on the videotape that Karen didn't know she was on camera.

Beginner's Luck finished its successful Dallas run.

*   *   *

Although Crane was not known to carry a grudge, he vowed he would never hire Jack DeMave again. The two men had not spoken offstage for the rest of the four-week engagement. Victoria considered Jack a Jekyll and Hyde. "He was nearly having a nervous breakdown. Jack was like one man and then another, but we adored him for what he was. And Alan and I really went out of our way to help him. Jack was on his own. We were sort of holding him together. We were very close. I mean, if it wasn't for us, I don't think he would have gotten through."

DeMave never wrote Victoria as he had promised, and when he spoke to her later he was cold. "I wish you luck," he said. "I'm sorry you're not going on a better production than you're in because that's shit." It was a statement fueled by jealousy, she thought. "Oh, he hated Bob."

As for Crane, his love affairs began to become a relentless daily hunt. He dispensed with secrecy and began to shape his career around the sexual possibilities available in certain areas. The press would later refer to his "orgiastic exploits," "dangerous and twisted compulsions," "eager partners of both sexes."

On May 25 Carpenter paid his Dallas hotel bill with his Carte Blanche card and flew back to Los Angeles. Three days later Ernie Braun drove Bob to the airport for his flight back to California. Rehearsals would be held in Beverly Hills for the Scottsdale production of *Beginner's Luck*, set to open at the beginning of June.

On June 29, 1978, Ernie heard over the radio that Bob had been murdered in Scottsdale. Tearfully he called his friends to discuss the tragedy. "Bob told me on the way to the airport that he was scared to go to Phoenix because of an incident that happened years ago," said Ernie. It seemed to have something to do with the suicide of a girl in his bed.

Then, remembering Patti's urgent calls to Bob, Ernie later told the police, "Patti might have had him murdered because if she couldn't have him, then no one else could."

PART THREE

The Third Prison: The Dungeon

The blow had struck her on the very crown of her head.... He struck her once more in the same spot with the blunt end of the ax.... Then he took out the keys...all on one steel ring.... He was even beginning to laugh at himself when another alarming thought suddenly struck him. He suddenly began to imagine the old woman was still alive and might actually come to....

He ran back to the body.... He saw clearly the skull was fractured and even slightly battered in on one side. He suddenly noticed a string on the old woman's neck and pulled at it.... "Good God! I've got to run, run!"

But two men were outside. He was trapped. Finally, spotted with blood, Raskolnikov ran to the canal to throw away the weapon.

Crime and Punishment
FËDOR MIKHAILOVICH DOSTOEVSKI

15
THE CORDOBA

Teaser—The scene that comes at the opening of a tele-play to capture the attention of an audience.

When Officer Darwin Barrie parked in the front lot of the Sunburst Motel at 11:20 A.M. on June 30, 1978, the day after the discovery of Bob Crane's body at the Winfield Apartments, it was already hot.

Dean had called in the seven officers working with him and given each of them an assignment. Barrie's was to find out if Crane's best friend, John Carpenter, had rented a vehicle from the Avis counter at the Sunburst during the time he was in Scottsdale.

The regular agent, Darla Preston, was not at the desk, so Barrie asked her replacement, Joe Pickard, if he could call up the rental on the computer terminal. Pickard was unable to work the machine and told Barrie he would have to wait until Darla returned at noon.

Carpenter's rental, Preston told Barrie when she returned,

had been a brand-new white Chrysler Cordoba. It had been rented on June 27 and returned the morning of June 29 at 8:30. "He said the lights weren't working properly," said Preston, "so I called up the Avis service lot and they sent Joe Pickard over to pick it up. He got here at three-fifteen P.M. to drive it to the lot at Twenty-third and Buckeye. He drove so fast he got a ticket and so rough he broke down at Thirty-second and Thomas."

Pickard left the Cordoba at the shopping center on the northwest corner of the intersection and called B&B Towing. Tow driver Bob Walsh arrived at four and had the Cordoba at the dealership half an hour later.

"Where is the car now?" asked Barrie. Preston located the Cordoba at Lanker Chrysler Plymouth on East Camelback. "I want you to call your office," Barrie ordered, "and make sure nobody touches the car until I get there." Then he called Lieutenant Dean and filled him in.

"Go to the dealership," said Dean, "and check it out." Barrie found the Cordoba, double-checked the license number (VTR 437) and the Avis ID number (8020561), and then walked around it, looking for damage or markings. He found none.

The outside of the car was dirty, as if water had dried on it; the passenger door was locked, the driver's door was unlocked, the keys were in the ignition. Barrie opened the door, saw nothing unusual, took the keys, and went to the trunk. The trunk was clean; it appeared it had not been touched since the car was made. Carpenter had been only the second person to use the car. The odometer read "00330.6."

Barrie removed the wing nut and took out the base to the jack, which was painted black and was covered by a thin layer of dust. The spare tire was pulled from its foundation, and Barrie laid it on its side in the trunk. All of the tire-changing equipment, including the jack assembly and lug wrench, was in place. All appeared new. Barrie returned everything and closed the trunk. Once again he walked around the car and saw nothing out of the ordinary.

The policeman took a closer look at the driver's door and then at the carpet. He inspected the backseat on the driver's side and saw nothing out of place in any of these spots. Suddenly he tensed and leaned across the front seat—there was dried blood on the interior of the passenger door!

He saw blood on the rocker switch for the electric window on the passenger door as well and a three-inch-long line, more a scratch, of what appeared to be blood on the padding of the door two and one-half inches from the door top. Several other small spots of blood were on the door. Barrie got out quickly, locking the door after him to secure the auto.

Barrie walked to the outside of the car on the passenger side and looked in. There he saw a stain of what he also took to be blood on the seat belts of the shoulder assembly strap. He raced to phone Dean. Dean said, "Get a tow truck. Tow it right down to the state laboratory at the Department of Public Safety. Once you put it in their compound, that's a piece of evidence that you've sacked up and carried there. You follow the tow truck—to keep the chain of evidence."

While Barrie was calling the Department of Public Safety, Dean phoned DPS criminal lab officer Bill Morris to join Barrie at the dealership. In the meantime Barrie was trying to discover who else had touched the car. One such person was tune-up mechanic Kevin Beaty, who had driven the car from the service area to the service bay. Beaty had done no work on the auto's interior, only under the hood.

"Did you cut yourself or injure yourself at any time?" asked Barrie. Beaty thought. He had not.

When Morris arrived he looked at the stains and agreed they might be blood. He decided to move the auto to the DPS lab before he did his examination. By phone Dean okayed the request, and the Scottsdale Tow Association transported the Cordoba to the DPS latent print processing area while Barrie followed in his cruiser.

DPS lab technician Bruce Bergstrom examined the stains on the door panel and found them to be type B human blood. "A quite rare blood type group which only ten percent of the population have," he said. According to the autopsy report, Bob Crane's blood type was B, the same as the bloodstain in the car. "Further characterization of the stain," stated the lab, "was inconclusive due to insufficient quantity." The sample, now in a plastic bag, was labeled "Item #116." The car door was removed for further study. It might be retained as evidence.

Much later Borkenhagen spoke about the blood in the car. "The panel was off the car and on a bench in their lab. On that door panel was a long scratch, three inches or so, and underneath, a very thin line of blood. I assumed the murder instrument was thrown out the window and scratched the panel. You could feel the scratch. It left a trail kind of like a pen—a thin line."

Dean added, "Remember, Dennis, how bloody that toggle switch was. A lotta blood. He wanted to get the weapon out that window."

Barrie told Dean the car was so new that only one person before Carpenter had rented it. Dean knew they would have to take blood samples of everyone who had come in contact with the car as driver, passenger, or repairman. Dean sent Barrie back to Avis to find out the name of the other renter of the car and to talk to Pickard.

"I only touched the car in the driver's area," said Pickard. "It was running bad and broke down. I got a ticket because the accelerator was sticking."

"Did you cut yourself or bleed in the car?"

"Definitely not."

Tow driver Bob Walsh told Barrie he too had handled the car only in the driver's area. He had not bled in the auto. He was certain. Under the seat of the Cordoba the lab found a Marlboro cigarette package. Neither Crane nor his friend Carpenter smoked.

Back at Avis, Darla Preston informed Barrie that the first driver of the Cordoba had been Peter Mars, with the L. B. Foster Company in Houston, Texas. Barrie rang him up. Mars explained that he had come up from Dallas to Phoenix with his wife to attend a wedding and do a little business. He had rented the car from June 21 to June 26, when he'd brought it back in. Mars had not used the jack, spare, or lug wrench, he said, and in four days and eleven hours he had driven it 243 miles. Mars said the Marlboro pack was his. "The car was clean when I got it," Mars said, "but it was relatively dirty when I returned it. My wife and I are positive, though, that there was no blood in or on the passenger door of the vehicle."

Barrie made a list of the car's occupants. There had been eight of them while Mars had the car. It was crucial that he check each one to see if he or she had left the type B blood traces. Mars had been the sole driver and could account for every passenger who had been in the car.*

Later, Mars called Barrie back. "I asked my in-laws, and they said they did not bleed in the car. *Nobody* was cut or injured. Besides, I looked the car over prior to returning it, and I noticed no blood."

"Carpenter didn't drive it much 'cause he was with Crane," Borkenhagen told Dean. "On his last night Crane drove Carpenter to the Windmill Theatre."

The discovery of the blood put Carpenter at the top of the list of suspects as far as Dean and Borkenhagen were concerned. "Some of the pieces wind back to Carpenter," said Dean, and he ticked them off.

"Carpenter's date was interviewed, and she could only provide an alibi for him on the night of the murder up to a little after two in the morning, which isn't good enough because it is the next hour that is critical.

"Carpenter appeared nervous and agitated when he checked out of the hotel earlier than necessary. The hotel people were all wondering why he wanted to get out of there. And as we gradually pieced those things together, that's what we call 'taking flight.' Even though he already had his tickets, he left for his plane earlier than he had to. What's he in such a big rush for?"

"And the Cordoba," added Borkenhagen. "He wrote it up for a lot of things that needed servicing. He wanted it to go into that service center because he figured once it was

---

*Peter Mars and his wife; his in-laws, the Sidney Kowowskys; a business associate, Harold Case; and four flower girls who rode in the backseat and never were in front. None had bled and none had type B blood. All four Lanker Chrysler employees who had come in contact with the auto, Jim Guza, Kevin Beaty, Jim Nolen, and Vince Giggliotto, also proved negative.

over there, they'd clean it up and wax it. Actually, none of those things he said were wrong with the car *were* wrong. In my opinion he just wanted to get it away from that hotel where he rented it, that hotel where he was staying."

Although Dean didn't know if Bob had been swimming the day of his death, he was certain that Carpenter had. "Carpenter's swimming trunks were just sitting there in Crane's apartment. They should have gone back to California with Carpenter. They didn't. I had to ask myself, 'Why?' I was already suspicious of him because of his unusual phone calls back to the Scottsdale area, coupled with other items. Once the number gets up to fifteen or twenty odd things, it's no longer a list of odd things—it becomes circumstantial evidence. There's just too much of it.

"He wanted to get that car off the lot at the Sunburst, conceal the fact that it had blood in it. And he was trying to get out of the hotel hours before he had to leave. All of this brings to mind—flight.

"I called him in California and said I wanted to talk to him. He said he wouldn't be available and would be going up to northern California. But he didn't do that. He wasn't on any planned vacation. He was, in fact, in the area. Part of the time he was at Richard Dawson's, and part of the time he was just doing normal routine."

On June 30 Carpenter rang up Bob's close friend Ronni Richards, in New York. She was irate.

"Where were you?" she said. "Why couldn't you help?"

"Oh, well, you know, Bob and I split, and I went back to the motel with a girl and Bob went back with another woman to his place."

Ronni thought about the conversation and told the police in a later interview, "It just didn't dawn on me to call him on it, to say, 'What do you mean, a motel?' I just wasn't thinking. Because when they picked up girls they usually never split. They usually did it in the same bed with the girls or in the same apartment, so it didn't make any sense to me. I'm just telling you what I know. I'm not condemning John or anything. I couldn't even stand the thought of a friend killing Bob. I mean an enemy or a stranger, but not a friend."

After speaking with Ronni, Carpenter went over to Richard Dawson's to spend Friday night. He had arranged to stay over, a not unusual occurrence, when he spoke with Dawson immediately after Bob's body had been found. During that conversation, John concealed his close friendship with Crane by saying that while on business in the Phoenix area he had read that Bob was in a play nearby.

Friday night there was little time spent discussing the murder. "It's done, it's done," John said, "and why be morbid over it or talk about it." Dawson, one of his sons, and Carpenter played video games, Pong, Breakout, and a new Fairchild game, all evening and into the night.

John left Dawson's early the next morning and went to his mother's house to stay. In the afternoon he called Richard and asked, "Has Rita been looking for me?"

"No," said Dawson. John then asked to stay over at Richard's again that night.

On Saturday, July 1, 1978, Dean and Borkenhagen flew to Los Angeles. There they were met by Ken Pollock of the L.A. County Sheriff's Department. Pollock was to be present throughout all the L.A. interviews. Dean and Borkenhagen met with Bob Jr., and he took them out to a baseball game, where, between innings, they discussed the death of his father. Afterward Pollock drove the detectives to Carpenter's residence.

Dean was surprised by Carpenter's home. He seemed well off financially. "I think he still works for one of those video companies," said Dean. "He probably makes a pretty good salary, but he hadn't stayed at a very classy apartment in Scottsdale." While it was still light, Borkenhagen took photos of the house. Golf trophies John had won were in the window.

At 6:50 P.M. Rita, John's live-in girlfriend of five years, opened the door. To the officers she seemed shy and quite a bit younger than Carpenter—no more than half his age.

Rita was twenty, 110 pounds with brown hair and hazel eyes. "We felt that she did have some suspicions of something going on in Crane's relationship with John," said Dean. "She didn't know where John was. She was supposed to be away for the weekend but had returned early and unexpectedly."

"John knew about Bob's death on the afternoon of June 29," Rita said, "but I don't know how he found out. I think he got a phone call about the death. John then called Bob Crane's number in Scottsdale and spoke with Lieutenant Dean at the apartment. He told me, 'I thought somebody would be there.'"

Dean and Borkenhagen watched glumly as Rita called several places where she thought John might be. "Wait," she said, "he might be over at Richard Dawson's. He was an actor with Crane on *Hogan's Heroes*." Before she could call, the phone rang. It was Carpenter.

"John," Rita said, "the police are here." She handed the receiver to Dean. Carpenter agreed to return home within the hour. "I'm out at my mother's house," he said, "about seventy miles away." Dean checked his watch, and he and his partner left. They would return at 8:40 P.M.

As Dean, Borkenhagen, and Pollock made their way back to Carpenter's, they were passed by a speeding black Lotus. Dean noted the license, 259 UKE, and stayed behind the taillights the entire way back to the suspect's home. The car matched the description Rita had given them of Carpenter's vehicle. The Lotus pulled in just ahead of them and John got out.

Immediately after entering Carpenter's home, Dean advised him that they were investigating the death of Bob Crane and because the motive and suspect were still unknown it would be necessary to read Carpenter his Miranda rights. Dennis took out his wallet and removed a well-worn card imprinted with the warning and read it aloud.

Carpenter acknowledged that he understood, waived the right to remain silent, and agreed to answer any questions. "Yeah, sure," he said, "but remind me so I don't forget later, ask me about urine." He then recapped his activities during the time he was in Scottsdale visiting Crane.

"Did you injure yourself at all during your stay in Phoenix?" asked Dean. "Any injury that might cause any bleeding?"

"No," said Carpenter.

"Did Mr. Crane injure or cut himself during the time you were in Phoenix?"

Carpenter thought. "Well, Bob cut himself frequently. Cut himself while shaving."

"Did you loan the Cordoba to anyone?" said Dean.

"No."

"Did you leave the car unsecured or did you give it to a valet while you were in custody of the vehicle?"

"The only persons who entered the vehicle while I had it were myself, Bob Crane, and my date, Miss Newell. I kept it locked at all times."

"Did you ever stay overnight with Crane?"

"I never stay overnight with him," said Carpenter, "because it would cramp his style."

Later Borkenhagen said, "So we ask him a bunch of questions and finally we get around to 'What about urine?' 'Bob says a doctor told him that after you have a piece of ass you should urinate: It cleans you out and you won't get VD. So it was always Bob's habit after he had a jump, he'd go take a leak.'

"What the hell are you talking about?" Borkenhagen said, but the detective was thinking to himself, He knew! He knew there was semen on Crane's leg. Borkenhagen later said, "I think he had a mind-set—he was saying to himself, While those guys are asking me questions, I'm going to be thinking about urine and then they're never going to catch me off guard 'cause I'm going to concentrate on one item and not go goofy."

Dean, Borkenhagen, and Deputy Pollock asked Carpenter to accompany them back to a Los Angeles County police substation where they could make reservations for Carpenter to come back with them to Scottsdale.

Dean said afterward, "I was ready to arrest him then. He holds out his wrists like they had handcuffs on them and began giving Rita his personal items and jewelry. 'I don't need this stuff where I'm going.' And he was *serious*."

"Wear your old watch, John," said Rita. The old watch was a very cheap digital, unlike John's new LAD watch, which she had given him for his birthday.

"No," said Carpenter, "that's not necessary. A watch is a watch."

Dean thought Rita was scared. As John left to get his jacket, he said directly, "You know he did it, don't you?" She shrugged her shoulders.

At the substation, away from Rita, Dean asked John if he had appeared in any of Bob's videotapes. Carpenter said he had, but long ago in Texas or Cincinnati, he had forgotten which.

Finally Dean told Carpenter that they had found blood in his rental car and that it was the same type as Crane's. John appeared puzzled at first, then shaken.

"Why did you kill Bob Crane?" Dean asked.

"I didn't. I didn't. That's impossible. I don't know where that blood came from. I don't even know how much there is. When you say to me, 'Why did I kill Bob Crane?' I can tell you right from the start that I didn't and I would never do such a thing. I have substantial people throughout the whole industry that know that Bob and I were extremely tight friends. I just wouldn't; I'm just not that type of person."

"What were you wearing the night he died?" asked Dean.

"I was wearing a dark blue short-sleeve button shirt and light blue pants."

"Was it a pullover shirt?"

"No, it was button."

"You might want to bring it with you to Phoenix," Borkenhagen said.

Borkenhagen hadn't picked up any body language from the suspect that would have revealed he was lying. "But," he said later, "it was always my opinion and Ron's that he was a deceptive person. He was cool. He was really calm. Could bullshit his way in."

At noon on July 2 they flew to Phoenix. At City Hall Dean asked Carpenter to take a seat. "We had the microphone sitting at the head of a long polished table with twelve chairs," said Dean. "I was sitting at the head and Carpenter was to my left."

Between the two men was the mike and a sheaf of papers. Dean folded his arms and took off his dark glasses. He looked at John. Carpenter gazed back coolly. "He was sitting very straight up," Dean recalled. "Composed. His hands in his lap." Facing the suspect from across the polished table, and to Dean's right, were Borkenhagen and Larry Turoff of the Maricopa County Attorney's Office. It was hot in the large conference room in spite of the air-conditioning.

Dean started the tape machine. "This will be an interview with John Carpenter . . . the date is July 2, 1978. The time is sixteen hundred hours," he said into the mike, and then to John, "We talked to you last night in California, and you voluntarily came back to Scottsdale, Arizona, just to continue the investigation into the death of Bob Crane. We have told you that we are investigating a murder. We do know that you were with him and you did volunteer . . . to clear up some discrepancies with your stay with Crane in the days prior to his death. Last night Officer Borkenhagen read you your rights. You waived your rights to an attorney. I will read from the same rights card that he read to you last night." Dean read them.

Carpenter appeared stoic. "I understand the rights," he said. "The way you read them . . . I was under the impression, correct me if I am wrong, before I make my statement to you, that I was coming out here to help you *out*, not put me *in*. And I am really very apprehensive about this."

"What we need from you," said Dean, "is, will you voluntarily answer my questions? And can you stop voluntarily answering my questions? Of course you can."

"Yes, I understand the rights, one hundred percent."

"Okay, again, at any time, you can stop, walk out of the room—leave," repeated Dean. "You understand you are not under arrest. You are not in custody."

"Go ahead, then. I'm here to help you."

"So that we fully understand for the tape what we talked

about last night, let's just run through it. I think we could start with Wednesday."

John Carpenter recalled for the investigators the events of Crane's last day. He reached the point where Bob left the Windmill after his last performance. "After the theater was out late," he said, "we found the car with a flat tire."

Dean's theory was that someone had tampered with the tire, since there were no punctures at the valve core. Possibly Crane was to have been hit in the back of the head in the darkened parking lot so that it would look like a street crime.

Carpenter finished his version of the events of Crane's last days. "It's basically the way I can remember it now unless there's something that you'd like to ask me about that I might have forgotten."

"During the time he was here," asked Dean, "did Crane have any arguments with anybody?"

"Not a soul," answered Carpenter, "from the day I got here till the day I left everything looked great." There was no mention of the disagreement between Bob and John at Bobby McGee's.

Turoff interrupted. "What was his relationship with this Victoria Berry?"

"They had done two shows together."

"Just friendly?"

"As far as I know," said Carpenter. "Let's put it this way: When I was with Bob, Victoria was kissing him in the dressing room like most theatrical people do. She never went out with us because Bob told her, 'Now, look, when we go into a place, don't hold on to me, because everybody will think that you're with me and it doesn't allow me to pick up some chicks.' Victoria, of course, understood this."

"No romance?"

"No."

"We talked about what you were wearing that night," Dean said.

"You told me to wear this costume. This is what I had on that night."

"Did I tell you to wear it?"

"We probably suggested he could bring it with him," said Borkenhagen.

"Yeah," John said, "so I said fine."

"I recall that," said Dean. "I didn't recall anybody ordering you to wear it." Carpenter was wearing light blue pants, certainly not the type of pants a person would wear on the night of a planned murder; the light color would show any stain.

"I hadn't unpacked it Friday," Carpenter said. "It was still hanging up the way that I took it off, and so this is identical, the same suit that I had on." There was no trace of blood. Dean noticed that the suspect had called the outfit a costume, and it was his theory that John was seeing himself as an actor putting on a performance.

"Where's your old watch?" asked Dean.

"My old watch is the round one, push-button, and that's all it is. I got this one on the twenty-fourth, on my birthday."

"Where is it?"

"Home. It's a very cheap digital. It's not a liquid quartz."

"Like where, specifically?"

"I don't know where she put it. After she gave me this for my birthday she put the other one inside the box and that was it."

"Was she coaxing you to wear the other one last night?"

"Yeah. She wanted me to leave this good one since she just got it for me. I said, 'No, that's not necessary. A watch is a watch.' "

"Did you tell her that the other one was not there?"

"No. No. She knows it's there 'cause she put it away."

Dean's theory was that during the murder the killer might have gotten blood *inside* his watch.

He asked Carpenter about Bob's habit of locking the door, and Carpenter explained about the dead bolt. "Did Bob have another set of keys?" said Carpenter. "I think one of you asked me this. Now, I said I didn't know, but his wife made a surprise visit here without her being invited. If there was another set of keys—this is hypothetical—she would have it to get in and out of his apartment while he was out, or use the pool with the kid, or bring the kid over and wait for Bob. When you were asking me about another set of keys it didn't dawn on me till today that she might have it."

The detectives believed that Carpenter was continually trying to mislead them by pointing toward other potential suspects, such as Patti. Dean observed the suspect as he talked. He had a theory: "When he's looking up to try to remember, he's telling the truth. When he looks down at his shoes, he's lying. When he's being truthful he says 'Ah' before he speaks."

The detective asked him, "Had you ever stayed at Crane's apartment?"

"Never. We've always been separate because he says it 'crams' his act. You never know when he's gonna have a thing going and I might be in the way."

Is he talking about the breakup of friends? thought Dean. Maybe John had begun to "cram" Bob's style.

"How much did he pay the girls?"

"Bob never paid for anything in his life. It's all gratis."

"He didn't pay the girls anything?"

"Not a dime. Bob says he don't need to, and he tells them straight out, 'I get so much for free, why should I pay for it?' "

"What was the relationship between Bob and Richard Dawson—were they friends?"

"They worked together for seven years, you know, on the *Hogan's Heroes* show."

"Has that relationship continued between them? Is there some reason they don't socialize together?"

"Not that I know of. I don't think they follow the same channels of hobbies or whatever you do."

Dean thought, Carpenter's dancing around.

"You can't think why anybody would do this to him?" asked Turoff.

"No."

"Do you think any of those girls ever showed up really late? Somebody knocking on the door?"

"They might. They would. They're that type."

"Do you know who it would be?"

"I don't know who. I'm just saying somebody."

"If a good-looking chick came to the door, Crane'd let them in, wouldn't he?"

"Yeah . . . like I say, when I talk to you, you people here, I really and truly want to help, one hundred percent. My mind is yours if you just let me. You shook me up with [your remark about] the blood on my car."

Dean took a deep breath. "Was Bob Crane into anything that was illegal, hiding anything? I don't even know what the hell it would be, but anything that might be illegal?"

"Not a thing. He never took drugs, never smoked dope."

"Do you know anything about any pictures he has, maybe of some girls? Do the girls want these pictures back? Have you heard of anyone?"

"I never heard of any. No."

Dean asked him when he last saw Bob's book of photos. "I saw it Wednesday afternoon," said John. "Wait. Wait. Was it Wednesday? Tuesday or Wednesday afternoon."

"Did he show the book off frequently?"

"Only to the people who were in it. Bob was discreet. He would have it with him on the road because he keeps increasing it."

Dean concluded the interview. "Before we get out of here," he said, "we were talking about a blood test. You do know we found some blood in your car."

"Right."

"Okay." Dean sighed. "There's a hospital right over there. Would you consent to a nurse drawing some blood?"

"Fine with me. Also, yesterday you said something about a polygraph. . . ."

Carpenter volunteered to take either a polygraph test or sodium pentothal immediately. Although he had never taken a lie detector test before, he had once been given sodium pentothal while he was in a hospital.

"I know what it does," he told Dean. "So if you people feel that you might get more information out of me—go ahead."

The officers declined.

"Even though Carpenter said he'd take a lie detector test," Borkenhagen said later, "I didn't want to put him on the polygraph until we got more information together because I thought he'd beat the damn thing—he's got a mind-set. His head is in a different place than the average person. To use a polygraph you really have to be into the investigation and you have to know a lot. It's not something you'd want to give without—"

"It has to be absolute," Dean interrupted. "We didn't have the blood test yet, and you have to know the answers one hundred percent to be able to check a lie. We didn't have enough to trip him up. At the very beginning he would have known that, too."

Dean had seen a convict lie about his own name and beat the machine. "Okay," he said to John. "That'll be all."

"What happens to me?" said Carpenter. They told him that he was going to be taken to the hospital to have blood drawn.

Long shadows were cast across the alabaster walkway. As they walked, Dennis Borkenhagen made random attempts to rattle the suspect.

"I'm not going to shit you," Borkenhagen said. "We've found blood on your rental car, Crane's blood type. Now Department of Public Safety is going to take it further and try the Kansas test enzyme breakdown. If Crane had measles as a child, it's going to show up as antimeasles serum; chicken pox, the same. If we can pinpoint that it's his blood, we'll come back and see ya."

While Carpenter was being tested and photographed, Dean drew Larry Turoff aside.

"I'd like to arrest him now."

"No. Wait for the blood."

"If his blood type comes back other than type B, will you arrest him?"

"Yes."

If Carpenter was the same blood type as Bob, a case could be made that he was the one who had bled in the Cordoba. If Carpenter was any other blood type than B (which only ten percent of the population has), then by process of elimination the blood in the car could have come from Crane. Forensic technology of the 1970s was not capable of proving incontrovertibly that the blood was Bob's and Bob's alone.

Even with the urgency the detectives put on Carpenter's blood test, the results would not be known for one to two days. Once Carpenter left the state he was beyond their reach without an indictment from the county attorney's office.

Dean watched in frustration as John's plane vanished into the evening skies. He had found no way to keep Carpenter in Arizona longer. He turned his back in anger.

"I wished I'd arrested him while he was here," he muttered.

It was a few days after the discovery of Crane's body that Dean saw Carpenter's room at the Sunburst for the first time. From the entryway he could see Crane's driveway at the Winfield half a block away. It would have been easy to keep watch from here, although the view of Crane's actual room was blocked by the tennis court and the tall trees.

Dean wondered if John's last call to Bob had really taken place. Carpenter was not a visual person, and the scene he'd painted for the detectives of Bob in his underwear editing a film sounded as if he'd actually been in the room instead of speaking on the phone.

"When you talk to somebody on the phone," said Borkenhagen, "and you are asked, 'Hey, what are you doing?' you don't reply, 'Oh, I'm here in my blue jacket and striped shirt and I'm at the table drinking a cup of coffee.' "

"And another thing," said Dean, agreeing. "He calls up Crane at three in the morning and says, 'You can go ahead and sleep late tomorrow, I'll get a ride to the airport.' But Crane would have had plenty of sleep by the time Carpenter was ready to leave—four to five hours. Junior told us the old man didn't need very much sleep.

"It's really ridiculous—to me, anyway—that he'd call Bob's apartment when he's with a woman or gonna go to sleep. And his calls to the Windmill Theatre made even less sense. Crane came in only minutes before showtime."

"Did you notice how he made a point of saying 'You probably have that photo album'?" said Borkenhagen. He laughed and imitated the suspect: " 'Am I gettin' through to you?' You're supposed to say, 'Oh! There's a missing album from the flight bag!' and 'Do you know anything about any pictures he has, maybe of some girls, and these girls want these pictures back?'

"Half of it may have been true. Crane may have had a short conversation on the phone and said, 'Come on over, I'll leave the door open for you.' Maybe that's the part of the conversation left out by Carpenter. He didn't want to say he was in the apartment. He all but put himself there in that apartment."

Officer Chris Bingham asked Robert Conway, the Sunburst's night desk clerk, if he still had the wake-up call sheets from June 29. "No," he said, "they are destroyed at the end of the last wake-up call of the day. I have no way of knowing if room 206 left a wake-up call for June 29. I cannot remember placing a wake-up call to that room."

Officers Bingham and Barry Vassall were assigned to knock on doors up and down the hotel, looking for anyone who might know something. It was they who found the maid who remembered John. She was a Native American named Geneva Davis, who worked for the Sunburst and various other Scottsdale hotels.

"He was short," she said, "and he was always dressed nice." She recalled making up the bed every day Carpenter had been staying there, lending credence to John's insistence that he had slept at the Sunburst and not at Bob's.

Until asked, Davis hadn't considered what she'd found in John's room of any importance. "Oh, yeah," she said. "I remember several days ago seeing a bloody pillowcase and bloody linen hand towels in the bathroom. . . ." Bloody towels or face cloths were not unusual in the hotels she worked, but there was enough blood on these so that she remembered. "Definitely more than if a guy had cut himself shaving," Dean said later. "She used check-off sheets on a clipboard, so she was very specific about the room they were in—a very credible witness."

"What did you do with the towels and pillowcase?" Vassall asked Davis.

"What I always do. Just threw them in the wash."

"By the time we got there," Dean said later, "they had been washed. She told us about them when they became significant to her. Prior to that, she didn't think nothin' of it."

Room 206 had already been made up again, and the present occupants were Lester Fraser and his wife from Woodron, Massachusetts, who had checked in about eight hours after Carpenter had checked out. Vassall and Bingham scrutinized the room's pillows for any blood residue, combed the room for any hidden weapon, and clambered up into the air-conditioning vents, looking there, too. But the search came up negative.

16
BOB JR.

Discovery—The revelation of something previously un-known, usually by the main character in the climax of a teleplay.

Over the weekend Crane's body had been returned to California. His funeral service was held on Wednesday, July 5, 1978, at St. Paul the Apostle Church in Westwood, an L.A. suburb where Bob had once lived. Four hundred mourners clustered together for the forty-minute service. Crane's first wife, Anne Terzian Chase, was there, accompanied by their children, Robert David, Deborah Ann, and Karen Leslie. The late actor's mother, Rose, Bob's brother, Al, Crane's present wife, Patti, and their son, Robert Scott, were there.

The service was conducted by Crane's longtime friend, the Reverend Bernard Lohman of Clemson, South Carolina, and actors Carroll O'Connor, John Astin, and Patty Duke Astin spoke, along with *Hogan's Heroes* regulars Larry Hovis, Robert Clary, and Leon Askin and the show's pro-

ducer, Eddie Feldman. Hovis and Clary were two of the
pallbearers, along with Bob Jr.

Victoria Berry sat, hands folded on her lap, in front of
John Carpenter.

Dean did not attend the funeral but was intrigued by
some of the reports he heard later from people who were
there. "There were some oddities in casual conversation
with Carpenter that came up," he said. "Some of the people
he spoke with mentioned mix-ups in times and things like
that. John kept telling his story over and over."

Carpenter told Victoria Berry that the police considered
him a suspect. "He was astonished," she said later. "He was
amazed. He couldn't believe they were accusing him."

After the service, Bob Jr. went over to Carpenter, who
was standing with Victoria at his side, and the two men
embraced.

"Why did this happen?" asked John.

Bob Jr. noticed that Carpenter was "trembling a slight
bit" but otherwise displayed no overt signs of emotion.

"Hey," said Bob Jr., trying to be light, "let's keep in
touch. You're going to have to help me set up the videotape
equipment wherever I live next."

Carpenter smiled back at Bob. "Yeah."

On Thursday, July 6, Borkenhagen phoned Bob Jr. in Los
Angeles and asked if he had noted anything of significance
at the funeral. "No," he replied. "Nothing seemed to be out
of place. John Carpenter attended the wake prior to the
funeral. Richard Dawson didn't come to the funeral."

Borkenhagen asked if Bob had experienced any trouble
with his business managers or agents. Crane's son said that
even though his dad had fired his two previous managers,
there'd been no argument or hard feelings.

"My dad felt they weren't doing enough for him," Bob
Jr. explained. Borkenhagen asked if Bob Jr. had ever seen
any of his father's videotapes involving sexual exploits. He
said he had.

"Did Mr. Carpenter appear in any of these tapes?"

"I've seen videotapes of John Carpenter, my father, and two women," said Bob Jr.

"Would you have any reason to believe that Mr. Carpenter had any homosexual or bisexual tendencies?" Bob Jr. answered that he had heard that Carpenter had participated in homosexual activities with another entertainer.

"When I asked him specifically, 'Hey, John, tell me about your phone conversation with my father on the last night,' he told me he had asked if my dad had scored that night and to tell what he had done with a lady friend of his," Bob Jr. told the detective.

Borkenhagen dialed Patti Crane in Los Angeles. She too knew of no animosity between Crane and his former managers. Patti said that Bob had called her in Seattle on June 28. The twenty-minute call lasted from 11:06 until 11:26 P.M. Patti knew that Bob was calling her from his apartment. She remembered the time because of a TV show that she was watching. "About twenty minutes after he called me," she said, "I tried to call him back, but I couldn't reach him."

"Did your husband say anything about editing a videotape for Scotty?" asked Borkenhagen.

"He told me that he had completed the editing of a tape from the movie *Saturday Night Fever,* and that the tape was ready to be given to our son." But Carpenter had told Dean that Bob had told him somewhere around 2:45 A.M. that he was still editing the film.

Borkenhagen got Carpenter's test results. He read:

> ITEMS: #M-2-blood sample (suspect)
> EXAMINATION REQUESTED: blood identification
> RESULTS: Analysis showed the blood to be type A.

In a call to Bob Jr., Carpenter said, "They say that there was blood on my car. A very uncommon type. This is bullshit. Boy, they're scratching my back hard, and I'm the one that's trying to help. If your dad had any best friend or whatever you want to call it . . ."

"It was you," Bob Jr. interjected. "I guess they're waiting for you to just break down or something."

On July 12, 1978, Dean and Borkenhagen returned to Los Angeles and were met by Deputy Pollock and driven to Carpenter's apartment. Once again Rita opened the door, and once again they read the suspect his rights.

"Are you always as nervous-acting as you are now?" Borkenhagen asked.

"No," said Carpenter.

"What was Crane doing on Wednesday, June 28, 1978, in the afternoon hours?" Dean said.

"He was editing *Saturday Night Fever* for his son," answered Carpenter. Earlier he had said Bob was taking a nap at the Winfield apartment, Dean thought. But Bob had really been at Terry's.

Carpenter told Dean that Patti and the kids were Crane's beneficiaries. John also recalled helping the gas station attendant change the flat at the Arco station near the Windmill Theatre.

"What did you think of Crane?" asked Dean.

"I thought he was a nice man, and I never had a disagreement with him."

Dean asked Carpenter if they could meet with him again either Thursday or Friday, July 13 or 14. "I can meet with you anytime," he said, "after five P.M."

Outside, Borkenhagen paused to take in the California afternoon. "You know," he said to Dean, "the last time we talked to Carpenter I hinted to him that we had high-tech blood tests that could conclusively match the blood in the Cordoba to Crane's. He understood it. He was acknowledging it. This time when we talked to him he never asked, 'How did that blood test come out?' That'd be number one with me: 'Hey! How'd you guys do?' He never mentioned it."

"Carpenter seems to be one of those types that wants to get you to suspect him. He dares you. He gave the two of us a lot of things. I've read over the transcripts of what he said. He *wanted* us to suspect him. He isn't going to confess, but he's going to make you know he did it and that you gotta catch him."

*   *   *

Deputy County Attorney Larry Turoff and investigator Ron Little were in California to do a series of interviews, gather additional information, and replow some of the same ground that Dean and Borkenhagen had worked over.

The county attorney's office was duplicating efforts out of routine and standard practice, their dissatisfaction with Scottsdale PD's results so far, their own theories about who might have committed the crime, and their still ruffled political feathers over not being invited to the crime scene when Bob's body had been discovered. Additionally, the solution to such a high-profile case would add luster to any department that produced it.

At a little past noon on Thursday, July 13, they met with Bob Jr. on the eighth floor of a Wilshire Boulevard office building in Beverly Hills. Bob's oldest son was working as a freelance writer for *Playboy, Penthouse, Oui,* and other magazines. Also present were William Goldstein, Bob Jr.'s attorney; Lloyd Vaughn, Crane's business manager and attorney; and Chuck Sloan, Bob Jr.'s stepfather.

"Let me start," said Ron Little. "I have some questions that Officer Borkenhagen wanted me to ask you. First, do you know of any incident involving your father and a married woman which occurred in Phoenix approximately five years ago?"

"No," said Bob Jr., "I don't."

"Do you know if Mr. John Carpenter, at any time, wore a mustache?" (There were several witnesses who had inexplicably described John as being an "Indian with a mustache.")

"To my knowledge," said Bob Jr., "he did not."

"Even including a fake or play mustache?"

"No."

"You and your father lived together, correct?"

"Yes."

"And where was that at?"

"Six thirty-four Midvale Avenue. That's in West Los Angeles."

"How long do you know, or if you know, had Dawson known Carpenter?"

"It didn't seem that long to me, but I have no factual knowledge. It seems like Carpenter and Dawson maybe had known each other a couple of years previous to my dad meeting Carpenter."

"Was your father a sound sleeper?"

"I woke him on occasion in our apartment."

"Just by simply walking in?"

"By simply being a presence in the room."

"Let's say he'd gone to bed about two A.M., gone to sleep, and somebody walked into the room at three or four when he'd been only sleeping for an hour or so," said Turoff. "Had you ever been in a situation like that, where he's asleep for maybe two hours, and attempted to wake him up or walk into his room?"

"Yes," said Bob Jr., "and for shorter periods of time. Thirty minutes of sleep and he would be almost rejuvenated."

Little said, "What Larry specifically is getting at is the situation wherein your father wanted to sleep for a long period of time and you had to wake him up because something important came up while he was sleeping. Was he still as easy to wake up then as you had previously stated?"

"Yes," Bob Jr. said without hesitation.

"He was a light sleeper?" asked Turoff.

"Yes."

"Do you have a dead bolt on your apartment here?"

"Yes."

"Did he always lock the dead bolt?"

"Yes."

"Did he indicate to you that he had an argument with anybody in Phoenix? Had any problems in Phoenix?"

"No indication of any problems."

"Did he indicate to you who was with him?"

"Yes. John Carpenter."

"Did your father ever talk with you about his relationship with Victoria Berry?"

"Yes. If you mean in terms of sex, I could only speculate on that. He had no love interest or anything like that in her."

"Did he ever mention any boyfriend or individual or husband or anything like that Victoria Berry had?"

"No."

"Did you have any knowledge through either John Carpenter or your father that Richard Dawson was involved in making any type of home video programs?"

"Yes," said Bob Jr., "I got that knowledge through my father, who got it through Carpenter, who got it through Dawson."

"Okay," said Little, "and what type of videotapes was Dawson making? Were they TV programs? Were they movies?"

"They were straight copies of programs off the television and also tapes involving women."

"Do you know who might have been involved in those videotapes?"

"Women? No."

"Do you know which men might have been involved in those videotapes?"

"I'm sure Dawson was. Possibly Carpenter."

"Okay. Would your father have ever appeared on any of those videotapes?"

"To my knowledge, no."

"Did your father, in his sleeping habits, wear pajamas?"

"No. He wore underwear . . . undershorts. That's it."

"Okay. Did he always wear undershorts while he was sleeping?"

"Every time I've seen him go to bed, he had undershorts on."

"Okay. When he was with a woman, after engaging in sexual intercourse, would he sleep nude?"

"I would assume in that situation he would sleep nude."

"In the middle of the night, how many people would your father open the door for? In other words, if it was a male, your father would have to be extremely well acquainted with and feel comfortable with him?"

"Yes."

"Let's take a hypothetical situation. I'm talking about predawn, after midnight. A female knocks at his door, whether here, California, Dallas, or whatever, and states that she is a friend or a friend of a friend or has seen him previously at a bar someplace. Would he open the door for her? Would he allow her to come into the apartment?"

"It's very possible that he would open the door for her."

"What makes you think that?"

"Basically he enjoyed women."

"What percentage of the time would Carpenter actually live in the same apartment that your father did?"

"I felt a hundred—I assumed a hundred percent of the time."

"Okay. What percentage of the time were you actually told that Carpenter was with him?"

"I was told that a couple of times. Every time my dad called me back in L.A. or I called him at whatever city he was in, it always seemed to me that Carpenter was in the background. I could either hear him, or I could hear video-tapes going. My dad would say, 'Yeah, John's here,' or that kind of thing. So I always assumed they were together for the four or five days that Carpenter would pop into a town."

William Goldstein interrupted. "I'd like to point out that I asked that question of Patti and she said to the best of her knowledge Carpenter *did* stay with Bob."

"During the Scottsdale performance," asked Turoff, "did your father indicate that John was going to be staying with him or that John was with him at the apartment?"

"Yes," said Bob Jr. "My father indicated that John would be coming into town, and then when John did come into town, on my birthday, when I last talked to my father, there were videotapes going or a television going in the background, and Carpenter was there."

"Let me ask you this," said Turoff. "Do you know any reason why Carpenter rented the hotel room at the Sunburst?"

"I didn't even know that he had rented a room. Once again, I assumed he was with Dad."

"Your father never indicated to you that they had an argument of any type, so that he told him to get out or

'You can't stay with me' or anything like that?"

"No, not in that particular time, but there was an indication before Phoenix just in a passing conversation with my father that Carpenter was getting to be a bit of a pain in the ass. No big physical-type things or verbal things between them, but my dad expressed that he just didn't like Carpenter kind of hanging around him."

"Cramp his style?" said Turoff.

"Yeah. It was fun for maybe the first half dozen or dozen times or how many times Carpenter visited him, but now it was like, yeah, cramping your style kind of thing. You don't need Carpenter hanging around."

"Point-blank," said Little, "do you know of anyone (and can you articulate the reasons why you think so) who would have a motive for killing your father?"

"I have two people in mind."

"Sure, go ahead."

"Kick out my amateur theory? To me Carpenter is a possibility in terms of a kind of second banana–type relationship. Maybe it caught up to him. To me there could be a jealous-type motive behind it. Once again he's hanging around with my dad. They go out to a club: 'Hey, it's Bob Crane.' Girls come over to my dad, and Carpenter's the second banana, getting the sloppy seconds if you want to be blunt. That kind of relationship might have caught up with him. He might have been jealous of that. They might have had words. My dad may have expressed, 'Hey, John, it's no longer kicks, it's no longer fun.' What I told you guys, maybe he did tell Carpenter, and Carpenter took offense.

"To my knowledge Carpenter has engaged in some bisexual activities in the past. For all I know he could have been in love with my father. But my dad never expressed any homosexual activity between them or between my father and any male ever in his lifetime. He was the all-American male to me and to everybody in my family. There was never any doubt of that. But in Carpenter's past there was at least one incident I knew of that was homosexual."

"Let me ask you this," said Little. "I want to stay on Carpenter for a minute since you brought all this up. You say you knew of one incident of Carpenter engaging in either homosexual or bisexual activity. When did this occur?"

"The incident that was told to me by my father occurred early on in the relationship of my dad and Carpenter. So we're talking about ten years ago, approximately."

"Who was involved in that?"

"[A well-known entertainer] and John Carpenter."

"And what was the sexual activity involved?"

"Sexual activity as described to me by my dad in passing was that Carpenter in effect went down on [this guy]."

"Fellatio."

"Yes."

"Was there any sodomy involved in the activity?" asked Little.

"No. That was the only action described to me."

"Okay. Is there anything more recent that indicates bisexual or homosexual activity on the part of Carpenter?"

"No," said Bob. "This is just all speculation. I didn't see anything in terms of tapes or any of that kind of thing, but I know he had a great respect for my dad, and that's why my mind wanders to a kind of a homosexual love or envy or whatever. I think he really dug the guy. I mean, there's one kind of male-to-male love and then there's another kind of male-to-male love. I'm not sure."

"I understand. Did Carpenter have any girlfriends, steady girlfriends, that you know of?"

"Yes. He's living with a lady right now. I think her first name is Rita. I don't know her last name."

"How old is Rita?"

"I assume young. From everything I've heard and gathered, Carpenter has a liking for pretty, young-type females, meaning under twenty-five, and he is a man of around forty-eight, maybe forty-seven. We used to kid around and call him 'Kinky John.' I've heard of some incidences in terms of sixteen-, fifteen-year-old girls."

Dean had considered arresting Carpenter during the time he was in Scottsdale for corrupting the morals of a minor because of a complaint filed by a young girl.

"How was Carpenter's luck with the ladies without your father being present?" asked Little.

"Well, it's tough for me to know because I relate everything through my father in terms of Carpenter. I wouldn't know Carpenter if my dad weren't my dad."

"Let me ask you this. Did your dad ever tell you anything that Carpenter had related to him about picking up a chick without your father being there?"

"John on his own, I know, got into some kind of swing-type or group-type sex things and related that to my dad, and I think he and my dad in Houston or Dallas got involved in that kind of thing a couple of times. So yeah, I know John got out on his own. For the most part, there was always kidding around between them. For instance, the last phone call. Carpenter didn't make out with this Newell girl, and he wanted to know how my dad did. So there was always a kind of kidding 'Yeah. Hey, we struck out again.' "

"Presumably Carpenter knew that your father had left the Safari Hotel with a female, because he was present, was he not?" said Little.

"Yeah, the way Carpenter told me, Carpenter was with Newell, my dad was with the fifty-year-old lady, which is old. They always seemed to go out with younger girls. Carpenter left with Newell, leaving my dad in the parking lot. So it eventually turns out when Carpenter called my dad at two forty-five, 'What happened, Bob?' My dad says, 'The chick didn't want to come back here with me, and didn't want me to come back with her to her place.' Nothing happened, in other words."

Little asked Bob Jr. whether, if his father was occupied with a woman, it would be out of character for Carpenter to call him, compare notes, and even ask to join in. He would have called out of curiosity, said Bob Jr., and it would not have been unusual for him to have called.

"It was the following morning, though, that he called you," Vaughn said.

"Carpenter called, I would say, around three P.M.," said Bob Jr. "I remember because I tried calling my father approximately a half hour later, to thank him for a birthday card that he had mailed and I had just received. Answering the phone at his apartment was Victoria Berry."

"He called you at about three?" Little said.

"Carpenter? Yes."

"Could it have been possibly after three-thirty?"

"No."

"What would your father's feelings be toward homosexual activities?" asked Little. "Let's assume that John attempted to pull something either with your father or somebody else, would he condone that? Was he tolerant of that? Or would he tell him to 'bug off, you little creep'? Have an argument which could have tarnished their friendship?"

"If they had not engaged in any homosexual activity up until the time of Phoenix, I don't see it beginning then."

"Well," said Turoff, "maybe your father found out that Carpenter is going back to his old ways or he never left his old ways. Would he have tolerated the fact that this guy, who's a hang-around anyway, is a homosexual?"

"My image is as long as Carpenter didn't try to pull anything on my dad, he'd tolerate it."

"Now," said Turoff, "you said you have two people in mind who might have a motive for killing your father. Who's the second person?"

"My stepmother."

"Why?" Ron Little said.

"Well, where would I begin on that. . . . I just recently found out about the will. It's totally one-sided in favor of Patti, Melissa, her daughter, and Scotty, my half brother."

In the twenty-two-page will, dated January 30, 1975, Patti was named executor and beneficiary of the bulk of the actor's half-million-dollar estate. His children received only five thousand dollars apiece and various meager possessions.

"When was this will made?"

"The main portion of the will, January 1975. But the codicil completely cuts my two sisters and myself out of it."

"Who drew the will?" asked Turoff.

"Lloyd Vaughn. What I'm getting at is Patti saw the end

in sight. My dad was not going back to her. He had, in fact, bought a house of his own. There was no sign of them reconciling. Patti had dropped in on my dad in Phoenix. She was with Scotty. My dad was kind of uptight about that because there was no notice and the fact that my dad was going out with other ladies in Phoenix."

"Which he told me Patti was furious about," said Bill Goldstein.

"Yeah," said Bob Jr. "Patti was furious. Patti had a glass of wine and it made her reveal her true feelings."

"The home on Tilman," said Turoff. "Was that purchased after their marriage?"

"No," said Bob Jr. "Just before."

"I'm getting at the community property. California's a community property state, isn't it? As far as you know, it was purchased just before the marriage by your father?"

"Yeah. Lloyd Vaughn can tell you better for dates and technical things."

"If I can interject something," said Goldstein, "Patti claims to have a document that says Bob granted to her all interest in the property and said he would never challenge that it was hers."

"Did you ever see it?" asked Turoff.

"I didn't, but I know about it. The way it came about was that they were having some marital problems and went away to Newport to try to resolve them. It was a couple of years ago."

"Uh-huh," said Turoff. "What I was going to get at, she got a piece of the action whether he's alive or dead, but of course she gets all of it under—"

"Well," said Goldstein, "in the domestic action she claims that the house was totally her property."

"I know what she was claiming," said Turoff. "We'll get to that."

Bob Jr. began to expound on his theory that Patti jetted to Phoenix to confront Bob, was rebuffed, and returned later to kill him.

"All right," said Turoff. "Do you know where she was between two A.M. and two P.M. on the twenty-ninth?"

"According to Carpenter, my dad called Patti in Seattle.

She had gone up there the Thursday before. It's conceivable to me that she would hop on a jet, fly to Phoenix. Maybe she leaves at twelve-thirty, one, gets into Phoenix two and a half hours later . . . and she lets him have it.

"It's all over. She knows what's in the will. There's really nothing to be lost at this point, and a lot to be gained financially and otherwise. And she'd get rid of my side of the family. I know it sounds like a Poe novel. Anyway, thanks for putting up with my theory."

"That's as good a theory as anybody's got in this damn thing," said Turoff.

"Yeah," Goldstein said. "You can say anything about the lady, most of which is probably negative, but the one thing she wasn't is stupid."

"I gather that," said Turoff. "All right, let's assume she got to his rooms and they went to sleep together. If she had gotten out of bed, he would have awakened."

"I assume so, yeah," said Bob Jr.

"So she wouldn't have gone out to her car, picked up a tire iron, and walked back into the apartment because he would be awake by that time."

"Right."

"Unless," said Goldstein, "she told him she was leaving, so he was expecting a sound—he was lying there and not sleeping."

"But she had to come back into the apartment," Turoff argued.

"He could have just been lying in the position."

"Yeah, I know. I'm not saying he's asleep," said Turoff. "His eyes are closed, but that doesn't indicate he's asleep before he gets rapped."

"As I said earlier," said Bob Jr., "from everything I've heard there was no forced entry. If somebody had a key, even, he would hear. I know for a fact according to Carpenter that he positively dead-bolted. So I assume the person at the door—"

"Just walked in," said Turoff.

"It was somebody he was comfortable with."

"Yeah," said Turoff. "Let me ask you: In your relationship with your father is there indication that he had any gambling debts?"

"No. He didn't gamble at all."

"Did your father have, to your knowledge, anything going for him in Las Vegas or any type of business that he was trying to set up or some deal he was trying to get going?"

"Nothing."

"Did he have any contacts with any people in Vegas who were heavies?"

"The only contacts I ever knew of were during the time of *Hogan's Heroes*. Somebody from a hotel approached him to appear in Las Vegas, which he declined because he's not a nightclub comedian."

"Okay," said Little. "I want to specifically direct this to Lloyd, because I think he might be able to better answer it. I heard that Bob owed some money to some Chicago heavyweights."

"To the best of my recollection," Vaughn answered, "absolutely not. I never got a call from a creditor."

"We're not talking about normal creditors," said Turoff.

"How much are we talking about?" Goldstein said.

"Enough to knock a guy off for," said Turoff.

"Impossible," Vaughn said. "I would have known about it. Bob's earnings were deposited into a business account. I used to give him a two-hundred-dollar allowance check at the beginning of the month, and that's all he ever used. If he had debts, he'd have asked for more."

Goldstein had another theory. "I think it's as simple as he slept with the wrong lady. Or had a film on the wrong lady."

"We're exploring that."

"On the other hand," said Goldstein, "that's a bullet in the head or a violent struggle or a man busting through the door, not someone he's going to let in the apartment and then lie down."

"What we've got is a bunch of circles," said Little. "We start at one point and work our way in. If it doesn't work out, we go for another route and try again."

17

DEAN

Emotional line—Main emotional line of development in a script, usually involving the protagonist and one or more other characters.

Larry Turoff and Ron Little left Bob Jr.'s office and by 6:00 P.M. were at Victoria Berry's Sunset Boulevard home. Alan Wells, her boyfriend, sat on a couch next to her, offering moral support. Little began the questioning: "You were interviewed previously by the Scottsdale Police Department, correct?"

"Yes, I was," said Victoria.

"And did you make a handwritten statement to the Scottsdale police?"

"Yes, but the handwritten one was not together at all. I wrote it directly after I'd found Bob."

Little handed it to her. "Maybe if you read it again, you might be able to explain some of the things that you meant."

"It's disjointed," said Turoff, "but we understand why."

"I got all his family mixed up. I know his oldest son, I don't even think I mentioned him," said Victoria.

"No, you didn't," Turoff said.

"But I know him. I couldn't think of the name Carpenter. I was just blank. Bob was having a lot of difficulty with his wife, which I'm sure you all know." She paused. "I'm thinking about what John told me at the funeral. He said that Patti had called and they had a really violent argument that night."

"Do you know of anyone who would have a motive for killing Bob other than his wife?"

"No."

"In a case like this," said Little, "we get cuckoos coming out of the woodwork and we get rumors and we've got to eliminate these things. We have a lady by the name of Rozella who claims that she was imported from Sacramento to Phoenix by a black male by the name of Ron-Ron, apparently hooked up with some underworld-type, syndicate-type figures, to do a setup on Bob Crane. You know anything about that?"

"Not a thing."

"We would appreciate your not repeating this conversation," said Turoff. Quotes attributed to Victoria had shown up in the tabloids.

"Are you kidding?" said Victoria. "I'm not saying anything to anybody."

While Wells was out of the room, Little said, "I want you to come down to my car in a minute and see if you can answer some personal questions out of earshot of Alan. I'm going to say it's for the purpose of examining and identifying some of Bob's photos."

"Sure," said Victoria.

Downstairs, Little questioned Victoria about any sexual relationship she may have had with the victim. She declined to answer, but because of Bob's openness she was knowledgeable about his sexual habits.

After sex, one woman told her, Bob would always get up and clean his person. He was in the bathroom on one occasion for so long that she felt extremely peculiar. After sexual relations he was an extremely clean individual.

Crane believed that if he went into the bathroom, urinated, cleaned off his penis thoroughly, and washed his hands, he would never get VD.

Victoria further told Little that it was not unusual for Crane to masturbate and watch the pornographic videotapes he had made. "Bob told me about this on several occasions, but he had never done this in my presence." She knew of absolutely no homosexual or bisexual behavior on Bob's part.

"However, many of Bob's girls were bisexual," she recalled, "and he'd joke about that to me." Several other friends of Crane's had stated that Bob "often liked to go to gay bars and try to pick up women."

Victoria did look at some photos of Crane's but was able to identify only Patti Crane and Ronni Richards, whom, she told Little, she did not like.

Just two weeks after Bob Crane's murder, Ron Dean told the press, "We feel we are making headway, but there are still many people to interview both in and out of state. Police agencies in California and other states have been extremely cooperative, assisting us with interviews in their area.

"Each witness questioned seems to lead to another. We cannot know all that is needed until the loose ends are tied up. Right now we're stepping it up and pursuing as many leads as possible. Unless we get some kind of break—such as the killer walking in and confessing—we expect to take whatever time it requires to make our investigation as complete as possible."

Using a number found in Crane's phone directory, Chris Bingham finally contacted Jack DeMave, Bob's costar in the Dallas production of *Beginner's Luck*.

"I didn't see Crane after the play closed in Dallas. My relationship with him was strictly business. We had no social contact," DeMave said.

Bingham asked him about the blowup with Bob. "It was a verbal argument. Crane wanted to change some of the dialogue. He wanted to interject certain lines that were not in the original play. I objected." He told Bingham that the other actors in the play had backed Bob up.

DeMave had been in New York doing a commercial and visiting from June 17 until July 25 and then had gone on vacation in Georgia with his wife. When asked about other people who might have had an argument with Crane or who might have had reason to harm him, DeMave could think of no one.

Dean and Borkenhagen went back to Los Angeles. As usual, Kenny Pollock drove them to the locations of their interviews.

"The more I thought about it," Dean explained, "the more it seemed that Mrs. Crane's alibi was just a little too pat, a little too perfect. She and Bob were having some big trouble. The day of Bob's death she just happened to be on an island off Washington.* To me that was suspicious.

"She called Bob many times at his friend Ernie's house in Dallas. Bob told Ernie how concerned he was over Patti's emotional state and the ill effect the split was having on her and Scotty. Bob didn't know what she would do if he didn't come back to her. Among his many theories, Ernie thought Patti might have had Crane killed. There was always the possibility that she could have hired someone to kill him even if she didn't do it herself.

"Richard Dawson's got his reason why he'd want Crane done—professional jealousy, I've heard. Patti does because of arguments and estate settlements. And that argument the night of Bob's death. Why did that particular phone argument take place right at the time Carpenter was there? Some people think Mrs. Crane has more to do with it than is apparent. This can't be shown unless there was some kind of conspiracy. But I think Carpenter's the guy who did it.

---

*On July 26, 1978, Borkenhagen contacted Western Airlines. They informed him no airlines had flights out of Seattle with connections to Phoenix after 7:30 P.M. or before 7:15 A.M.

If the Mrs. sent him to do it, I don't know. But nobody has any evidence to that effect."

Dean, Borkenhagen, and Pollock spoke with Patti Crane at the office of her attorney, Lee Blackman, in Beverly Hills on July 13, 1978, at the same time Turoff and Little were speaking with Bob Jr. Borkenhagen began the questioning. He asked if Bob had been meticulous in keeping his apartment clean, and Patti stated emphatically that he "definitely was not, and his property was usually scattered about, so much so that he always had difficulty in locating specific items."

"Did Mr. Crane usually sleep wearing undershorts?"

Patti explained that Bob usually slept naked, adding that he also walked around the house naked unless the children were present or they had company.

"Did he sleep wearing his wristwatch?"

Patti said that he never did. Yet Bob was wearing both his shorts and his wristwatch when he was found dead.

"Where were you prior to Mr. Crane's death?" asked Borkenhagen. Patti told him that she and her son were at Mrs. Buck's house on Bainbridge Island in Washington State, where they were on a two-week vacation. She confirmed that the call she had gotten from Bob on the night of his death at 11:06 P.M. had turned into a fight. On Thursday, June 29, it was Lee Blackman who had called and advised her of Bob's death. Patti had canceled her vacation and returned immediately to Los Angeles.

Patti told the officers that she was well aware of Bob's porno videotape library and had seen numerous tapes of Bob and other women performing sexual acts. It turned out that Patti and Blackman had gone to Crane's L.A. apartment and confiscated several of his photos, films, and videotapes. They now produced them for Dean and Borkenhagen.

As Patti was going through Bob's L.A. apartment she discovered a photo developing tray containing pictures and negatives. She held some up to the light and thought she recognized Ronni Richards. She thought there might be additional snapshots of her.

Apparently the photographs went back quite a few years.

Bob had always denied to Patti that he had anything going with Ronni. "She's just a good friend," he would say, "that's all." Patti believed it was Ronni in the photos and drew several conjectures from the negatives of an unknown blond woman. She came to the conclusion that the woman in the films was more than a good friend.

Patti also brought out a battered cardboard box that included a photo album that held eighty Polaroid photos of various females performing sexual acts. Patti theorized the photos were from a recent trip Bob had made to Hawaii.

Blackman said he would hold the photos and negatives in the tray in *his* safe, would make them available to the Scottsdale police if needed, but only then. Dean had been told that Mrs. Crane was in some of the photographs, and he suspected this was why Patti and Blackman wanted to keep them locked away.

"So Patti gave us the photo album of Hawaii," said Dean. "We didn't need it. But I think the killer just *had* to have taken one."

The officers' next appointment was at noon with Richard Dawson on the set of the television show *The Love Boat*. Even though Dawson had been a star in two hit shows, *Hogan's Heroes* and *Family Feud*, he was given little respect by the *Love Boat* crew.

"It was maddening," said Borkenhagen, "the shabby way those poor actors were treated." He and Dean watched a scene being shot, waiting for Dawson to be free to talk. "Dean and I waited and waited, and they just had no consideration for the actor's time. The scenes were done over and over. Dawson comes out as a waiter. He's got a platter with a bird in flames on it. It was some sort of plaster bird doused with lighter fluid.

" 'Who ordered the goose well done?' says Dawson. He looks at a little boy, who folds his arms, looks at his plate, and snarls 'I don't like Brussels sprouts.' 'Cut!' shouts the director. They replace the little boy with a little girl. They do it again. They light up the bird and shoot the scene right from the top. 'I don't like Brussels sprouts,' says the little girl. 'Cut!' says the director. 'Do it again.' "

Finally the detectives got to speak with Dawson. He escorted them to his cluttered trailer. The actor explained that he had worked with Crane on *Hogan's Heroes* for six years and had known him well but did not socialize away from the studio. The last time Dawson had seen Bob was when they were at a November 1977 luncheon for Tommy Lasorda.

Dawson said he had known Carpenter for about thirteen years. "When I go away on vacation," he said, "John usually stays and maintains my house." Borkenhagen asked about Carpenter's family life. "To the best of my knowledge," said Dawson, "Carpenter has not been married during the thirteen years I've known him." The actor did know of an ex-wife named Diane, and he knew about Rita.

"Was it routine for Carpenter to stay at your residence overnight?" asked Borkenhagen. Dawson said it was not an unusual occurrence.

John had told Richard that he had been with Bob just before Crane was killed and had returned to Los Angeles on June 29, where he heard the terrible news. "John came over on the evening of June 30," said Dawson, "and stayed overnight. He left early on July 1."

On Friday, July 14, seventeen days after the discovery of Bob's body, Dean, Borkenhagen, and Ken Pollock arrived at Carpenter's house to take him to a sheriff's substation in an unincorporated area of Los Angeles for another interview.

Before the interrogation Dean once more accused John of the killing. He started the tape. "Okay, John," he said, "we've had several talks. Some out here in California. At one time you did go back to Scottsdale with us. Do you recall being advised of your constitutional rights, per the *Miranda* decision?"

"Yes, sir."

"Okay. You have the right to remain silent. . . . Do you understand these rights?"

"I do, sir."

"Will you voluntarily answer my questions?"

"If I can."

"Okay. As you know, we've been out in the Los Angeles area for a couple of days and have interviewed quite a number of people, and so to fill in what we need to know we have to talk to you about several things. John, can we try to do this chronologically? Can we get back to Dallas?"

"Dallas, Forth Worth?"

"Before Mr. Crane came to Phoenix," said Dean. "Does May 20, 1978, sound right?"

"I would have to check other records that I have."

"How about American Airlines, flight 122?"

"That flight sounds familiar."

"Okay, if that sounds right, then would May 20, 1978, sound about right?"

"Possibly."

Dean showed John some of Bob's photos. "I don't know where this picture was taken," Carpenter said, "but she was a good-looking girl."

"So as far as you remember, you haven't seen any of those girls in these photos?"

"No, not straight out. No, definitely not there, there, and there, and there."

"And I'm right in saying that as far as you know, Mr. Crane did not have a timer on his Polaroid."

"Not that Polaroid that I know of. He was very good with a Polaroid."

"Is there anything else you should tell us about Texas?"

"Why?"

"Since the last time we talked, we came up with a lot of stuff that should have been fresh in your mind, but you didn't bring it up."

"I thought we were talking strictly from the time that I got to Phoenix."

"But you know now what we're trying to talk to you about?"

"No, I have no idea."

"We're trying to talk to you about the murder of Bob Crane that occurred in Scottsdale."

"This I understand. This I understand."

"And that means we have to learn everything. We thought that being a friend of his for about twelve years, you would help us out."

"All right."

"What do you think about that?"

"I think it's a great idea, but when you sit across from me and accuse me of killing my best friend, one of my best friends . . ."

"Well, I'm still thinking that you did."

"All right, then, fine. . . ."

"Because I think I would be able to prove that you did."

"Then fine," said Carpenter. "Then I'm not going to say another word. I'm sorry."

"I don't know if you should say another word or not."

"Then I'm sorry."

"What do you mean, 'You're sorry'? You're sorry you killed him, are you? *Or* do you think he deserved it? Why don't you tell me about that? Let's get right to it! I think you're about ready to tell us about it. What happened in Scottsdale, Arizona, to cause you to kill Bob Crane? You know damn well you can't live with it, so let's hear about it."

Dean still believed that Carpenter, under the pretext of buying a sunscreen for his Lotus at various auto supply stores, had bought a valve core remover in order to deflate Crane's car and strand him in the darkened theater lot, where he could be killed with a tire iron.

"Valve core remover," Dean said abruptly. "Did you buy one in Phoenix? How did you get that valve core out of Bob's tire? Want to tell us about that part?"

Carpenter said nothing.

"John, I think it's about time for you to tell us about it. I really do. Let's not play games. We could play games forever, and of course, we have forever to do it, too. But I'd rather have this over with, and I'm sure you would, too."

Carpenter remained silent.

"I'd like a statement from you. All it can do is help you."

Silence.

"Are you going to tell us about it, John? It's your opportunity to give a statement."

Silence.

"What do you say, John? We're talking about serious consequences. We're talking about a murder. Arizona still has the death penalty."

"I don't know if you're getting any feedback, John," said Borkenhagen, "but there were two other guys that came down with us, the guys are a deputy county attorney and his investigator. They've been out covering the same things we have. The county attorney, when we talked to him this morning, said he was pretty happy with the way the investigation was going, but you gotta know a little bit about the law. You know at this time we don't have enough to arrest you."

"Thank you," said Carpenter. "Can I leave now?"

Neighbors in Glendale, Arizona, had noticed a Century 21 Realty sign in Brenda Broyles's front yard starting June 25. There was high grass around the sign. Brenda, who had a passion for parties and celebrities, was one of Bob's lovers and a friend of his for five years. She lived at 5350 W. Maui Lane with her seven-year-old son.

Brenda's friend, Julie Brinker, had told Officer Barry Vassall that Brenda knew somehow that one of her friends had died and "felt much remorse the day of the twenty-ninth," so CA investigators Ron Little and Kate McCormick made a follow-up visit to Brenda at her home at 1:30 P.M. on August 1.

Little began. "Brenda, my name is Ron. I hope you don't mind if I call you Brenda."

"That's all right."

"Okay. This is Katie."

"Hi," said McCormick.

"We understand that you are a friend of Bob Crane's."

"I was introduced to him by a friend of mine at the Ivanhoe five years ago. I was modeling there at the time."

"Uh-huh, I see. When Bob was here the last time, how many times did you see him?"

"Twice, I believe. The first time we went back to his place, where Julie joined us later."

"That evening that you went back to Bob's apartment, was Bob using his videotape machine that evening?"

"Yes, that's the night he got the pictures with me in them."

"When was the last time you saw Bob?"

"I ran into him at Bogart's."

"How long after the first time you saw him?"

"Oh, a week, I guess."

"You didn't see him again after that?"

"I talked to him on the phone a lot. He was supposed to come over to my house one afternoon and he never—never made it." The last time Bob had called her, Sunday, June 25, the day John had arrived, he had canceled his plans with Brenda.

"He called me a lot," she said.

"Oh, he called you? I see. Okay. Are you working any place now?"

"No. I'm trying to get with a band right now."

"Now Julie Brinker had a conversation with one of the Scottsdale police officers," said Little, "and she said that right after Bob's death you mentioned something to her."

"Yeah, about the pictures."

"Anything else? Well, I'll tell you what she said. That you told her that you felt some remorse on the twenty-ninth and then found out that Bob had died that day."

"You don't understand. I'm a psychic. Each night I have a preview of the next day's events. When the moon has a type of energy level, and if I get lots of sleep and get this high energy level going, I can read thoughts. It's like a whisper.

"The day before his accident—I'm into music a lot, and I was playing a lot of Jimi Hendrix and Janis Joplin, and the music was telling me that a friend of mine had died and I was mourning someone. A week before, I spent the night at Bob's place, and I was hearing atmospheric disturbance in the place. I could see it on the wall like a shadow. So I drove all the way over to Bob's to try and find out if I could help him, but the police wouldn't let me in. I tried to offer my services. The officer was so stupid, man. You sit there and tell her something four times, and it still doesn't soak in."

"We'd appreciate your help," said Little. "To be perfectly honest with you, I don't know what the Scottsdale police position is on this. As a matter of fact, I would appreciate it greatly if you didn't even mention to them that we were out here talking to you. But I would really appreciate it if you do have that psychic ability—"

"They weren't listening to me. I know that if I'd been able to see his body and to touch some of the things around there, I could have given them more information."

"Maybe there's something that we missed in this entire investigation here," said Little. "This is why I come over here to talk with you about it. Did you get any other particular vibrations from the apartment while you were there?"

"Just a disturbance. I have a female spirit guide who talks to me, and she told me a man is involved . . . Bob's wife. . . ."

"Bob's wife?"

"Yeah. Knows him."

"Knows the man?"

"Uh-huh. Maybe they're in it together, but . . . she'd been fighting with Bob about property and trying to take everything he had. And she's been a violent type and—"

"How do you know that?"

"Pardon?"

"How do you know she's been a violent person?"

"Well, Bob used to talk to me about it. He was really bothered. He told me several times how she attacked him, and how they had to send the kids away because she was getting so out of hand."

"Did you say you went over there?"

"Yeah, and I sat outside the door, and no one told me about the cord being tied around his neck, but I had found a piece of rope tied around another piece of rope."

"Do you think you might be able to pick up any impressions by going back over to the apartment now?"

"Is it in the same condition it was?"

"No."

"The spirits say I can help," said Brenda.

"Okay," said Little, shutting his briefcase. "Just wondered, you know. We might need you. We're exploring all the possibilities. I think that should just about do it for now. I'll give you one of my cards and—"

"The spirits have told me the murder was for no reason. It had no purpose. It shouldn't have happened. Did they find the murder weapon, or did they discover what it might be?"

"I'm not at liberty to say that. Did you have any impressions on what the murder weapon might be?"

"Well, no." Brenda paused a few seconds and then said, "Iron . . . steel . . ."

"Steel? Any size, thickness?"

Pause.

"Manager," said Brenda.

"Huh?" In Dallas Bob had often introduced Carpenter as his manager.

"I think," said Brenda, "I really would have to go down pretty deep. My friend is sensitive too, and she told me that they had already talked to the guy who did it . . . It would take me half an hour of meditating to get low enough to really get any good impressions. I can do that some night this week, possibly."

"Super," said McCormick, "that will be great."

But Brenda was no further help. In another interview with the Scottsdale police, she became irate and refused to talk further. Was Brenda the woman with long blond hair seen leaving Bob's hours before the body was discovered carrying a paper-wrapped parcel? Could she also be the "sickie" Crane suspected of having gangland connections?

Soon after Little and McCormick's visit, Brenda's house was sold. She left her son with his grandparents in Illinois and disappeared. She has yet to be found. Persistent rumors have indicated that she went to Mexico to make a film and was killed in the desert.

*   *   *

Patti was sleepless and fearful, sweating over the seem-
ingly endless leaks to the media and the insatiable public
interest in the unsolved mystery, especially in the tabloids.
On July 18 she picked up the *National Enquirer*. The headline read WIDOW COMFORTS SON. A picture of Patti, Bob,
and Scotty (taken when he was much younger) was there,
along with other photos of Bob with Victoria and Bob with
Rose "Terry" Lange.

In the *Midnight Globe* there was a cover headline trum-
peting AN EXCLUSIVE INTERVIEW WITH PATRICIA CRANE.
Why, she thought, I've never talked to the press. Patti began to breathe rapidly. She wondered how the information
in the article, which was accurate, could have been discovered unless someone with the police or CA's office had
leaked it.

The article mentioned her argument with Bob on the
phone and that Bob was wearing his shorts and wristwatch
when he was killed. It told of her discovery of the box of
photos of women. Patti had some suspicions she wanted to
share with the county attorney's office, but everything she
had said so far had ended up in print, and she was afraid
it would happen again. Nevertheless, she asked her attorney, Lee Blackman, to call Ron Little on July 19 and tell
him her theories.

Blackman began by complaining about the leaks. Little
sighed. "There's a lot of leaks, and we've got a very good
indication where they're coming from. We're trying to
close those sources off."

"Good," said Blackman, " 'cause Patti really panics over
things like this. She brought up an interesting thought—she
thought if you guys know how the mob does a hit and the
mob wanted it to look like it wasn't them, then they could
have done it messy, the way it was done."

"Yeah," said Little, "that's entirely conceivable."

"Anything developing?"

"There's a lot of questions that have to be cleared up,
and to rush through it and do a half-ass job on it is not
going to do anyone any good."

The suspects that Patti floated through her lawyer were
an old girlfriend of Crane's and Ruth Walters, the wife of

Warren Walters,* the man whom Bob suspected was having him tailed. A negative of Warren had been in the box Dean and Patti had gone through. "That's Warren Walters," she had said to the detective. "He's big in construction in the southwest area. This guy would be heavyweight enough to create some real problems. You should check his wife, Ruth, out."

The next day Blackman called Little again. "Patti's really starting to panic about the names. She was scared to death to even mention Ruth Walters, but she figures she's got to tell it. She's talking about getting police protection and things like that. So if you could be real discreet with this stuff, we'd appreciate it. Don't tell anyone except Larry Turoff where you got it from, 'cause, dammit, she's just shaking in her boots."

The previous week John Carpenter had been calling Bob Jr. frequently. "I can't believe what's happening," John kept repeating. "They're asking me if I killed Bob!"

Abruptly the calls stopped. Carpenter was the one to break contact. Simultaneously, Pat O'Brien at L.A.'s channel 2 rang up Bob Jr. "The news hasn't broken yet," he said, "but the papers are going to identify John Carpenter by name as the suspect in your father's murder." In fact, the *Arizona Republic* had already run the news.

Once the *L.A. Times* learned that John Henry Carpenter was the "prime suspect" in the Crane case, they phoned John at his office at AKAI to tell him what was going on. "I'm shocked, completely shocked," Carpenter replied, and said he would call his lawyer, Beverly Hills attorney Gary Fleischman.

Meanwhile Dean began proceedings against their top suspect. Chris Bingham was assigned to draw up the complaint summary.

The next morning, July 24, Bob Jr. called county attorney Chuck Hyder in Phoenix. He said that Ronni Richards

---

*The names of Ruth Walters and Warren Walters have been changed.

had been on the road with his dad fifty percent of the time, and he suggested that Hyder talk with her. "She talked to my father the day before his death. She told me my father said that John Carpenter was staying at the apartment with him. But Carpenter told me differently. I don't know what he's told you folks at all."

"Other than Mr. Carpenter, do you know of anybody who might have a motive to kill your dad?" Hyder asked. Bob Jr. mentioned his Patti theory.

"Yeah," said Hyder, "Larry ran that by me. I thought maybe in the meantime you had discovered some other information. Might have thought of something else."

"No. As I told you, Carpenter has been calling here, kind of sticking close. But that's all. How does the investigation stand?"

"I'm waiting for more information," Hyder said. "Right now it's not enough to act on. Legally and factually the proof is just not sufficient."

Bob Jr. agreed. "I wasn't sure if it was Phoenix or Scottsdale coming out with the name of John Carpenter as suspect. How could they if there's not enough evidence?"

"Don't ask me. I'm very perturbed about it."

"Was it Scottsdale?"

"They claim they didn't do it."

"It just seems odd that one suspect is being singled out, yet there's not enough evidence to issue a warrant or anything like that."

"I wish it were otherwise. But we'll have to get all the leads we can and follow them out."

"So nothing else? No other potential suspects?"

"Not that I know of."

"Because I was asked a couple of questions in terms of my dad's gambling, which he didn't do, and buying land in Phoenix, which I have not heard of. It was like Carpenter to hang out with my dad for three to four days on the road, and perhaps it was no longer kicks or fun or whatever it originally had been. But it doesn't mean he killed my father."

Hyder assured Bob Jr. that he would call Ronni "and just

forward our work product over to Scottsdale." Ronni told Hyder exactly what Bob Jr. had reported.

In Scottsdale, PD Major Gannon put the pressure on to find the leak; he called the *Enquirer* and asked where they were getting their information. "We're the police. We need to know and we expect you to tell us."

"We're getting it from the county attorney's office," said the reporter.

"Who?"

"The county attorney, Hyder. He's our source," they claimed.

Two days later the Scottsdale police received an unsigned letter with an unlikely return address of 555 5th Street, Los Angeles, California. It was handwritten, dated five days earlier, and read: "I watched Bob Crane being buried three weeks ago, and the police department is one hundred percent correct to suspect John Carpenter. If you need additional information, place an ad in the *Herald Examiner* classified of the personal section for August 6, 1978."

An hour later Chris Bingham placed an ad in the *Herald* that read "Friend of Bob, call me about John tomorrow at 10:00 A.M. (602) 994-2314. Chris." The letter writer never called.

18
THE WALL

Collaboration—Cooperation with one or several other persons in the making of a television drama.

The schism between the county attorney's office and the Scottsdale police grew. Begun by errors at the crime scene, the split was further widened by the release of the suspect's name before an indictment had been approved and prepared.

In his office a put-upon Ron Dean reflected upon the "good ol' days" when the prosecutor's office and the Scottsdale detectives worked together harmoniously. Now charges of incompetence were being leveled against the Scottsdale PD. Neighboring Phoenix policemen were calling Scottsdale's investigation "very inept," and there was widespread concern about the smaller police agency's "ability to handle the high-profile and complex murder investigation of such a prominent person."

Dean said to the press defensively, "We've been charged

with incompetence because our department does not have a regular homicide detail. But our town doesn't have that many murders, only about two a year on an average, and all our officers are trained in basic police investigation."

Scottsdale detectives even came in for criticism from their own department. "Scottsdale police threw all their evidence into one garbage bag, contaminating anything that might have been admissible in court" was one of the charges. Dean knew this to be untrue. Page after page of their recovery list showed dozens of cataloged items that had been bagged in individual plastic bags. Even garbage had been bagged.

"Just 'cause a crime occurs," said Dean, "you don't take every single goddamn thing out of the apartment as evidence—we had every piece of evidence of value. We impounded damn near everything in that apartment, every piece of film, of course, all that camera equipment."

What was especially damaging was an *Enquirer* story saying that Bob Jr. and Lloyd Vaughn had been allowed to take clothing, wine, and beer out of Crane's apartment. "There were two suitcases," Bob Jr. said, "kind of a brown leathery suede. We cleaned out a couple of drawers in his bedroom. Things like his underwear and his drumsticks."

"Each person in the case," said Dean, "had his own motivations. Lloyd Vaughn had a secret reason to be poohpoohing things, we later learned. He started feeding Bobby information, and then both of them said things to the *Enquirer*. The higher-ranking officers left me holding the heat. Maybe that was smart because the county attorney's office was ready to hit anyone who stuck their head up.

"Hyder just ran with the *Enquirer* story," Dean recalled. "The county attorney began a series of statements to the media about an inept investigation. We did have some problems, I think, at that scene that first day. I don't think Victoria Berry should have been allowed to roam about, for example. At the same time she didn't damage anything. Hyder or Turoff, somebody from the county attorney's office, kept talking about evidence that was contaminated, but nothing like that happened."

Part of the continued criticism was that Victoria had been

allowed to handle the phone before it had been checked for
prints. "Not true," said Dean. "I let her answer the phone,
which had been ringing, only after it had been dusted for
prints. I had her answer and act like nothing was wrong. I
couldn't very well answer and say 'This is Lieutenant Dean
of the police department.' They might have hung up. As it
turned out, suspect number one and an early suspect [Kathy
Reid] were the two callers she spoke to.

"Anyone who has read the volumes about the case hasn't
criticized the investigation. We made some minor mistakes,
but nothing terribly wrong. I don't get critical of the men
for making a mistake that any human could make. It's so
easy to criticize. Being a critic is an easy job."

Chris Bingham completed the complaint summary, nam-
ing John H. Carpenter as the defendant and, as witnesses,
Dr. Thomas B. Jarvis, deputy medical examiner; Bob
Crane, Jr.; Geneva Davis, the Sunburst maid; Linda Robertson, the cocktail waitress at Bobby McGee's; Jack Lindsay, McGee's bartender; Carolyn Jean Baare, Crane's date;
and Officer Dennis Borkenhagen, Lieutenant Ron Dean,
and Officer Gene Richards of the SPD.

As complaining witness, Dean listed available evidence:
"A vial of blood from the victim, blood from the suspect,
an electrical cord found around the victim's neck, blood
scrapings from the victim's apartment doorknob, blood
scrapings from the suspect's rental vehicle, a photographic
lineup, and photographs of the crime scene." Bingham concluded the complaint with a synopsis of the homicide investigation.

Charles Hyder was concerned by Bingham's summary.
He called in Larry Turoff. "They've got tunnel vision," said
Turoff. He believed that the Scottsdale PD was so convinced Carpenter was their man that they were not considering other theories and other suspects.

"They had nothing," Turoff said later. "They had a spot
of blood that was the same type as Crane had. To my recollection that was the only link they had."

Hyder agreed. "I think," he said later, "they were committed to one person and one theory early on and had nothing to substantiate the person and the theory and never did. They just didn't do a good job of investigation." He believed that they not only failed to produce strong physical evidence, but had not established a motive. "The investigation was so sloppy," said Hyder, "it would have been impossible to get a conviction. It was so bad that even if someone had confessed and then changed his or her mind, I don't think we could have gotten a conviction."

Borkenhagen shed light on the relationship between prosecutors and police. "On one of our initial meetings after we had issued the complaint, after we had submitted the case, the county attorney's office gave us a list of 'furthers,' which is common practice. I would guess that in approximately seventy-five percent of the serious felony cases we submit, they will come back with a 'further,' and it's usually some small item such as 'We need an estimate on the value of the property.'

"This was an *extreme* 'further,' pages and pages of 'Do this, contact this person, find this, get that. . . .' We jokingly referred to it as 'Bring me the broom of the Wicked Witch of the West, now go back and get all the straws you missed.' But, anyway, we got this 'further,' and we went out and did what we could."

Hyder thought the summary was "incomplete and grossly insufficient." He said, "I gave Scottsdale chief Walter Nemetz a letter containing more than two hundred things and people to check out in relation to the murder." The county attorney said he never heard whether those items were pursued.

Nemetz disagreed. "He didn't give me a list. If he gave it to anyone, it was to the investigators, and I'm sure the things on it were investigated. It was a difficult case because we never came up with any evidence to link the suspect with the crime. But I think it was properly investigated."

"Chuck Hyder has real strict rules," said Dean. "With robberies it has to be a hundred percent case or they don't take it on. They win, I read, ninety-eight percent of their cases—but if you have the kind of rigid guidelines he has,

you're really going to have to screw up not to have a
ninety-eight percent rate of conviction. You'd expect a hundred percent conviction rate if you always have to have a
confession or a fingerprint."

Hyder made his decision—he would reject the murder
indictment and arrest warrant Dean had requested. On
Thursday, July 20, he called in the press and announced,
"There was simply not enough evidence to charge anyone
with the crime. Information provided by the investigators
was insufficient to show probable cause that the suspect
committed the crime. The evidence they've shown us to
date is insufficient to file a complaint or even to show probable cause.

"Some of our people talked with the Scottsdale detectives, but the matter was referred back for further investigation." He refused to reveal who was named in the
indictment.

Meanwhile, Dean was back in Los Angeles (he had already wasted one trip there—subpoenas for documents obtained from a Maricopa County judge were faulty and could
not be served in California) and was proceeding with his
plans to arrest Carpenter and bring him back to Arizona.

"We were going to move right away on Carpenter," he
said. "If anyone else was involved with him, we could dig
around for them later. What you do is take off the number
one character, the guy who used the club. You get that
person, then you can grab any other people around him. If
you can do it real quick, you can really shut down a case
and have all your evidence where it can't get away from
you. But if anything slows you down, you lose it."

At the Los Angeles sheriff's station, Dean briefed the
deputies on the facts he had learned in the case. Many were
as convinced as he was that Carpenter was the killer. "They
were ready to grab him, so we go over to his place," said
Dean.

At Carpenter's they parked beneath a shade tree on Lime
Street. Carpenter's residence wasn't fully visible from the
street, and it wasn't until the officers turned into an alcove

that they could see his front door. Rita answered and invited them in. Carpenter was in the living room standing with his back to them near the door. He turned, and Dean saw that the expression on his face was one of confidence.

With a gesture of triumph the suspect held up a late edition of an L.A. newspaper that contained Hyder's statement to the press that he would reject the indictment of John Carpenter. "The prosecutor ain't going to prosecute me," said John.

Furious, Dean left. He said, "You just don't do that in a murder case! Carpenter's being defended by the prosecutor. Carpenter's own attorney *was* going to turn him in to us. He called me and said, 'Hey, let's make this easy. I'll just bring him in. I want to be right there and try to get him out myself.' He's more cooperative than the guy who's supposed to be on our side! I can't believe what we're up against!"

Dean was bitter and angry. It was a battle between two strong men. "I don't know why Hyder is acting this way," he said. "Maybe somebody was lying to him and he went off on it, just went wacky on this one case and never backed away. It creates other problems when the chief prosecutor goes public—people willing to talk before are frightened off. And it creates a lot of internal problems in the system and department from the chief on down."

Dean and his supervisor, Major Mike Gannon, said to the press that an indictment and warrant were being sought so the suspect could be brought to Arizona for further questioning. Neither Gannon nor Dean would confirm that the suspect was John Carpenter, but they did imply that the indictment was a strategic move, possibly with the intention of placing pressure on the prime suspect.

"We're only asking for a complaint," said Dean. "The evidence *is* sufficient to show probable cause." Borkenhagen's personal feeling was that "we did have enough evidence, but we were in a political battle at the time." He felt the CA's office was still smarting over not being called to the crime scene. "I think that was, believe it or not, the basis of most of our problems. But if you do it their way, the prosecutor at the scene becomes a witness who can't prosecute, too. The judge would say, 'You were there, you've got to testify.' The defense attorney says, 'Anybody at the scene, I get fair game at.' "

"They were actually playing the game wrong, and we eventually were to pay a penalty for them to discover they were screwing up," said Dean.

On July 24 Hyder said, "We don't have a case to issue subpoenas at this time. What they think and what can be proved in court are two different things. When the evidence is sufficient for a complaint, it will be filed. Nobody wants this murder solved any more than I do."

Dean disagreed publicly. "We know who did it. The facts are there, ready to prepare for trial."

On Friday, August 4, the two warring camps met again to review the case. "So Dean and I went down and had another meeting with Chuck Hyder and Larry Turoff," Borkenhagen recalled. "Chief Nemetz was there, too. It finally got down to the point where we asked, 'Just exactly what do you want to issue a complaint?' "

"Look," said Dean. "There's a blackboard right there and some chalk. Why don't you get up and list the reasons for us?"

Hyder reached toward the chalk, then thought better of it. "I'm not going to do it."

"Come on," said Dean. "Give me one reason or several. Write them on the board."

"We want the murder weapon with the suspect's fingerprints on it," said Turoff, "or else we want a confession. That's what you need."

"But we have circumstantial evidence here," said Dean.

"We don't do circumstantial cases. We will not prosecute circumstantial cases."

"That," said Borkenhagen, "is the biggest bunch of bullshit I've ever heard in my life! A lot of people have gone to the chair on circumstantial cases. You don't always have an eyewitness to a crime." They just don't want to touch this, he thought.

*   *   *

Carpenter had told Dean of his repeated June 29 calls to
Scottsdale from both his business and residence phones. In
order to verify the sequence of these calls, Chris Bingham
requested a search warrant for the suspect's billing records
from Diane Eagan of the Los Angeles County District Attorney's Office. Bingham believed that the string of calls
"appear[s] to have been attempts to learn whether the killing had been discovered as well as establish Carpenter's
noninvolvement . . . apparently calculated to divert suspicions from himself."

On August 24, the warrant was signed by a magistrate
of the Los Angeles District Superior Court and served on
the Pacific Telephone Company at 1010 Wilshire Boulevard. Requested were any credit card–charged calls, home
calls, or calls from AKAI Limited, where Carpenter
worked, as well as the phone records for Crane's Scottsdale
apartment from June 1 through August 18, 1978. One of
Carpenter's calls to Bob's apartment, the one Victoria answered, was timed at 3:05. Dean believed that the other
calls were made from Richard Dawson's house or from
phone booths.

Since July 14, Officer Mark Salem, on loan from the
Scottsdale Special Enforcement Unit, had been on tempo-
rary assignment to the Scottsdale PD to screen each of the
thirteen videotapes and six reel-to-reel tapes that had been
impounded from Bob's Winfield apartment. Salem had
made a careful outline of the contents of each and used the
tape counter to mark the different scenes. Using names and
numbers found in Crane's address and phone directory, he
spent all of July tracking down the women Bob filmed in
Dallas.

Salem completed his transcriptions of the videotapes on
July 27, at 11:10 A.M.; the last was tape "L," which was
labeled "Hope" and showed a smiling Crane taking pictures
of his wife and son Scotty while they were all celebrating
Father's Day. Then the tapes were packed away in a box
and placed on the top shelf of the evidence room (along

with the taped call from the anonymous motorcyclist), where they would remain until the case was solved.

The Arizona Canal could be dried up by shutting off the water flow at Granite Reef Dam. In December a second search of the canal was made. "When we went in," said Dean, "we really checked things out. Something like fifty or sixty tire irons were turned in, but none could have been the murder weapon." During the winter the canal would be drained again by the Salt River Project and searched once more, to no avail.

By January 6, 1979, the papers were saying, "Even luck—which law enforcement officials acknowledge always is a vital element in any investigation—has eluded police."

The *National Enquirer* hired Phoenix private eye James Vance to look into Bob's death. At the end of May Vance sent a copy of his fifty-seven-page report on to Hyder. In it he named two men who frequented a "swinging singles bar" with the actor and who, he claimed, had been hired to kill him. Their weapon, Vance hypothesized, was a heavy wrench. "This looks like the breakthrough everyone has been waiting for," said Vance. "The next step is to find out who hired the killer—and why."

At first Hyder embraced Vance's findings, but then he discarded the theory. Borkenhagen had dismissed it from the beginning. "Vance was adding two and two and coming up five," he said. "Jig-Saw John," the famous L.A. bounty hunter, was also called in to the case as a consulting detective, but his findings were largely ignored. No copy of his report survives, but he did tell newsman Pete Noyes of KNBC-TV that he thought the murder weapon was a camera tripod.

Exactly one year after Bob's murder the *Scottsdale Progress* said, "Scottsdale police know for certain how Crane was killed and they claim they know who killed him. But investigators don't know why."

"Anger, greed, a desire to silence Crane," said Dean on the eve of another fruitless trip to Los Angeles to attempt to see Carpenter. "Motive's a difficult thing to establish in this case. The pornographic material could not in itself, if at all, account for a motive."

At September's end Hyder said, "Dozens of people around here were involved with Crane. Detectives had enough leads for a dozen murders.* We'll never stop looking, but it appears we're at a dead end."

By early 1980 the police were using the talents of the FBI, a local law enforcement agency, and an Arizona psychiatrist, all attempting to arrive at a motive for their "number one suspect." "We believe we have physical evidence to link the suspect to the scene and have enough evidence based on probable cause for an arrest," said Dean. "If an arrest was made, we could obtain more evidence that we otherwise wouldn't have access to. We would have, for example, the opportunity to take fingerprints of the suspect."

Dean knew that if Carpenter ever appeared in Arizona, Scottsdale would have the jurisdiction to make an arrest. Turoff met with Dean and Borkenhagen, and as far as he was concerned nothing had changed.

About a month and a half after the murder of Bob Crane the FBI had developed a psychological autopsy of the victim. "They didn't want to come out publicly with their findings, so they gave us the results verbally," said Dean. "They agreed that our suspect, Carpenter, fit the FBI profile. They gave it to us as sort of an investigative lead.

"I was invited by the FBI Academy to present the Crane case to the students there," Dean said. "The FBI not only

---

*Danny Stewart, twenty years a Texas cop, and now a PI, had a link with Bob's murder: "A Houston detective, Ron Phillips, had a death down here in 1979," he said. "Cheryl Wright, a homicide victim. Her husband went out and came back. Bingo! She's there—dead. When the detectives went through, they found some of the missing videos with Crane. I don't know if they were taken out of Crane's apartment or just floating around. Houston sent them up to Scottsdale. We ran it by them and said, 'Maybe you got the same killer in Scottsdale we have in Houston.' "

trains its own agents, but they have what we call the National Academy, which teaches police chiefs and officers from around the country at a special building in Quantico, Virginia, the marine base there. Being an old marine, I felt right at home.

"I was there a week and talked to people from the psychological lab who reviewed the Crane file we had mailed to them earlier and all the visual tapes we had sent them. They were able to reach some conclusions on it.

"While other detectives from around the country also presented unsolved cases, the Crane case elicited the most interest. Officers were there from Florida to California, and all wanted to know about it. We had an overflow lecture.

"After a detailed presentation we asked the jury of students and professionals, 'Well, who do you think did it?' Most thought the same major suspect we had did it. That's John Carpenter. Also, the people at the psychological lab felt the same."

On June 29, 1980, the second anniversary of Crane's death, the case was still unbroken.* Dean, now the only detective assigned to the case, was limited to spending four hours a week on it, but on the anniversary, he met with his men and talked over the current events and modest progress of the year. As for Bob Jr., his close contact with the county attorney's office stopped.

Lloyd Vaughn, Crane's former business manager and attorney, had always been an enigma to Dean. He remembered that on the day Bob's body was found, Vaughn had been noticeably nervous and distracted. Crane kept acting on the dinner theater circuit because he was having cash flow problems, he had told Berry, but actually it was Vaughn who had created them. After the actor's death, Vaughn, fearing the truth was bound to come out, contacted

*The Crane file, almost a thousand pages, weighing fifteen pounds in three six-inch-thick binders, contained over a hundred interviews, the fruit of two thousand man-hours.

Lee Blackman, Patti's lawyer, and requested a private conference. Vaughn confessed that he had embezzled money from Bob because he had gotten in over his head financially.

Vaughn promised Blackman he would make restitution of some $102,000 to $110,000 to the Crane estate, plus interest and penalties. Vaughn made the first payment on schedule, but a promised payment of $75,000 was not made by the due date of December 1979. Patti went to the Los Angeles District Attorney's Office and filed criminal charges against Vaughn.

In March of 1981 Vaughn pleaded nolo contendere to the theft of $75,000 and agreed to pay to the Crane estate a total of $108,000 including legal fees and interest. He was sentenced to one year in jail and five years' probation.

"If it had not been for Crane's murder, the discovery of the embezzlement would not have been made at that time," Dean said. "Crane might have gone on acting for another four or five years before he found out that Vaughn had stolen over a hundred thousand dollars from him."

Since Hyder still found the evidence against John Carpenter insufficient to take to court, the Crane murder became a campaign issue in 1980. Popular Phoenix attorney Tom Collins decided to run against Hyder for the county attorney's post with the pledge, "We'll take another look at the Bob Crane murder case."

The Scottsdale police eagerly threw their support behind Collins. Before the election, Borkenhagen stopped Collins on the street and complained of the current CA's office. "You can't get anywhere with Hyder. It's like he's our adversary instead of trying to work with us."

"The prosecutor has put together the finest bunch of defense attorneys I've ever seen," said Collins.

In November Collins successfully replaced Hyder and on the seventeenth of that month the Scottsdale Police Department asked the incoming prosecutor to keep his promise. On January 28, 1981, he requested Chief Nemetz to take a more in-depth look at all the evidence in the Crane case. "I would hope," said the chief, "that we would at least be able to take the case to the grand jury." To the investigative team they added Cecil Kirk, a former forensics expert with the Washington, D.C., Police Department and the man responsible for identifying Lee Harvey Oswald as the person who fired the rifle that killed JFK. "We are going to apply some techniques to the case," he said, "that even if they were available were not widely used at the time of the murder."

However, the same attorneys were in the CA's office and the same medical examiners, Dr. Karnitschnig, Dr. Jarvis, and Eloy Ysasi. On June 10, 1981, Collins ended his new look at the case and, to the chagrin of Dean and Borkenhagen, on the following day also passed on an indictment of John Carpenter.

"All one can say," said Collins, "was that he knew Crane and was around that night. That's the totality of the evidence. There were others who had the motive and opportunity."

"Dr. K and Ysasi were at direct odds with Collins," said Dean, "and with each other. There were instances of them fighting *during* an autopsy. They would not help with the Crane case."

So strained were the relations between Collins and the medical examiner's department that in 1985 the county attorney sought to have the entire staff removed. He said that at times Dr. K overrode requests for tests because he didn't think they were necessary, accused Dr. Jarvis of numerous technical errors, and claimed that Ysasi was performing autopsies without a medical license. Collins was unable to have them removed.

Even by 1985 forensic technology was not sufficient to make an incontrovertible match of the blood in the Cordoba with the victim's. Dean was a patient man (small towns had a luxury big cities don't—detectives can give tough cases all the time necessary to solve them), and he settled back to wait for science to catch up with what he knew in his gut. "Our investigation does continue," he said. "Theoretically, it will be kept open forever or until it is solved. We get leads from time to time and still send people all over the United States. But after this long it's difficult."

In Dean's mind he saw an unscalable wall that effectively separated him from his quarry. It seemed to be growing until the top was obscured. Dean retired. Borkenhagen retired.

Almost a dozen years passed and still Dean could find no better suspect, nor a motive for Carpenter.

19

MURDERERS NEVER REST

Blind spot—Something important that the protagonist of a drama is unaware of in his struggle toward a goal, but which is removed in the climax.

It was January of 1989 and I was deep in the writing of this book. Tacked on the wall above my desk was the first photo I ever saw of Bob Crane. It accompanied a *TV Guide* article entitled "A Man in Pursuit of Himself" and showed Bob racing through the rain-slick Hollywood streets with his briefcase in hand, feet flying over the pavement, trying to catch up with the image of Jack Lemmon. Crane's own image was reflected in the puddles, but it was distorted and unfocused.

I recalled the first time I saw *Hogan's Heroes*. I had recently moved to Stockton, California, to start a job on the *Record* and was unpacking in my living room as the credits to the premiere show began rolling. In the excitement of the new job I had lost track of the TV season; September 17, 1965, was also my twenty-third birthday. I was completely unprepared for a comedy about a German POW camp. I was alternately mesmerized and astounded.

In the eleven years since Crane's death the face of television had changed dramatically. All three networks had been sold, CBS no longer dominated the top ten, and the number of TV households had doubled to 92 million since *Hogan's Heroes'* debut. One thing had remained constant: sitcoms.

"It is in fact true there are more people in the U.S. watching *Hogan's Heroes* than there were at the time it came out," Werner Klemperer told me, "because the syndicated market is so strong. It is run on all the local stations five days a week—in places back to back—two segments. We have a whole new generation of young people who were small children or not born when we did the show."

Since I like to act as my own detective, I almost always select unsolved cases to write about. You've read what I learned up to this point in the preceding pages. The beginning process often consumes an entire year—I try to learn enough about the case in order to ask informed questions when I seek out the principals in the investigation. I draw maps, illustrations, and diagrams, most of which will not be used but serve the purpose of making me feel I am part of the story.

A true crime book gives value to the individual human life in a world that sees so much senseless violence—I look for that moment when truth is revealed, the questions are answered, there is a possibility of justice being done and a balance being struck. As I've often said, a subject chooses me, not the other way around. Once I've begun I am tenacious, and the project occupies all my thoughts until it is completed.

A reporter with the *Scottsdale Progress* later told me, "Here in Scottsdale the Crane murder takes on a much different stature than it would anywhere else—here, it's legendary."

By phone I spoke with Ron Dean, who had retired from the force the year before. Dissatisfaction and emotion over the stalled case still colored his conversation. "Even after all these years," he said, "I feel very strongly about it. It's a critical time right now. These days I run a private investigations agency and do consulting to small police departments. I work for several defense attorneys and do everything from homicide on down."

Scottsdale had altered greatly since Bob's death. "It was a growing, thriving city then, but now it's exploded. It's still a beautiful area. But it's really changed. I took the road through that neighborhood around the Winfield Apartments the other night. Before, you could see from the driveway of Crane's apartment to the Sunburst. But now that's going to be closed off by the larger building being built behind it. I went up to the old Windmill Theatre—of course, it's changed now, too, it's now a big Liquor Barn, well lit where Bob had his flat tire."

"Absolutely nothing was happening in the case last year when I started my book on Crane," I said. "I feel like my job is to get the facts out there, maybe jog someone's memory."

"If you turn the heat up high enough," Dean said, "you might be surprised. Somebody did it, and he shouldn't get away with it."

"Absolutely. I don't know how a man could hold together all this time. The act entailed a certain amount of premeditation. Still, how could he blot out what he had done?"

"He just justified it in his mind," Dean said thoughtfully. "And you don't feel any remorse about it or guilt or anything like that. If you ask somebody like him—if he finally does get caught, and he was willing to tell you—he'd have to say, 'Oh, yeah, I did it for this very just cause.'

"If you have a conscience and feel guilt, you can't get away with things in your own mind." He paused. "People's memories are still good considering how much time has passed since Bob was killed, but they are less emotional now. Any time murder is involved, emotions can be intense.

"There are investigators who are still interested. It would be nice to solve it, but at least we have to put everything together and let people reach their own conclusions, if the state isn't willing to. Let's hope there are some objective people in the county attorney's office now."

Dean invited me to come and see him and Borkenhagen. "We'll run this thing by and piece things together." I said I would.

For the last decade the Crane investigation had been virtually moribund, but then a new Maricopa County attorney was elected to replace Tom Collins: Richard "Rick" Romley, like Dean, an ex-marine. He too vowed to solve the murder.

"By the time Ricky came along," Dean told me, "he didn't have all this baggage. That's why he had a clearer mind. All he was interested in were the facts."

In June 1989 Romley appointed a team composed of fifteen expert prosecutors and experienced investigators, including the head of his investigative bureau, to review complex, difficult, high-profile cases and bring the different disciplines of each expert into play.

"I put together my personal review board for a lot of different reasons," he told me later, "not just to investigate ongoing, current cases, but to look at some of the older cases that we have." Heartened by his success in two unsolved past murders, Romley decided to take a crack at the Crane homicide. He had gotten bags of mail from Bob's fans urging him to do it.

The board did an "instant review" of the material on the Crane case and made presentations of different angles of the investigation. Then the group as a whole had to determine if the evidence had any merit. "We brought together all the information, the basic issues, and decided it definitely warranted a continued moving forward," Romley told me.

"I put Myrna Parker, a special assistant DA, in charge. She is thorough. She is a very brilliant lady. She's a detail person, extremely aggressive. She doesn't have anyone else do it, she goes out and reviews the material, talks to the witnesses, and looks at the evidence."

On a board composed of devil's advocates, Romley was the biggest advocate of them all, aggressively questioning and challenging. He loved the intellectual sparring.

"It does get heated," he said. "One meeting ran for six hours." Romley would let each board member take the case from a particular perspective and then, when the discussions ceased to be productive for that day, call a halt with "Hey, let's do more research on this by the next meeting."

He told me, "Legal issues lead to additional investigation and so forth. We came back from another briefing and the excitement that came out of that was just awesome. We had a more in-depth look at the case. It was quite astonishing."

Sometimes Romley would call in the initial investigating officers to give a presentation in the big conference room so the group could try to get into their frame of mind in 1978. Darwin Barrie, now a sergeant with a squad of his own, conducted interviews with people who had known Crane and spoke with Bob's family members. He contacted all the people interviewed in the original Scottsdale police file. For instance, Rita and John had broken up years ago and were no longer living together. John was back with his wife, Diana. He had moved often since then and was traced through the DMV.

Romley also had Barry Vassall assigned to his office on a daily basis. "It's a very frustrating thing to be right on the edge," Vassall said. "We've been on the edge for the last twelve years."

In October of 1989 Vassall and former Phoenix police detective Jim Raines began sifting the evidence and contacting witnesses, rebuilding the case from the evidence Dean, Borkenhagen, and their men had preserved.

Science had finally caught up with the scant amount of biological evidence: it was now possible to take "genetic fingerprints" from blood samples. At last there was a chance of proving that the blood in the Cordoba was Bob Crane's.

Only eight months earlier the FBI had established a national lab in Quantico, Virginia, to refine DNA profiling, a process of identifying a person's genetic makeup, which had been developed in England in 1985 by Alex J. Jeffreys, a University of Leicester molecular biologist.

The critical question to the detectives was, Could an exact match be made between the blood sample in the Cordoba and Crane's genetic makeup? To the technicians at the Selmart Diagnostic Laboratories, a private lab in Germantown, Maryland, where the small scrapings were sent, the question was, Is there enough of the sample to test through the new and complicated process of genetic fingerprinting?

A source in Scottsdale phoned me and said, "The Scottsdale police will be using a sophisticated DNA test on the blood samples. This should settle the question of whether it's Crane's blood once and for all. I would think an arrest would come soon if the tests go as hoped."

Now it was just a matter of waiting.

Romley said of the DNA test, "We were excited about it. We were hoping that it would give us additional evidence that would allow us to move forward in this case. To be quite frank, I had some hesitancy about this. DNA [testing], for example, requires that the specimen be preserved in some manner. Over the years the blood wasn't refrigerated. We just didn't know any better. You hope against hope."

The eleven-and-a-half-year-old blood flecks from the Cordoba received by the Maryland lab were prepared for testing at the beginning of November. The small size of the sample concerned the technician. Romley soon got his answer: "Inconclusive." The forensic lab had been unable to determine the DNA of a specific individual from the dried blood specks found on the auto door frame because they were too old and there was not enough of a sample.

"We were told there just wasn't anything to test," said Dwane Hilderbrand, head of the SPD crime lab. "Who knows, though, maybe a new technology will come along someday, and we can do some other tests."

On January 29, 1990, Romley announced the result to the press but declined to speculate whether there would have been enough evidence to file charges had a blood match been made. He was not daunted. "There is no new evidence per se, but we'll look at this case this spring, brainstorm, and see what can be done." To his team he said, "Keep looking," and set April as the deadline. Romley was looking for another kind of blood test that would work on unrefrigerated blood.

On the advice of his lawyer, Gary Fleischman, Carpenter avoided the public eye. Fleischman advised him not to discuss the case with either the police or the press. He was appalled that police from Scottsdale had attempted to interview Carpenter without first coming to him. "They know that I have represented him . . . and going directly to his house was highly unethical. They were trying to pull a fast one."

Bob Jr., now a Hollywood publicist, spoke with the *Arizona Republic* to say he was elated after all this time to find attention turned once again to his father's murder, but he had expressed serious reservations that it was focused on the right party. He had not seen John Carpenter since his father's funeral and could not think of any clear-cut motive for John to have killed his friend. Bob Jr. had compiled his own suspect list. "I'm not saying who they were, but all three of them were friends of my father, both on a professional and personal basis. I can think of three people, two men and a woman, who had strong motives. In fact, I asked the police to investigate two of them, but they were convinced Carpenter had to be the one who killed my dad."

Although Bob's family had never stopped hoping for a solution in the case, they were surprised at the amount of interest that had been rekindled in the investigation. Bob Jr., however, wanted to be positive that when an arrest was eventually made it would be the right person.

"I was twenty-seven when he was killed, and we had almost a brotherly relationship. Gosh, I'm nearly forty now. My sisters are married and have families. My mother is happily remarried. But there remains that void of not knowing who killed Dad. It bothers us all."

Romley used Crane's own medium, television, to warn Bob's assailant on *Entertainment Tonight*, "You killed Bob Crane, but don't rest easy just because ten years have gone by, because we're still going to pursue you. I don't care how old the case is, we're going to take another look at it." Co-host John Tesh cautioned, "However, after thousands of pages of reports and nearly a hundred interviews, there is

no weapon, no motive, and no hard evidence linking
Crane's death with the prime suspect."

From the air Camelback glowered an angry red streaked
with orange. The distant Superstitions were tinged with
blue. It was September 1990, and I was on my way to
Scottsdale.

Ron Dean met me at the airport, extending a beefy hand.
I shook it, noticing how the desert sun had lightened his
hair. He returned quickly to his truck and started it up.
"When you live out here in the desert," he told me, "you
don't think about the heat. You just go from an air-
conditioned car and try to get to a cooler place."

Dean drove me to the crime scene, then to show me the
changes in the Sunburst Motel area. I looked at the corridor
leading into Carpenter's room and then at the now paved
road leading to Bob's apartment a quarter mile away. During the day we visited all the nightspots Bob had frequented.

Later Dean and I sat down at the booth at the Safari
Restaurant where Crane had eaten his last meal that night
in 1978. The long brown menus were probably the same,
and I guessed that several of the waitresses were, too. Then
Dean drove me to the new house he had built on a hillside.

Stowed away in the garage, polished and still in pristine
condition, was his blue Corvette, the same car he had driven
to the Winfield when Bob's body was discovered. "I golf,"
he told me, "fish, play softball, and ride. In fact, I can see
the horse stables from my house, even though I don't have
horses. As I said, I do private consulting work for quite a
few attorneys and accountants these days." Dean was also
now the marshal of Fountain Hills.

"The case is not dead. Dennis Borkenhagen retired last
year, but he's interested. We'll talk about Crane from time
to time when we go out golfing and he'll tell me the latest.
Dennis and I still want to see the case go, 'cause it should
have gone. We were told by the newest prosecution team
that if they had it at the time they would have filed by no

later than the third day out. That's what *I* wanted—I wanted it by the second or third day out."

Dean asked me if I had seen Scott Crane's interview on *A Current Affair* a short time ago. I said I had. I remembered it well. On the show Scott held the flier's cap Bob had worn on *Hogan's Heroes;* it was one of his few mementos of his father. Scott was now in a rock and roll band and had written a song called "Dear Dad." On the screen he was the image of his father, but with long black hair.

"Somebody took my father away from me, and I'm jealous, in a sense, of other kids with fathers," he said. "Down deep I am—I mean, it's sad."

As a result of that appearance a local Arizona man had been deeply touched, Dean told me, and come forward, after all these years, to tell the authorities what he and his partner had seen.

Then Dean delivered a bombshell. "He says he was at the Winfield that day and it was independently verified that he was. He will make a good key witness—*he puts the number one suspect at the scene.*"

20
ROMLEY

Tight on—Very close shot.

"**We actually have** someone at the scene within an hour or two of when the crime occurred!" said Dean. "It's a perfect piece of evidence. He worked for a moving company. To verify that the witness was really there, that he wasn't just saying it, we checked his company. Their records show that he was there."

A moving company! I remembered that the man in the apartment almost directly above Crane's, Mr. Billera in 225A, had told the police that he had heard nothing because he was moving in that day. "The drivers were there outside, when Crane was killed," Dean said. "They were just waiting for daylight so they could unload, more toward a reasonable hour."

"They were there at four A.M.?"

"Probably. It gets light here in the summer quite early—

four-thirty to five A.M. Plus it's cooler then. Anyone who's into that kind of business starts out early—truckers, construction men. They all go out in the early morning when it's really cool. They quit their day about one or two in the afternoon. When the witness saw Scotty on *A Current Affair*, he felt sorry for him. Decided he was going to help. That's why he came forward after all these years. Otherwise he didn't want to get involved.

"There was no sign of the killer washing up at the murder scene. But he had blood on his hand when he parted the drapes to look out front. He may have seen the movers and thought, I've got to get out of here anyway, and just walked right by them, trying to look really cool as he did it."

The movers later said that they saw a man peeking through Crane's drapes, where the bloody print was found. When the man exited, carrying a jacket over one arm, he asked them to move their van so he could leave. He then drove away in a white car.

A second piece of information Dean told me was equally important. "We've always felt the murder weapon had been thrown out of the window of the Cordoba. There was a scratch there." In 1978, on the day the door was removed from Carpenter's rental car, Borkenhagen had noticed a thin, blurred line several inches long hidden beneath the blood. "Remember?"

"I do. But if a person was driving a car and wanted to throw a murder weapon out, wouldn't the Arizona Canal have been to the driver's side?"

"*If* he threw it into the canal. He knows he was seen by the truckers and he wants to get rid of a murder weapon. He has to do some heavy-duty thinking, and he doesn't want to be driving too much. Cars stand out at that time. There are cops out. The last thing he wants is to be seen by a cop car this early in the A.M. with a bloody weapon in his hand. He couldn't have gone far. Very little mileage was put on the Cordoba."

"What I can't figure," I said, "is why he would drive his car at all. He was within walking distance."

"Probably so he wouldn't be seen walking down that wide open dirt street behind the Sunburst with a weapon in his hand. Anyway, the task force people were going over the 1978 evidence. They were looking at an eleven-and-a-half-year-old photo of the Cordoba; DPS had taken a series of twenty-one pictures of the car door. And they saw for the first time that a piece of human tissue had been caught in the groove of the scratch left by the murder weapon. It could still be there. Now we've got to find the Cordoba!"

My heart pounded. After all these years, were they getting close?

During June 1990, Myrna Parker and investigator Jim Raines had continued their search for evidence in the Crane homicide. By July Raines was back to asking himself some basic questions. He had seen color slides of Bob's apartment taken from every conceivable angle but no pictures of the Cordoba.

"As I'm reading through the case there are references to some black-and-white photos that had been taken of the scene," he told me afterward, "so I started looking for these black-and-white photos, not knowing that the car photos ever existed. I can't find them anywhere, so I went to my supervisor, Ray Howard, and asked him if he had read this part in the reports about these black-and-white photos and if he'd found them or knew where they were.

"He said, 'No,' and I said, 'Well, they've got to be somewhere. Scottsdale didn't have them.' And I asked him where he had retrieved all those old files before I started to work on the case. He took me to a closet on the third floor of the old courthouse. It was a secured closet and he says, 'Well, that's where I found the stuff originally. Let's go back and double-check and search that closet again.'

"And, lo and behold, we went back and found a box marked CRANE HOMICIDE. In the box there were three notebooks and in one of the notebooks there was a series of black-and-white photos from the scene. And then—bingo! I hit twenty-one color photos of the car and that's when the tissue was found. The three-by-five normal 35-mm-size photo is what I found."

One DPS photograph was a close-up of the odd scratch, blood smears and streaks on the interior of the passenger side door of the Cordoba.

"As soon as I laid eyes on that I knew exactly what it was," Raines said. "I knew exactly what it was at first glance. You could see the yellow fatty deposits in it, the red muscle fiber. I could see this with the naked eye, you understand. There's a ruler in the photograph, and it measures about an eighth of an inch. Between an eighth and a sixteenth of an inch. It's a little piece. But since it's a close-up photo, as soon as I saw it I knew what it was."

"A small portion of unidentified material appears on the vinyl section of the inside of the right passenger's door," Raines wrote in his report of what he saw caught in the groove of the small scratch and mixed with dried blood. "This material appears to possibly be tissue. The status of the substance is unknown at this time."

Only one-sixteenth of an inch in diameter, the speck was so small it had been overlooked in 1978. In fact, no notation was made of the tissue in any of the initial reports, although Pete Janik, presently a Tempe, Arizona, police sergeant had a "vague recollection of someone placing a tissue speck in a vial."

"We started with our local medical examiner," said Raines. Raines showed the close-up photo to Dr. Karnitschnig who concluded that the tissue captured in the photo was a "a fragment of matter consistent with human adipose tissue [fat]."

Apparently, tissue samples had been taken from Crane in 1978, but had subsequently been destroyed. If it was brain matter in the groove captured on film, where in the world would the detectives get samples of the victim's brain matter to compare it with?

Two weeks later, Raines and Vassall were going over the twelve-year-old physical evidence. They came upon the yellowed pillowcase where Crane's bludgeoned head had rested. Here were actual fragments of his brain tissue captured in the fabric.

"When I found the tissue I knew that we had him," Raines told me later. "And what makes that tissue so strong is the fact that at the scene on the pillowcase I also found a piece of tissue that looked just like the piece of tissue in the photograph."

This sent Raines scrambling back to the old photos of the scratch on the door. He hadn't imagined it. The speck of tissue looked very much like the brain matter found on the pillowcase. The two sets of tissue apparently were consistent with the kinds of wounds Crane had suffered—brain matter, or fatty tissue of the kind that would have come from a head wound.

"To be perfectly honest with you," said Raines, "Scottsdale had never had that pillow examined. So now I've got tissue in the car. I've got tissue on the pillow where the murder happened and then I'm going through the autopsy photos one day and here's a chunk of identical tissue stuck in his hair. So I've got a three-way connection. That's what brought it together."

"I saw plenty of good color photos of the scratch and the blood droplets on the door," Dean told me. "About ten, but I never saw any of the black-and-white photos. I had my own set of photos that zeroed in on the blood specks and scratches plus a close-up of the scratch. Of course, I made sure I had those because that's what my investigator saw.

"In a way you could say there's two separate sets of photographs. To the best of my recollection I don't think I ever saw the Department of Public Safety's photos. They stopped their series early and then gave the whole set all the way through to the county attorney's office. DPS may have been assuming that they shared those things or that they would bring them out to Scottsdale. Doug Ferguson, a former DPS print examiner, had his set and Ron Little, the county attorney's investigator, had their set, but what they failed to do was give Scottsdale P.D. a set of those same twenty-one photos. The first time I saw those was when Borkenhagen and I met with Myrna Parker and Jim Raines in 1992."

At one point, back in 1981, shortly after Collins had become county attorney, the tissue photo had been at

Dean's feet tucked snugly inside Little's briefcase. After Raines' discovery of the close-up photo, Dean said that if he had seen that picture he "would have jumped through the roof."

It's doubtful that Chuck Hyder saw the DPS photo in 1981, but if he had it hadn't made much of an impact on him. It was in October of 1990 that Jim Raines asked the former county attorney to take a closer look at the spot of red in the photograph.

"It looks like tissue or skin...," said Hyder. "If we would have seen that, we would have been talking a whole new ball game."

Raines showed the same picture to Little who at first thought that the speck was a piece of debris or grease. Raines reported that Little kept looking at the spot and asked, "Is that flesh with a hair in it?"

"He sat there, mouth open, staring at the ceiling," recalled Raines. Little then said, "I never at any time suspicioned it to be tissue. All I can say is we blew that one."

In December three medical examiners in Texas and New Mexico were consulted. "It is my opinion that this is a fragment of tissue, most likely blood-encrusted brain," Dr. Vincent Di Maio, chief medical examiner for Bexar County, Texas, wrote back. "Though I cannot absolutely rule out subcutaneous (fatty) tissue." The others also concluded that "based on photos of tissue found in John Carpenter's rented car [the speck] was a piece of human tissue."

"First a trail of blood," said Dean, "blood on the doorknob, the curtain, blood on the Sunburst towels. Now there is a trail of brain matter from that pillowcase out to that car. Two trails leading toward the same guy.

"Within six months it is expected there will be an arrest. The county attorney's office is out locating all the witnesses and searching throughout the West for the Cordoba." I returned to San Francisco, as chill as Scottsdale was ablaze. They *had* to find that car.

*   *   *

Two days later, September 29, 1990, I spoke with Richard Romley by phone.

"What have you heard that is going on?" he asked.

"Rumor," I said, "but it's a pretty good one. That you've got about the best possible evidence on the leading suspect."

He evaded my question. "Who do you think did it?" he asked.

"In the lecture that Ron Dean gave at the FBI Academy they seem to have come to the conclusion it was the L.A. friend. That's what I've always believed, at least until a better suspect comes along."

"Carpenter?"

"Yeah, but I don't like to use names. I try to be careful."

Romley laughed. "I've got immunity, you don't. I'll give you a little bit of information."

"What's that?"

"We found the Cordoba again! And we're bringing it in. It was abandoned in New Mexico."

I made another trip to Scottsdale on October 19. "I spoke to Rick Romley," I told Dean. "He seemed excited. They found the car, tracked it down."

"Trial preparation is going on right now," Dean said. "Investigators flew to L.A. to reinterview Bob Jr. and find the other witnesses. Bob Jr. knows something's up. The review board is talking to Dawson now, and I'm sure he'll be on the phone to his friend Carpenter right away."

Two weeks earlier Romley had secretly conducted a dry-run trial for Carpenter in front of twelve experienced southwestern prosecutors and lawyers. At the end of the mock trial their verdict was "guilty." All said, "The case will fly." Romley's own attorney had suggested that he indict Carpenter, but he only took this on advisement. The ultimate decision would have to be his alone. There was still no motive for the murder.

By November 2 the case was still under review. "There's still several months of work to do," said Bill FitzGerald of Romley's office. "We've been talking to a lot of people and are still gathering information. There is no specific time when it will be concluded." Dean wondered if it would ever be over.

On Thursday, November 8, I sat with Dean and Borkenhagen by the pool at the back of the newly remodeled Sunburst Motel. Wind stirred the colored umbrellas, waiters were setting up, music was in the distance. I could see myself reflected in Borkenhagen's dark glasses. "I hear they have two witnesses now," I said.

"I don't know if that's coming off as well as it's hoped," Dean said.

"The mover had a partner. They were there. Records show it. There's no doubt about that," I said.

Borkenhagen sighed. "I understand some things one of them said just don't match up too well." He would not tell me what. Perhaps they had gotten cold feet about testifying. Even the existence of the two witnesses was highly confidential.

"Carpenter's so distinctive looking. They were in a truck. . . ."

"Moving van."

"The only time Carpenter actually described a scene to you—Crane is in his underwear and the film is being edited. It sounds as if Carpenter is there in the apartment while this is happening. But at eleven-fifteen Crane had told Patti that the editing on *Saturday Night Fever* was already finished."

"You've seen the crime scene photos," Dean said to me. "Bob Crane piled up the reel-to-reel recorder of Bob Jr.'s, the edited tape, and on top of that, those two-tone blue trunks of Carpenter's. These were things that were supposed to go back to California with John, and he placed them where he could not overlook them in the morning. That pile was a reminder to him to take them to the airport when he took Carpenter. It's only because Crane was killed that they didn't go to the airport together."

"And the edited tape was *under* the swim trunks Carpenter had dropped on the floor at two P.M.," I said.

"That was one strange call Carpenter made to SPD the day after the murder, changing his time."

"Right," said Dean. "He's thinking, What can I do to adjust this time? An innocent person doesn't have to concern himself with that." He paused and looked into my eyes. "When he called Crane's apartment and spoke to Victoria and then to me, he never asked why the police were in Crane's home. That made him a suspect immediately. How come he didn't say, 'Hey, what happened? What are you doing there?' He returned to the scene of the crime—by phone.

"Crane may have said, 'Come on over, I'll leave the door open for you.' Maybe that's the part of the conversation John left out. He didn't want to say he was in the apartment. He all but put himself there."

Victoria Berry was now Victoria Wells. She'd married her boyfriend, Alan Wells, and was working as a drama coach in Los Angeles and writing a screenplay of her life, *Can't Kill a Weed*.

"She cared about Crane," Dean said. "She suspected Carpenter. Wasn't she the one who was telling us how Carpenter was almost trying to lead her on sometimes?"

"Bob Crane, Jr., was a decent guy," said Borkenhagen. "The only problem I got with him is when we talked to him, he gave us a lot of information that sounds like Carpenter did it, but in recent interviews that I've seen on TV, he's telling them, 'I don't know, it could have been this broad.' " Borkenhagen was very angry over the case. " 'It should have been filed two days after,' is what I've been hearing," he said. "That's kind of interesting since I've taken twelve years of shit on this case, and it just irritates the shit out of me! . . . My friends tell me that the Crane case is my albatross, that this tag will go with me to the grave.

"Here's another thing that makes me totally convinced that Carpenter's our man—Crane is dead, and after Dr. K finished the on-the-scene examination, we get to looking and there is what appears to be a couple of blobs of semen on Crane's left thigh. We're assuming it was *not* Crane's semen. Here's *our* theory: Carpenter whacked Crane in the head and then beat off over him. The thing about the cord—

it's typical of the homosexual murder, but I keep an open
mind about that."

I asked Borkenhagen, "Have you ruled out a woman as
the killer?"

"No, I wouldn't say so."

"Wouldn't Crane have had to be struck when the room
was brightly lit for the wounds to be so close together?" I
asked.

"I don't think so, there was enough illumination," said
Borkenhagen. "The indentations in the skull are side by
side." Borkenhagen drew the marks' actual size on my
notebook:

"Then what was the instrument?" I asked. "The one that
left the scratch on the car door. What was the murder
weapon?"

"I don't think it was a tire iron," said Dean. "That doesn't
make any sense to me. I think the weapon was a golf club.
If you picture a golf club in someone's hand, you're going
to bring it down with two hands—control, accuracy, and
leverage."

"Dr. K had pretty much indicated it was a heavy instrument with a turned-up end on it, which would fit either a
tire iron or a golf club," Borkenhagen added. "Myself, I'm
hung up between the golf club and the tire iron. One or the
other."

Almost at the same time we were speaking, Ray Gieszl,
a Phoenix Police Department criminologist, was in the

crime lab discovering that the long-sought weapon was not a crowbar, poker, tire iron, or golf club.

Using all these implements, Gieszl tried to duplicate the bloody imprint on the sheet at the foot of Bob's bed, but he failed. Dean believed the killer had used the sheet to wipe blood off the murder weapon, but Gieszl wondered if the murder implement had instead been rested against the end of the bed. Then he had an inspiration. He remembered that although Crane owned two large camera tripods, only one had been removed from apartment 132A.

Gieszl bought a tripod of similar size and type to Crane's missing one and by striking a life-size clay head was able to duplicate Bob's wound. Plaster casts of the wounds on Crane's skull matched perfectly! When he laid the tripod against a sheet the stain was similar to the one in Crane's bedroom.

"Some really minute detailed configurations in the blood-stain is what led our criminalist to the tripod," Jim Raines later told me.

John Carpenter had sold Bob Crane the VCR that the cord wrapped around Bob's neck had been cut from, and he had sold the actor the tripod that had evidently killed him.

Romley, Parker, and the team had exhaustively screened and rescreened the videotapes taken of Crane's body at his apartment in 1978. They knew that Dean and Borkenhagen had discovered a long black hair on Crane's back when he was rolled onto the gurney for transport to the medical examiner's morgue. Myrna Parker was looking for more because their principal suspect had long black hair.

In one of the video shots, there was, she noted, "a single piece of hair on the victim's forehead that looked different from the rest. It was longer and blacker." It was not Crane's hair but was lost when the coroner did his on-the-scene shaving of Crane during the preautopsy at the apartment. Apparently also lost was another black hair, root still intact, caught in blood in the ball of wires behind the videotape equipment and the curtain.

*   *   *

For years Dean had considered the motive for the murder—jealousy, envy, killing the object of one's affections. These were all at the top of his list. He told me that the motive was similar to the killing of John Lennon by Mark David Chapman. "I was looking for a way to vent all the disappointment, my anger, my rage," Chapman had said. "I saw him on the roof of the gabled, luxurious Dakota apartment. And I became hurt. Enraged at what I perceived to be his phoniness."

Bob's increasing boredom with his friend intensified a frustrated love-hate relationship fueled by jealousy, theorized Dean. "These were very strong feelings," said the detective. "This guy was a hanger-on. He just wanted to be with Crane because of the actor's attractiveness to other people. Bob could pick up two or more women at a time, and John could get one of them.

"The appointment book that Crane had, that's really interesting to me. It didn't dawn on me until I had read all the reports and done all the interviews that Carpenter didn't score one single time in Scottsdale. More jealousy. And Crane had 'X'-ed out all his future meetings with Carpenter after June 29."

Bob Crane, Jr., told the press that his father had told him he was getting tired of having Carpenter around. "My father mentioned to me two days before the murder that Carpenter was getting to be a nuisance," he said. "It was no longer kicks or fun or whatever it had originally been."

Some believed that Carpenter was in love with Bob and killed him in a jealous rage after propositioning Crane and being rejected.

Bob's close friend, actress Ronni Richards, now living in Boca Raton, Florida, put forth a story to the press that was different from her 1978 statement. She claimed that the actor and Carpenter had a falling-out just before Crane's death. Ronni attributed the split to two incidents. In one, she said, Bob saw Carpenter beating up a woman, and in the other Carpenter approached Bob sexually. "Bob told me that Carpenter tried to put the make on him," she said. "Bob was one hundred percent straight. He wasn't interested in men."

As a rule, Carpenter set up the complex video equipment for Bob, but in Scottsdale Crane had already set it up himself, including the elaborate wiring behind the curtain. While John was out looking for a sunscreen, Crane hooked up the SL-8200 from Dyna-Tronics. John was becoming dispensable to Bob.

Therefore, from all angles, it appeared Carpenter was being cut off, and this rejection may have been the catalyst for the murder.

Rick Romley's office was on the eighteenth floor of the First American Title Building. The forty-two-year-old prosecutor leaned toward me on his carved cane, a strong and appealing figure, his hand extended. His grip was firm. Romley was injured as a marine in Vietnam; a single parent, he had raised both his sons, who were now marines. He was concerned that they might be on their way to the Persian Gulf and war.

I told Romley what I had learned over the last two years. "Jesus Christ," he said, "you've got good sources." We sat down.

"When you go over a case," he began, "you can draw a lot of conclusions in a review or a subsequent review, but there does come a point when it looks like resources shouldn't be allocated to continue the investigations."

"Do you still have a deadline for reviewing the Crane case?"

"Yes, we do. It would be at the end of March 1991. If we decide not to go ahead, it's over."

There was more blood in that car than had been known. When detectives opened the door of the recovered Cordoba, they found some caught in the doorjamb. I asked Romley about future tests on the blood.

"A new technique has created a bit more hope," he said with a smile. "We came up with another process for the blood sample out in Oakland, California. The first two questions I asked them were. 'What about sample size?'

and 'What about the preservation of it?' The Oakland lab said that size was no obstacle, it will work with smaller samples, and it doesn't require preservation. We're looking at that process right now.

"I think when it comes down to it, motive is going to be a big issue," Romley told me. "We continually hope to find additional witnesses. As you know, we've found two. They were there all the time. We have been very successful.

"The investigation was done very well initially, but there was a problem. When the Cordoba was being towed to DPS, an officer should have gotten in the car. There's just some standardized police procedures."

"Get inside?"

"Just driving along with the car while it was being towed." I had understood that Officer Barrie had followed the Cordoba.

Looking into his eyes, I could see that he was a man who loved what he was doing, and he was not wary of circumstantial cases, the most difficult to try. "A pure circumstantial case with all its parts is awesome—I'm not afraid to put one forward," he said.

"Would you have prosecuted in 1978?" I asked.

"If I had been in office in 1978, I would have worked more hand in hand with the Scottsdale Police Department," Romley told me, "ensured that the investigation was full . . ." He paused.

"It's a tough question," I said.

"Would I have prosecuted—that's the bottom line. With just the blood, with just the blood? You see, now we have more than just blood. It would have been a real close call. If there was no more evidence from right then—*probably not*. But you always hope with the no statute of limitations, you might . . ."

"And of course you wouldn't have had the technology then."

"Well, it's not so much that. People talk . . . people talk. You hope you can find some other type of information that might come forward. I would think waiting was better than taking a chance on losing it and never being able to bring it back again. You lose and that case is gone forever, even if the guy admits it later. Anyway, it will all be over by the end of April," Romley told me as I left, "one way or the other."

But May of 1991 came and Jim Raines, Barry Vassall, and Romley were still plugging away at building a case. "Raines and I," said Vassall, "just took this case apart. We worked it from the ground up, as if it were a new homicide." He said he thought the original investigation by Scottsdale police was a "slipshod affair." "They were inexperienced and hampered by conflicts with the prosecutors."

"If it wasn't for me saying I want that door panel secured, and had it wrapped in plastic . . ." Dean reacted. "They're acting like 'This is our case and we did the whole thing.' No, you didn't. We laid the foundation. If they go to trial, they're just going to dump on me and Dennis Borkenhagen almost as a strategy. I think that's a very bad strategy because they're going to damage the evidence."

Romley had missed his April deadline because of the "AzScam scandal," and on May 9 the papers were full of stories about the former county attorney, Charles Hyder, who was now a federal attorney in Phoenix. He had been accused by defense lawyers of allegedly suppressing evidence in a 1973 murder trial. The charges, even if groundless, would be studied by the Arizona State Bar, but their findings are not made public. More important, though, Hyder was beginning to reevaluate his feelings about Carpenter as a suspect.

At this time Carpenter granted his first interview (to the *Arizona Republic*) since the murder, revealing how he and his wife, Diana, had been harassed by the media over the years. "To me," he said, "it's very difficult to look at my neighbors after an article or a news broadcast is on the air. I always hope their television set is broken."

Diana, sobbing, later told how they had been pursued by the press. "If the dogs bark, I jump," she said. "It just goes on and on. This is the United States of America, and we haven't done anything!"

Gary Fleischman, Carpenter's lawyer, was told there was new evidence, but not what it was. He openly questioned whether it amounted to anything. "They haven't looked beyond the ends of their noses," he said. "If you get involved with celebrities, God help you—if you are a celebrity or a celebrity is a victim. I'm only afraid they'll indict him just to do something. They've been barking up the wrong tree for fourteen years, and it just nauseates me."

On February 6, 1992, Carpenter appeared on *Entertainment Tonight* with his wife and his lawyer, in order to plead his case. The trio seemed exhausted. "I just want to be left alone," said Carpenter, "I really and truly do." His mouth was drawn tight. "I, myself . . . my wife especially, that's it."

Diana insisted they had been wrongly persecuted for fourteen years. "People asked if I was told what was going on," she said. "Children are cruel. Teenagers are cruel. They don't mean to be. Two o'clock in the morning, driving by, screaming, 'Murderer! Murderer!' They egged our home. You see, that's just part of it."

Fleischman added, "I think the authorities in Arizona have literally, by continually bringing up his name, without ever doing anything about it, ruined their lives."

"Fourteen years I've been chased by the media, followed," said Carpenter. "Myself, I feel that I'm man enough to take this, because it's the media. These people are trying to get some type of a story. It's not journalism as far as I'm concerned."

Dean had watched Carpenter's appearance with a jaundiced eye. "It was a controlled situation, with the cameras there and his attorney telling him really not to say anything. He didn't say much other than protesting. He really didn't have a good script, either. You could tell he sort of winged it there and didn't show any outrage. You notice he never said anything about being not guilty."

21

DUST DEVIL

Climax—The peak of dramatic tension in a drama; the point where the plot is resolved, where the theme is revealed.

The climax of the fourteen-year-old case now lay in the hands of Rick Romley. He had to make the final decision whether or not to prosecute. If yes, it would mean that enough evidence finally existed to try someone for the murder of Bob Crane. If no, then the odds of ever trying anyone for the crime were virtually nil.

The prosecutor passed sleepless nights. His own attorney had said, "Prosecute." Finally in May of 1992, a year behind schedule, he entered the large conference room for a confidential meeting with his team. His face was unreadable. He spoke a single word.

The word was "Yes."

"You have to decide. Do you go with something that has problems, that may be close, but you think the guy is guilty?" said Romley. "We decided to go with it."

*   *   *

From various sources I had heard on good authority that
the arrest was set. On Thursday, May 28, I called Romley.
He sounded spirited and then exhausted. I told him I had
heard things were about to pop. Legally he could tell me
nothing about the case at this point, but there was a long
silence.

"Next week, watch the papers," he said. "Watch the papers." Then he hung up.

On Friday Romley had Myrna Parker file a direct complaint affidavit charging Carpenter with one count of first-
degree murder. Since there was no grand jury indictment,
the county attorney's office would be required to lay out
their witnesses and evidence in open court during Carpenter's preliminary hearing.

Once Carpenter was arrested and extradited to Arizona,
a probable cause hearing would determine if the evidence
was sufficient to order the suspect to stand trial for murder.
Prosecutors sometimes prefer a direct complaint over a
grand jury indictment because they have an opportunity to
test the weaknesses and strengths of a case in front of a
judge, before an actual trial.

The affidavit, signed by Barry Vassall, read: "Subsequent
investigation revealed that Carpenter, in a described state
of anxiety, checked out of his room at the Sunburst Motel.
Carpenter made numerous telephone calls to the Scottsdale,
Arizona, area the afternoon of June 29, 1978, in an obvious
attempt to obtain information concerning the death of Robert E. Crane." A camera tripod, the affidavit revealed, purchased by John Carpenter, was the possible murder weapon.

Judge David Cole of Superior Court received the arrest
warrant.

Plans for the arrest were ready, but Carpenter had been
out of town until the end of May. Upon his return the suspect had been kept under surveillance, while Myrna Parker
flew to Los Angeles with Scottsdale policemen. They were
joined by Los Angeles County sheriff's deputies.

"We went over the day before and met with the LASO," Raines told me. "We had a squad of maybe four or five guys and staked him out in his house."

On Monday, June 1, 1992, at 6:10 A.M. Carpenter, now sixty-three, left his home on Doty Avenue in Torrance, a blue-collar South Bay neighborhood, wearing a white shirt open at the neck and black pants and began his drive to Carson, where he had worked as a stereo component service manager at Kenwood USA for the last four years.

Raines watched Carpenter's Mazda RX-7 on the road ahead. "For some unknown reason he pulls over to the curb, stops his car about two or three blocks from his job there and when he did that the sergeant who was in charge of the thing said, 'Go ahead and take him off,' " recalled Raines. "There were plainclothes guys that were surveilling him in these unmarked cars—Carpenter had absolutely no idea we were there—none, whatsoever. He claims he did, but he did not because I was right there and I saw the look on his face. I saw the whole thing come down and he had no idea."

Raines told him, "You're under arrest for the murder of Bob Crane."

John offered no resistance as he was taken from his car by police and handcuffed. Charged with first-degree murder, he grimly kept his head lowered as a photographer took his picture. However, by the time he reached the Los Angeles County Jail he was grinning broadly. Gary Fleischman, his attorney, joined him. Myrna Parker was at Carpenter's extradition hearing later in the day at Los Angeles Municipal Court, where Fleischman asked that the hearing be postponed a month. It was reset for July 1.

Outside the court he said, "My client is eager to speed his return to Arizona to clear his name. I can see no useful purpose in keeping him in jail here. He wants to get this behind him. This has been hanging over his head for fourteen years. He's glad that this has finally come to pass."

I called Ron Dean. He had been trying to reach Borkenhagen and retired SPD chief Walter Nemetz, both of whom were on vacation out of state. "I wanted to congratulate the chief for being right. We're really gratified that the case will now have its day in court. A good conclusion," he said.

"You gonna be watching the press conference?"

"You betcha! Romley's got to be cautious because it's an election year—somebody else still has time to jump up and run against him if he goofs. Romley's a good guy. I'm so glad someone picked up the banner and is going to run with it. It could have been a disaster. At least now it has a chance of being solved. Bob Crane is dead. He can't do it himself, and I'm sure if he could, he would say, 'Go find the guy that did me.'

"And it's fourteen years later—I don't care if it's fifty years later! They're still doing murder trials over in Germany and France from World War Two."

"Carpenter had a big grin on his face while he was being arraigned," I said.

"He is such a bad guy," said Dean, "he really is. Murder can happen to anybody. I always think, What if it happened to me? Would somebody go work the case and care about it?

"The police officers have done their part, now it's up to the attorneys and the courts. I knew it wasn't going to be anybody else but Carpenter. I was hoping this would break someday."

"This must feel so good for you."

"It does—and after fourteen years to the month!"

Romley's press conference was packed. A large American flag hung behind him. He gave credit to Vassall and Raines and mentioned the original investigators.

"We're working with new evidence they may not have had then," said Romley. "This is the culmination of over two years of intense investigation by several different departments and individuals. We've gone over all of the evidence and reinterviewed all of the key witnesses. I think this is an important statement to the community that homicides are never closed, that we in law enforcement will always aggressively pursue those who break the law.

"I think there is a lack of faith in the system, and the community just has lost their ability to believe in the criminal justice system and that it is out there protecting them," Romley told me. "I think society as a whole is our job. Cases like this require aggressiveness, and society has a right to have an answer."

On *Good Morning America*, Romley said, "If there was perhaps one significant thing, it was the brain tissue in Carpenter's car."

Rene Lynch, a *Daily News* reporter in Long Beach, called me and said, "I talked to Carpenter's wife, Diana, very briefly last night. She was not happy to see me. I got very little out of her. She said, 'He's innocent, absolutely innocent, and he will prove it. He's going to waive extradition. He has no criminal record. He has nothing in his background that would indicate anything like this. He's actually relieved now, he's tired of running. We've moved and he's gotten different jobs. He tried to stay one step ahead.' "

Diana told Rene the stories about her husband were vicious lies and characterized the neighbors and the press as "the worst."

I spoke with Steve Brennen of the *Scottsdale Progress*. "Romley has really taken a stand on this case, and certainly he's going to catch a lot of criticism about it. Vassall alluded to something about blood," he said. "It might be their trump card."

"That must be the results of the Oakland blood test. An LAPD officer told me that the test came out positive," I said.

Then came a shock. On June 9, 1992, Carpenter was arraigned before Judge Elvira Austin of Long Beach Municipal Court on three counts of lewd conduct with a child!

"It was a couple of young girls who were friends with him and his wife," Brennen told me. "The cops in Long Beach had put the case together back in 1988. Interestingly enough, there was some information that was uncovered by the Long Beach detectives that was used in obtaining the felony warrant in Arizona."

The case had not been prosecuted in 1988 because of insufficient evidence. The victims were Carpenter's girlfriend's ten-year-old daughter and her daughter's twelve-year-old friend. Carpenter's girlfriend was not anxious to prosecute, but the other child's mother insisted. Carpenter's girlfriend had also allegedly been molested by Carpenter when she was fifteen.

"John had her when she was fifteen," said an L.A. source, "and he followed her movements because of his obsession of having sex with the daughter of someone he'd had before. Apparently Carpenter shared her with Crane and another famous friend.

"If everything I hear is true, he had children, underage teenagers, and grown-ups.

"Even if the murder charge against Carpenter can't be proved, they'll hit him with the child molesting charge, keep him in custody for the rest of his life. A sixty-four-year-old man going down in L.A. for three counts of child molesting is not going to survive."

If convicted of the three counts of committing lewd and lascivious acts on a child under fourteen, John could be sentenced to up to twelve years. The fact that he had waived extradition to Arizona now meant nothing. Until the molestation case was resolved he would stay in California, held without bail.

One girlfriend of Carpenter claimed in the tabloid *Globe* that she and John made love three days after her thirteenth birthday. "I often had to have three-way sex or take part in orgies with as many as eight other men and women," she said, and alleged she'd made love with both Bob and John in a threesome.

When she spoke to John in 1990 about Crane's murder, she demanded to know if he had killed him. "He slapped my face and said, 'Don't second-guess me. I didn't kill him.' Then he walked out in a fury," she recalled. "In all the years I've known him, he'd never hit me before."

Dean was restless, but relieved. He still held a tremendous amount of anger because of the long battle he had been forced to endure in his quest for an indictment and arrest. He had done his part as a lawman, now it was up to the judicial system to reach a verdict in a trial that might be far in the future or never take place.

At the end of his fourteen-year journey, Dean pondered the steps that had brought him there. So much had changed in that time. Today, July 13, 1992, would have been Bob Crane's sixty-fourth birthday.

That night Dean watched *Hogan's Heroes*. Bob was captured on the show forever youthful, wisecracking, impudent, and sly. It was a form of immortality. Dean watched the TV until he dozed off. The station went off the air, and the room was illuminated with a silver light almost as bright as the desert toward Carefree, where Bob had watched the dust devils on his first day in Scottsdale.

Across the gravel wash amid the ironweed and mesquite he had been hypnotized by the devils spinning madly to the north. There was not a breath of air as he turned his eyes into the blinding light. These dust devils, *remolinos de tierra*, are plentiful in the summer, and since ancient times they have been believed to be powerful harbingers of danger and bad luck.

CHUCKWALLA

EPILOGUE

On Tuesday, November 10, 1992, in Los Angeles County Superior Court in Long Beach, John Henry Carpenter pleaded no contest to one of the three charges of sexual battery and sexual misconduct with a girl younger than fourteen years old. In return for this plea two of the three charges were dismissed and he was sentenced to three years' probation. The *nolo contendere* plea also allowed Carpenter to be returned to Phoenix in order to face prosecution in the Crane case. He had waived extradition in June on the day of his arrest.

In December, John's six-month emergency leave of absence from Kenwood USA came to an end and the firm was obliged to fill his position. Christmas Eve, Carpenter was released on $98,000 bail after putting up his two-story Torrance, California, house as collateral. However in the

months ahead, not only would John be forced to sell his
gun collection and Diana compelled to part with her dia-
mond wedding ring, but the couple, with their savings dan-
gerously depleted, would face the very real prospect of
losing their home.

No matter the outcome of the approaching pretrial hearing, the wasting away of John Carpenter had begun. The
black mane of his hair was shot through with white above
the temples and above his forehead. In the six months since
his arrest Carpenter's lined face had grown pinched and
pounds had melted from his once stocky frame. Depression
showed in his posture as he walked or slumped in his chair.
He was jittery and jumped at noises. The impish twinkle in
his eye that had been so much a part of his personality back
in the summer of 1978 seemed stilled forever.

A high-powered and high-priced Southwestern attorney
who had initially offered to defend Carpenter bailed out
and at the last minute was replaced by Stephen Avilla, a
deputy Maricopa County public defender. Carpenter's preliminary hearing began in February of 1993 in Maricopa
County Superior Court under the stern eye of Judge Gregory Martin.

Prosecutor Myrna Parker wasted no time in introducing
heartwrenching color photos of the actor's bloodied head
and detailed schematics of Crane's Winfield apartment and
bedroom. Avilla came out swinging too, pummeling the
police and prosecution with allegations.

He charged that integral items of evidence had been mis-
handled, misplaced, or suppressed, that detectives had lied
about a fingerprint report concerning work that had not
been completed, and that Exhibit #50, the DPS tissue speck
photograph, may have been fabricated.

Avilla based his conclusion in the later complaint on the
absence of any photo negative and on the presence of a
ruler alongside the red speck that appeared unlike the ruler
in the other photos. Fittingly, considering Crane's belief in
luck, the only numeral visible on the ruler was unlucky
thirteen. Avilla raised doubts about who had taken the
photo in the first place and when.

DPS criminologist Bruce Bergstrom, who had done test-

ing on the Cordoba door panel in 1978, could not recall
seeing the tissue or locate mention of it in any of his reports.

On March 3, an aggravated Parker said, "Avilla evidently
can't come up with anything in his case and so he is wan-
dering around the courtroom making accusations . . . that he
wouldn't dare make outside the courtroom."

Remarks made by attorneys as part of legal proceedings
inside a courtroom are shielded from libel suits. Under this
protective umbrella, Avilla said that he thought that Victoria Berry and her ex-husband, Alan Wells, not Carpenter,
were the murderers of Bob Crane. Lee Fetty, one of the
trio of movers who saw a man exit Crane's apartment the
night he was murdered and drive away in a white car, now
said that the car was a Cadillac with California plates such
as Wells drove, but that the stranger was neither Wells nor
Carpenter.

Judge Martin told Avilla that he "eagerly awaited the
evidence" that Berry and Wells were involved in the killing.
"It's one thing to say it, but you have to prove it," said
Martin.

During closing arguments Martin lashed "law enforcement" for doing "sloppy work" on the Crane investigation.
Inaccurately quoted in the press as criticizing Scottsdale
P.D. alone, Martin clarified his remarks the following day,
Thursday, March 11, 1993, as the three-week hearing came
to a conclusion. "The Scottsdale police were not the only
agency involved. I didn't single them out for criticism," he
said. He then read his three-page order that stated the "only
reasonable inference" that can be drawn from blood and
tissue found later in Carpenter's auto "is that the blood is
that of the victim and the tissue is body tissue of the victim
transferred from the scene of the crime to the defendant's
rental car . . . Probable cause has been shown that the crime
of murder . . . was committed by John Henry Carpenter. Mr.
Carpenter is therefore bound over for trial" on a charge of
first-degree murder.

Trial date was set for May 26, 1993, but later Carpenter
waived his right to a speedy trial and a new date was set—
January 18, 1994. Investigator Raines quoted a printed re-

mark of Carpenter's to me over the phone. " 'I didn't kill the son of a bitch,' he said. Your best friend for thirteen years that kept you in more women and booze and everything else you could shake a stick at. He turns up dead at the hand of some unknown person and you say, 'I didn't kill the son of a bitch.' "

Because of doubts raised about the authenticity of the tissue speck photo it was imperative that Raines find the negatives to the DPS photos. In late May, with the help of volunteers searching through mountains of boxes, he finally did.

"I've run across a new witness lately," Raines told me in June of 1993, "who was there at the Sunburst when Carpenter checked out, and this new witness described a piece of luggage that Carpenter had with him and knowing what the dimensions of the tripod were and then what the witness tells me about the dimensions of the suitcase it could have been inside the suitcase. He could have checked that very, very easily. This guy knows Kathy Nugent [the desk clerk] and was the night auditor. He told me that not only did John Carpenter come down at 8:30 A.M. to get out, he had called before Nugent had even come to work, about 6:30 A.M.

" 'Get my bill ready and call me a cab. I got to get out of here.' That was at 6:30 A.M. He claims that he was confused on his flight times."

In July, Bruce Bergstrom remembered seeing tissue from the door panel and told Raines in an internal memo that he had observed tissue in a test tube at DPS shortly after the Cordoba was examined. Then where was his sample and where were Bergstrom's notes?

Avilla's motion for a new pretrial hearing was denied and then, in mid-October, Myrna Parker left the county attorney's office to take a new job as the head of the Navajo County public defender's office in Northern Arizona where her husband had been transferred. Veteran prosecutor K. C. Scull, the chief of Rick Romley's Major Felony Bureau, was designated to replace her.

On November 3 the *Arizona Republic* reported that it had obtained a copy of an October 1990 report that disputed the stains found on the door panel were blood. Jennifer Super Mihalovich, a criminologist with Forensic Science Associates of Richmond, California, reported then that testing of the sample which Romley had sent her had "yielded a negative result for the presence of blood."

K. C. Scull responded, "It's absurd to say that there was never any blood on that door panel. There was. It was tested. And it was used up." In reference to an anonymous fax sent to the press, Romley denied that Parker had been forced to resign from his office for allegedly withholding evidence in the form of Super Mihalovich's report. "To anonymously distribute these accusations is cowardly," he said.

On December 21, Dean received a letter at his new home informing him of the "unforeseen illness" of K. C. Scull. Fortunately Scull was recovering but would be replaced by Robert J. Shutts, deputy county attorney, in the prosecution of John Carpenter. Assisting Shutts would be Jim Raines, attorney Alex Poulos, and legal assistant Dick Strobel.

Consequently the trial was again delayed and rescheduled. On February 21, 1994, Dean and Borkenhagen received subpoenas for their testimony. Dean called me shortly afterward and said, "The trial is now set for March 21, but I suspect that they will delay again. I'm predicting this not because of any reason why, but because I know they do."

And Dean was right. Over the next month he was restless and anxious. He continued his work as a P.I. and launched a new business. When the trial date rolled around it was reset for April 4 and then rescheduled for April 11.

The legal sparring continued, more walls and roadblocks sprang up and, finally, as June 29, 1994, approached, it seemed apparent that the sixteenth anniversary of Bob Crane's death would come and go without a verdict. It had been a long wait and with sixteen years of patience under their belts and their powers of endurance well-seasoned, the principals in the case continued to play the waiting game.

AFTERWORD

Finally, on Tuesday, September 6, jury selection for Scottsdale's most notorious murder trial commenced. Pretrial motions foreshadowed the shape of the prosecution's case. Shutts would depend weightily on photographic evidence, the portrayal of the defendant as "prone to violent rages," and Bob's loss of interest in maintaining Carpenter's friendship—a friendship that was enormously important to the former video troubleshooter. Judge Martin cautioned prospective panelists that the trial could last from eight to twelve weeks.

The first salvos were delivered in the form of opening statements the following Monday. Avilla's co-counsel was Candace Kent; Shutts would be assisted by Alex Poulos.

"By 1978, John Carpenter was wearing thin on Bob Crane," Shutts told the jurors. "Crane complained to his son that Carpenter was 'too much a hanger-on' and 'a nuisance.' There were all the elements of a friendship gone bad and, with the ending of that relationship, Carpenter would have to sacrifice the source of beautiful women he could never obtain himself, because Crane was a high-energy magnet to women. He fed off the fame and energy of the actor."

Shutts promised to prove that Carpenter crushed Crane's skull with a tripod in a violent fit because the wisecracking star wanted to end their long friendship, thus effectively canceling John's ticket to a life of easy sex.

The defendant, the prosecutor argued, had the motive to kill the actor, had access to his Winfield condo, and even told Bob, Jr., that he had "tunnel vision" that made him extremely aggressive when he got angry. Shutts explained away the fourteen-year delay in filing charges by blaming a lack of communication between investigating agencies and the clash of various lawmen's "egos."

Shutts related how Crane enjoyed "first choice" of women during their sexual romps, leaving Carpenter with the "leftovers." Understandably, this may have created animosity between the two intimate pals, and for this reason some of Bob's homemade sex videotapes would be shown in court during the trial.

These X-rated encounters showing the two men simultaneously having sex with the same woman would demonstrate the "secondary position" that Carpenter unfailingly took with Crane. One grim, grainy, black-and-white video showed Bob and John engaging in oral sex with a woman. Another showed Bob and a blonde on the old striped couch in his Winfield apartment. The tapes were informative on another level—the missing tripod, the possible weapon, was visible propped up behind the couch.

"As soon as legally possible," said Shutts with disgust, "we'll take those tapes and toss them in the garbage where they belong."

Avilla told the jury, "The only important question in front of you is whether the state proves John Carpenter guilty beyond a reasonable doubt of killing his friend Bob Crane."

The state's case hinged strongly on a 1978 photograph taken inside the rental car Carpenter drove while in Scottsdale and Phoenix, Avilla explained. The crucial photo included a speck one-sixteenth of an inch wide that prosecutors believe is the victim's brain tissue. Avilla scoffed at this presumption, saying that sixteen years ago that speck was identified as nothing more than "debris." Ron Little, now a Navy lieutenant, testified in a sworn affidavit that the speck was noticed by the police in 1978, but dismissed as "debris" unrelated to the case.

"There is no [brain] tissue because there never was," said the defense attorney. "Much of the evidence you will hear will astonish you as to the incompetence of the agencies involved."

Investigators failed to follow up on potential suspects, said Avilla, including a man seen coming out of Crane's apartment the morning of the murder by furniture movers, and a woman who saw Bob forty-five minutes before his death. He also contended that the crime scene was irreparably disturbed and evidence improperly stored, lost, or destroyed.

The rental car, said Avilla, was not seized by Scottsdale police until about thirty-two hours after the homicide. During that time other people had driven the vehicle. "Not one witness will say that those stains were there when John Carpenter dropped off his car," he said.

Victoria Berry took the stand as the first witness. A videotape was shown to the jurors, but it wasn't of the pornographic variety. It was only Bob and Victoria's rehearsal of a scene from *Beginner's Luck*, the reason the actress had gone to Crane's in the first place.

Avilla tried to cast the Australian-born actress in the role of Bob's killer by asking if police had ever searched a large purse she was carrying while officers questioned her at the apartment. Berry vehemently denied she was the killer or that the bulky murder weapon was concealed within her purse.

On September 14, Dr. Thomas Jarvis, who had performed the autopsy on Crane, told the court that the "mystery cord" was tied across Bob's neck while he was still alive. "I don't think it had anything to do with his death," he said. "Crane died within a minute after being bashed on the left side of the head with a rounded blunt instrument about one-half to three-quarters of an inch in diameter."

What was the purpose of the cord, then, unless it was symbolic? In some kinds of kinky sex, nooses are used to inhibit the flow of oxygen and increase pleasure. But would the actor have severed the all-important cord to his VCR? Surely, a lamp cord from next to the bed could have sufficed.

Over Avilla's objection Jarvis testified about dried semen found on the body and, under questioning by Shutts, said the victim could have discharged the semen when he died. The actual specimen had been lost.

Jarvis studied a photo of the speck and told jurors that it was consistent with fat tissue from the brain area. However, under cross-examination by Avilla, Jarvis admitted that he wasn't "absolutely positive."

"Terry" Rose Lange, Bob's girlfriend, told jurors on Friday, September 16, that during a lull in their two-hour tryst, Crane expressed to her that he was "kind of tired of having [Carpenter] hang around" and that he was on the "outs" with John.

"Bob said Carpenter was kind of jealous because Bob Crane got the first choice of all the girls," said Terry, "and he got the leftovers. 'He acts like a woman with PMS,' he said. I was surprised by Bob's comments. The impression I got was that they were very good friends for a very long time."

Avilla argued that Terry told the police that Crane never spoke poorly of Carpenter. "I did not feel Bob was speaking badly of his friend when he made these remarks," she answered.

Avilla doubted Crane mentioned PMS, an acronym not in general usage until 1981. However, under cross-examination Terry was unshakable and insisted that she was familiar with the term at the time she knew Crane. "I suffered from PMS in 1978," she said, "and was aware of the syndrome."

On Monday, Susan Marts testified to her recollection of

the defendant's actions in the Winfield swimming pool the day before Bob's death. Carpenter told her that he could "make me famous" and that he was Richard Dawson's manager. John, she said, demonstrated karate moves and explained how to get the most force behind a blow. "Always aim a few inches beyond the target when striking a blow," he said.

Linda Robertson, the waitress at Bobby McGee's on McDowell Road, who had waited on the two pals sixteen years earlier, was now Linda Davis. She testified next that she saw Crane and Carpenter having a "tense" conversation.

"They were not real friendly toward each other. They weren't interacting a lot," she said. Moreover, they were abrupt with her.

Carolyn Baare, the last woman known to have seen Bob alive, had joined the two friends at McGee's and felt that Carpenter was "not having a good time." Then, for the second time in five days of trial, Avilla tried to cast suspicion on someone else.

He asked if the Scottsdale police department had ever asked to examine the clothes Baare was wearing the morning of the murder for bloodstains.

"The police never made such a request," Baare replied.

"Did you kill Bob Crane?" Shutts later asked her.

"No."

"Did you go over to his apartment and bludgeon him to death?"

"I hardly knew the man," Baare answered. "I only dated him twice."

Crane had made sexual overtures toward her, but Baare said she never became intimate with him. She admitted to Avilla that she had claimed to have learned of Crane's death about 10:00 A.M. on the day he was murdered. That would have been almost four and a half hours before Victoria discovered the body. Baare now said she didn't find out until almost 5:00 P.M. that day and that her previous statement was in error.

On Thursday, September 22, Ron Dean put on his best tan jacket and went to testify. Asked to indicate the dark speck of tissue on the window button of the passenger-side

door and various stains on the vinyl interior of the rented
Cordoba, Dean knelt and studied the assortment of twenty
mounted color photographs.

"Surprisingly, after that many years," he told me later,
"I still remembered all the answers. If they asked me anything very specific I asked to see my original notes that I'd
typed up at the time. So then, with that, I thought from my
perspective my five-and-a-half-hour testimony went rather
smoothly.

"Shutts asked me some questions that he wanted to put
on record and they centered on those phone calls from Carpenter I received when I was at the Crane apartment. I was
wondering then, 'Why don't you ask me what I'm doing
here?' They thought that was quite crucial—why Carpenter
kept calling back when I told him I was going to call him
later.

"Later when I did try to contact John, and said, 'Well,
I'm coming over to California,' he made himself not avail-
able. In fact, he used the term, 'I won't be *very* available.'
When I said that on the stand there was a big controversy.

"There was a couple hours back and forth with the defense yelling for a mistrial and 'We don't want that in there'
and 'If they get that in there I want to say he offered to
take the lie detector test.' So they were going round and
round, but eventually they just said, 'Well, just don't say it
again and we'll go on.' "

Carpenter's trial was running at the same time as O. J.
Simpson's, and I was struck by eerie parallels between the
two high-profile proceedings. In both instances police had
observed spots of blood on a white rental car, and had been
unable to recover the murder weapon. Both were circumstantial cases in which blood testing played a part and in
which the defendant left the state immediately after the
murders, then placed a series of calls back home. Bloodstains were allegedly discovered in the Simpson and Carpenter hotel rooms and there were legal concerns about the
breaking of the chain of evidence during the towing of the
vehicles.

During the Crane trial, Judge Martin kept a tight rein on
the media. Dean noticed from the witness chair that there

were no cameras in sight, only a wood-paneled wall. But
they were there behind a type of screen, blended and colored like wood paneling, that allows the still camera and
video camera to filter through.

During the 1993 preliminary hearing, former DPS criminalist Bruce Bergstrom hadn't understood the importance
his work played in the prosecution—the case hinged heavily on the physical evidence. Shortly after returning to his
home in San Diego he read a *New Times* article that emphasized the crucial importance of the tissue specimen.

"I sat down to concentrate and meditate on what I did in
this case," Bergstrom told the jurors on Monday, September
26, "and remembered the tissue in the vial. I do not recall
the piece of tissue on the door panel. I remember it's very
possible that I received this piece of tissue [in the vial] that
was removed by somebody else. I don't know where I got
it or what I did with it."

Bergstrom told the jurors that the bloodstains were Type-
B blood, Crane's type and a type possessed by approximately one in seven people. Under cross-examination he
admitted that he hadn't recalled performing the bloodstain
tests until he reread his 1978 report.

Three days later, Bob's widow, Patti, took the witness
chair and quickly refuted Avilla's insinuations that she'd
had anything to do with her husband's murder.

"I love my husband," said Mrs. Crane. "I still love him.
I don't even date. I never remarried. I still wear my twenty-
dollar gold wedding band. It hasn't been off my hand in
twenty-four years.

"We had an open marriage. I told him I never wanted
him to miss anything in life because of me. Bob was con-
sumed by his hobby of photography and would videotape
any and all sexual encounters he could get his partners to
agree to. He never went on the road without a truckload of
video equipment."

Patti not only condoned her husband's unusual sexual
habits and many escapades, but occasionally viewed videos
of his conquests. They did not upset her and were not the
reason for their separation in 1977, although Bob had promised to seek counseling for his obsession during their brief

reconciliation. They split because they were not communicating anymore.

Patti denied to Avilla that Bob's womanizing angered her. Shutts drove the point home. "Did that ever become an issue in your marriage?" he asked.

"Never," Patti answered.

After their last phone argument, Patti had attempted to call Crane back at ten the next morning. By then Bob Crane was already dead.

On Monday, October 3, the fourth week of the trial began with Bob Jr., now forty-three years old, testifying. Until comic actor John Candy's recent death, he had been his representative.

"My father told me that Mr. Carpenter was becoming what he termed a 'hanger-on,' a nuisance to the point of becoming obnoxious," said Bob Jr. "He said, 'I've got to make a change here . . . [Carpenter] is becoming a pain . . . he's cramping my style.' "

Bob Jr., also commented on the strange call he'd received from Carpenter the day of his father's murder. "If there's anything you need, give me a call. Let me know," Carpenter had told him. During the considerable time he'd known John, Bob Jr. had never received such a call and it was so "awkward" it prompted him to try and reach his dad in Scottsdale.

"Bobby's testimony really helped to the point of his having a lot of knowledge of his father wanting to get this guy out of his life," Dean told me. "Crane was calling John a 'hanger-on.' It seemed to me Carpenter would come to town and just push himself into Crane's life."

Scott, Bob's son, now a recording studio owner in Seattle, told *People* that he remembered his father as a loving and playful man, and the day of his death clearly. "I was in total shock after my mother told me. It took me three years to start crying and then it took me three years to get it all out." He added, "I don't know if Carpenter did it. Only he would know." Though Patti had charged in court papers that Bob had shown six-year-old Scott some of his homemade porno tapes, he recalled none of it.

A moon-faced young man in a brightly colored, flowered

silk shirt was constantly in court looking out for his friend, John Carpenter. He was Richard Dawson's son, Mark, who'd first met John when he sold his father one of the first VCRs in the United States and installed it in the entertainer's home. He'd continued his father's interest in video and at thirty-four was a producer.

Mark brought his camera equipment to Phoenix. "He was making a tape of everything," Dean told me, "for a later movie or for appeals. I don't know which." Dawson denied that Crane and Carpenter ever had a serious falling out. "John has said to me more than once, 'No, I didn't kill my best friend. No one asks how it feels to lose your closest friend.' "

The following day, Dr. Karnitschnig testified about the speck. "It's yellowish," he stated. "It has a gelatinous appearance. It isn't muscle. It isn't skin." He found it similar to tissue visible on Crane's head wound in an autopsy photo.

Meanwhile, Judge Martin was having second thoughts about showing Bob's sex video. "I'm concerned about playing it to the jury. It's real problematic."

Avilla was willing to confirm the contents of the video, including the presence of a tripod in the background in order to avoid screening the tape in court. The defense feared that the video would "inflame the passions of the jury." Shutts replied to Martin, "If you like, I'll rethink it."

Avilla objected to Carpenter's estranged son, John Merrill, a disabled pipe fitter, testifying on October 6. He considered the testimony "character assassination" and "unduly prejudicial." Merrill had met with his estranged father at a Tillamook, Oregon, hotel two or three years before Bob's death.

"He was showing me pictures of my mom when she was young, back when they were together. He was asking about my character, how I reacted, was I violent," said Merrill. "He told me he had a violence problem in the past and he called it 'tunnel vision.' "

The son said his father described tunnel vision as a "focus on the person he was in combat with, to make sure they didn't get up again. During such phases, everything else was 'blacked out.' " Merrill said Carpenter told him that he would become obsessed with one goal—to take out the person who was giving him trouble.

The next day, a blood splatter expert, homicide investigator Ron Englert of the Portland, Oregon, sheriff's office, explained how blunt force affects blood droplets. The blow that killed Bob was delivered with "medium velocity," he said, one that would splatter blood not with the first hit, but on subsequent ones. He thought there might have been three blows.

"Bloodstains on Crane's bedsheet showed two parallel lines slightly curving inward to a 'V' that were consistent with a tripod. Hand smear marks on the victim's upper back indicated he was bludgeoned before the cord was placed around his neck."

Englert thought the missing blunt instrument was a camera tripod.

After much soul-searching, Judge Martin decided to show the video. On Wednesday, October 12, ten minutes of a fifteen-minute homemade pornographic scene were played back to the jury. It portrayed the star of *Hogan's Heroes* and the accused killer cavorting with a beautiful Dallas woman in May of 1978. Genitals had been electronically censored.

Judge Martin cautioned the panel that they should not consider the tape "evidence of bad character," only that it revealed "a relationship between Crane and Carpenter." Additionally, recent audio testimony from the woman performing in the threesome was presented.

"I met Bob Crane at a Dallas nightclub," she said. "He invited me to come back the next night and see his play, and so I took him up on his offer. I liked to drink and party, so we had some drinks at a nightclub.

"I could have had ten to fifteen drinks. I was going from Cuba Libres to Kahlúa and creams. I was pretty relaxed and was flirting with Crane. I was attracted to his celebrity. He was a soft-spoken man, while Carpenter was a big talker . . . name-dropping on other people. I have vague recollections that we were being filmed. I sensed no hostility between them. They were sharing a girl. I would have caught that."

The prosecution rested on Monday, October 17, and Avilla attempted to have the case thrown out. "There is no indication of any loud arguments between the two men. There is no indication of any hostility between the two," he said. "The court should end this farce, end this fiasco and find there's no evidence to take this case to a jury."

Judge Martin ruled down the request, saying that enough circumstantial and physical evidence existed linking Carpenter to the crime to allow the trial to move forward.

Avilla began his defense with a truck driver who reported seeing a man other than the defendant exit Crane's apartment the morning of the murder. Walter Ferry said he saw a man look around, then reenter Bob's room.

On cross, Ferry told Shutts that he couldn't recall much about the times he saw the man. He'd arrived at the Winfield complex around 5:30 A.M. and was there roughly six hours.

The following day, Dr. Roger Fossum, an expert witness for the defense, said he'd ruled out the speck being fat while thinking over the case on his flight to Phoenix. "It occurred to me on the airplane," he said, "that when fat melts, grease comes out." Inside a sun-baked auto, fat should have been excreted, but there were no grease streaks around the speck in the photo," he said.

Dr. Fossum doubted a tripod was the missing weapon. "My opinion is that a camera tripod is not the type of instrument that, certainly on the first blow, could ever cause this type of damage," he said. He believed that Crane was struck three times because of an unusual incisionlike cut. Under cross he admitted that this incision could have been caused by a light, rodlike item like a tripod leg.

The defense rested on October 19, after a single day of testimony and without the defendant taking the stand to testify. Closing arguments were scheduled for Wednesday, October 26, after prosecutors presented a rebuttal witness and legal instructions were drafted.

The jury had been out for two and a half days when word came at 10:30 A.M. on October 31 that they had reached a verdict. In thirty minutes a question asked over sixteen years earlier might be answered. As I waited, I studied a tabloid interview with the woman Patti had replaced on *Hogan's Heroes* as Colonel Klink's secretary. Cynthia Lynn told the *Star* that she'd had an affair with Crane and that he'd taken photos of her.

"In the photos," she said, "Bob insisted that I be stark naked—except for one little thing—the U.S. Air Force cap he wore on the show. I think taking shots of me in that little brown cap gave Bob more of a kick than actually making love to me."

I recalled how Crane taped sex sessions with women and immediately watched them afterward. One woman commented that this excited him more than the act. In those ghostly, flickering black-and-white images, Bob, the eternally visual man and perfect choice as a television star, found a greater reality. To him, the image was more real than the actual experience. It had to be more than coincidence that the network that gave Crane his greatest fame had as its symbol a gigantic eye.

Before the trial, Werner Klemperer had said, "It seems the prosecution's case is so circumstantial, I have the feeling that this crime will never be solved." And he was right, the verdict of the jury was for acquittal.

But I realized that this greatest of all Hollywood mysteries, in lacking a final word, would give Crane an immortality far greater that *Hogan's Heroes*.

In 1992, another attempt to bring *Hogan's Heroes* to Germany failed. But decades after World War II, revisions would make the sitcom palatable to modern German viewers. In 1995, a private network, Cable 1, rewrote and redubbed the show, renaming it, *A Cage Full of Heroes*. By 1997 the show was a cult hit throughout Germany. Under German law the phrase "*Heil* Hitler" was forbidden as was the "*Heil* Hitler" salute. Producers replaced them. From then on when the Nazis saluted each other, arms extended, they were dubbed as saying "This is how high the cornflowers grow!"

In June 1997, more than one thousand *Hogan*'s fans gathered in Arizona to hold the world's biggest séance.

Their intent was to contact Bob Crane. The bizarre séance began at the stroke of midnight at the Windmill Dinner Theatre where the actor had given his final stage performance shortly before his death. Psychic Jan Ross tried to reach out to the slain actor's ghost, but failed. Cynthia Lynn claimed that Bob's ghost was now haunting her in terrifying predawn dreams. "Bob's not at peace because police still haven't found who killed him," she said. Fans held out faint hope Crane would make his presence known at a bash to celebrate his birthday on July 13, 1997.

Bob had acted on Seattle stages during the sixties and seventies and kept a second home on Bainbridge Island. Scotty Crane, following in his father's footsteps, was now a popular radio DJ on Seattle's KQBZ-FM. "He was definitely a sex addict," said Scotty. "He was very open with his sexuality, and that was what got him in trouble. . . . The thing about Bob Crane is his life doesn't need any sensationalism. It was a sensationalistic life as it was, and to try to make it more sensational is just so dumb, because the truth is *amazing*."

Bob's legacy took a decidedly trashy turn in 2001 as Scotty publicly exhibited Bob's black-and-white pornographic video clips and nearly fifty explicit photos on his Web site. "This is just like all-American fun," said Scotty. When the site proved extraordinarily popular, he set about publishing *The Faces of Bob Crane*, a coffee-table book he considered "a pretty good tribute to his father."

"This is all the faces of Bob Crane," Scotty told reporter Robert Wilonsky. "The guy wore many hats, and so this isn't just a slash-and-burn, sleazy pornographic book. It's actually the true-life story of Bob Crane. There is some writing in the book . . . but the photographs tell the story more than anything else. Pictures speak a thousand words." In the book are two pages of drawings of naked women and men Scotty had done when he was between four and seven. His wife, Michelle Ahern-Crane, told the *Seattle Times* that when she saw them for the first time, she cried. "I thought his innocence was stolen," she said.

Bob Crane Jr. and his sister, Karen, a California antique dealer, considered the book and Web site a disservice to their father. Karen told the *Arizona Republic* in June 2001 that her half-brother "is using our father disgustingly to try to benefit himself." Bob Jr. concurred. "This is not a celebration of my dad," he said.

Things were winding down. On Friday, September 11, 1998, twenty years after Crane's murder, John Henry Carpenter, friend and suspect, died at age seventy. The wonderful actor Werner Klemperer died at his New York home on Wednesday, December 6, 2000. Colonel Klink was gone.

"Escaped?" Klink once said on *Hogan's Heroes*. "No one has ever escaped from Stalag 13. Sound the alarm. Let loose the dogs. All guards turn out and search."

"There is no escape from Stalag 13," said Sergeant Schultz. "That's an order by Colonel Klink."

SELECTED REFERENCES

Books

Allman, Kevin. *TV Turkeys*. New York: Putnam Publishing Group, 1987.

Austin, John. *Hollywood's Unsolved Mysteries*. New York: Shapolsky Publishers, 1990.

Barnouw, Erik. *The Image Empire*. New York: Oxford University Press, 1970.

Bedell, Sally. *Up the Tube*. New York: Viking Press, 1981.

Boyer, Peter J. *Who Killed CBS?* New York: St. Martin's Press, 1989.

Brown, Les. *Television, The Business Behind the Box*. New York: Harcourt Brace Jovanovich, 1971.

Castleman, Harry, and Walter J. Podrazik. *Watching TV, Four

Decades of American Television. New York: McGraw-Hill Paperback, 1982.

Collier, James Lincoln. *Benny Goodman and the Swing Era*. New York: Oxford University Press, 1989.

Crockett, Art, ed. *Celebrity Murders*. New York: Pinnacle Windsor Publishers, 1990.

Cross, Wilbur L. *Connecticut*. Cambridge, Mass.: Riverside Press, 1938.

Fabe, Maxine. *TV Game Shows!* New York: Doubleday and Company, 1979.

Freberg, Stan. *It Only Hurts When I Laugh*. New York: Times Books, 1988.

Grote, David. *The End of Comedy: The Sit-Com and the Comedic Tradition*. Connecticut: Archon Books, 1983.

Heyworth, Peter. *Otto Klemperer, His Life and Times, Vol. 1, 1885–1933*. London: Cambridge University Press, 1983.

Kaminsky, Stuart M., and Jeffrey H. Mahan. *American Television Genres*. Chicago: Nelson-Hall Publishers, 1983.

Klemperer, Lotte. *Klemperer on Music: Shavings from a Musician's Workbench*. Great Britain: Short Run Press, Ltd., 1986.

Levinson, Richard, and William Link. *Stay Tuned*. New York: St. Martin's Press, 1981.

McNeil, Alex. *Total Television*. New York: Viking Penguin Inc., 1984.

Metz, Robert. *CBS: Reflections in a Bloodshot Eye*. New York: Signet, 1976.

Morgan, Ted. *An Uncertain Hour*. New York: Arbor House/ William Morrow, 1990.

Munn, Michael. *The Hollywood Murder Casebook*. New York: St. Martin's Press, 1987.

Osborne, Charles, and Kenneth Thomson, eds. *Klemperer Stories*. Great Britain: Robson Books, 1980.

Paley, William S. *As It Happened*. Garden City, N.Y., Doubleday, 1979.

Paper, Lewis. *Empire*. New York: St. Martin's Press, 1987.

Peck, Stephen Rogers. *Atlas of Human Anatomy for the Artist*. New York: Oxford University Press, 1978.

Recreation Map of Phoenix and Central Arizona. North Star Mapping.

Rovin, Jeff. *TV Babylon*. New York: NAL Penguin Books, 1984.

Rowe, Findley. *Great American Deserts*. Washington, D.C.: National Geographic Society, 1972.

Shanks, Bob. *The Cool Fire: How to Make It in Television*. New York: Vintage Press, 1976.

Shirer, William L. *Rise and Fall of the Third Reich*. New York: Simon & Schuster, 1959.

Slater, Robert. *This . . . Is CBS*. Englewood Cliffs, N.J.: Prentice-Hall, 1988.

Smith, Sally Bedell. *In All His Glory*. New York: Simon & Schuster, 1990.

Snyder, LeMoyne. *Homicide Investigation, Third Edition*. Springfield, Ill.: Charles C. Thomas, Publishers, 1977.

Sutton, Ann, and Myron Sutton. *The Life of the Desert*. New York: McGraw Hill Book Company, 1968.

Theroux, Paul. Quote from unidentified short story, 1977.

Periodicals and Newspapers

Arizona Highways: "Phoenix and Scottsdale" 50:4, April 1974; "On the Trail of the Devil," Sherwood B. Idso, 55:6; "The Salt River Project," Raymond Carlson, ed., 57:3, March 1981; "Arizona's Fabulous Resorts," Pam Hait, and "Dream Merchants of the Desert," photos by J. Peter Mortimer, 58:1, January 1982.

The Globe. 38:48, November 26, 1991; 39:30, July 28, 1992.

Inside Detective. Grass, Thomas. "Murder of Bob ('Hogan's Heroes') Crane." May 1979.

The National Enquirer. Michelini, Chuck, and David Wright. May 29, 1979.

The National Enquirer Special. "Murder, Mystery and Scandals." 2:3, June 1991.

The National Examiner. September 10, 1991.

New Times. Kiefer, Michael. "A Life Among the Dead." May 27–June 2, 1992.

New Times. Rubin, Paul. Three-part series on the Bob Crane murder case. April 21–April 27, April 28–May 4, May 4–May 11, 1993; "New Trails in Crane Case." October 27–November 2, 1993.

The Star. "Hogan's Corny Heroes." August 12, 1997.

TV Guide: "Bob Crane, A Man in Pursuit of Himself," Marian Dern, 15–17, February 27, 1965; "Hogan and His Heroes," Leslie Raddatz, 22–24, November 27, 1965; "His Podium a Prison Camp," Dwight Whitney, 22–25, January 22, 1966; "The Strange History of A-5714," Dick Hobson, 23–26, November 19, 1966; "TV's Most Huggable Nazi," Dick Hobson, 16–17, May 6, 1967; "Sigrid Valdis," 24–25, August 5, 1967; "Ivan Dixon," 35–38, September 16, 1967; "Richard Dawson," 27–27, December 23, 1967: "Hip, Flip, Cocky Bob Crane," Edith Elfron, 25–27, August 3, 1968; "Larry Hovis, Invisible Actor," Dick Hobson, 12–13, August 8, 1970; "Decade of Change, Decade of Choice," Neill Hickey, 29, December 9, 1989. "A peek at the seedy past of Heroes's Hogan," Williams, Tim. August 11, 2001.

Article on Robert Clary, "I've Been Married Nine Years, Going on 105," Dan O'Keefe.

Arizona Daily Star: Mary K. Reinhart.

Arizona Republic: David Cannella, Randy Collier, Abraham Kwok, Brent Whiting, Chuck Hawley, Jack Swanson, and Charles Kelly.

Boston Advertiser: Anthony LaCamera, November 11, 1965, March 2, 1975. Cynthia Lowry, April 20, 1969. Hal Humphrey, July 21, 1968. Dorothy Manners, November 30, 1969, April 19, 1970.

Boston News: Kay Gardella, August 29, 1965.

Chicago Tribune: Michael Coakley, August 16, 1978.

Los Angeles Times: Leslie Berger, Eric Malnic, Laura Laughlin, Ann Japenga, and Ted Thackrey, Jr.

Phoenix Gazette: John Schroeder, J. W. Brown, and Mike Padgett.

San Francisco Chronicle: Buck Biggers, Chet Stover, Al Stump. Terrence O'Flaherty's columns: January 28, 1975, "As Wilbur Said to Orville," and March 11, 1965, "Crane and Company."

Scottsdale Progress: Steve Brennan, Steve Wilson, and Dan Liefgreen.

Torrance Daily Breeze: Rene Lynch.

Dallasobserver.com. Wilonsky, Robert. "Klinky Sex." November 28, 2001.

Seattletimes.com. Zebrowski, John. "A distinctly different kind of dad. Son reveals the highly sexual life, death of Bob Crane." September 5, 2001.

Television Programs

A Current Affair: Maureen O'Boyle, May 19, 1992, January 28, 1991, February 8, 1991, August 6, 1991, June 1, 1992, and September 19, 1991.

Sources

The primary source for this book has been the 849-page, three-volume Scottsdale police file #78-08649 and the Maricopa County Attorney's Office follow-up investigation. Many of the conversations set in 1978 were based on the verbatim transcripts of taped interviews with the hundreds of people involved in the case. In most cases these quotes have been more accurate than more recent remarks of the participants because of the passage of time. I have tried to make this book reflect as accurately as possible the state of mind of all involved at the time of Bob Crane's murder.

As is my custom, I have visited all of the places mentioned in the book, photographed, sketched, and mapped each, and although much of this behind-the-scenes work does not see print, it is essential to me to understand the story. I have also studied unpublished crime scene photos of the victim and Winfield apartment 132A and viewed black-and-white copies of the private sex tapes. I have seen transcripts of anonymous calls, the property invoices, drafts for search warrants, blood type reports, Department of Public Safety lab results, investigators' notes, and DMV and phone records.

In addition to extensive interviews with many of those involved in Bob's life and the investigation, I spoke with cast members of *Hogan's Heroes* and writers for the sitcom. I watched all 168 episodes of the program, including the show's black-and-white pilot and read virtually everything written about Colonel Hogan and his band of heroes.

I was fortunate enough to have interviewed important officials in the investigation (such as county attorney Richard Romley and detectives Dean and Borkenhagen) before the suspect's arrest, at which time further remarks from them would have been improper.